Critical Praise for *Honor Bound*

★ ★ ★

"*Honor Bound* is an engrossing, first-hand account of military justice in an age of terrorism and what it takes to defend liberty as a JAG officer today. U.S. Army Captain (now Major) Kyndra Rotunda was at the center of the most important and controversial legal issues in the war, including the difficulties of detaining and prosecuting terrorists while traditional war is being redefined. Her fascinating and lucid story chronicles her journey from a Wyoming law school, through the shock of September 11th, to interrogation cells at Guantanamo Bay, terror trials, and to Walter Reed Army Medical Center deficiencies. And though she pulls no punches where criticism is due, she (and we) can be justly proud of the underlying integrity of our military services and the honor-bound system of our men and women in uniform."

— **Edwin Meese**, Former U.S. Attorney General

★ ★ ★

"The detention and prosecution of unlawful enemy combatants captured in the global war on terrorism will be the topic of debate for many years to come. A critical component of the debate will be the firsthand observations of those who were involved. Kyndra Rotunda provides a unique perspective, having served in three different capacities. She was the legal advisor in Guantanamo Bay to the detention camp commander in 2002–2003, where she provided legal advice to the Commander and worked with the International Committee of the Red Cross. Later, as a member of the Criminal Investigations Task Force, she was legal counsel to the military law enforcement agents who interviewed detainees and developed cases for possible prosecution. Finally, as a member of the Office of the Chief Prosecutor, she prepared war crimes charges against alleged Al Qaida and Taliban members designated for trial at Guantanamo Bay. No one else saw things unfold from these three distinct vantage points."

— **Morris Davis**, Former Chief Prosecutor for the Military Commissions at Guantanamo Bay

★ ★ ★

"This eye-opening inside account must be read by everyone who cares about balancing national security and human dignity."

— **Alan M. Dershowitz**, Professor of Law, Harvard University, and author of *Finding Jefferson*

✯ ✯ ✯

"Major Rotunda has written an immensely readable and stunningly valuable book about terrorism, terrorists and the extraordinarily difficult and demanding task our military faces in dealing with captured enemy combatants. I have twice visited Guantanamo, and participated in our government's defense against some of the legal challenges to our nation's efforts to protect us from another—possibly vastly more dreadful—September 11. Nevertheless, this book was a page-turning eye-opener for me. No American should miss the opportunity—and responsibility—to read it. Bravo!"

> —**Theodore B. Olson**, Former Solicitor General of the United States, Former Assistant Attorney General, Office of Legal Counsel, Department of Justice, and partner at Gibson, Dunn & Crutcher

✯ ✯ ✯

"Kyndra Rotunda's book, *Honor Bound*, not only is an interesting and well-written account of her experiences as a military lawyer, but reveals the surprising facts behind the Guantanamo Bay detainee stories, the problems with recent War Crimes prosecution trials and a host of other facets of the War on Terror."

> —**Joyce Malcolm**, Professor of Law, George Mason University, well known legal historian and Constitutional scholar and member of the Royal Historical Society

✯ ✯ ✯

"While much has been written about the America's War on Terror, *Honor Bound* is the first work to approach the conflict from the unique perspective of the men and women who fight on a little-known battlefront: the uniformed lawyers charged with detaining unlawful enemy combatants and prosecuting terrorists for war crimes. Not only does Major Kyndra Rotunda's book introduce to general readers the relevant legal issues in a thorough, but engaging, manner, she invites the reader to share her own fascinating journey through the military justice system, including her service as a legal advisor to the camp commander at Guantanamo and a prosecutor preparing cases against our enemies.... While not everyone will agree with this well-argued book's conclusions, anyone wishing to understand the upcoming detainee trials will want to read this fine account."

> —**Professor J. Peter Pham**, James Madison University, Senior Fellow, Foundation for the Defense of Democracies

★ ★ ★

"I quickly became an instant admirer of this spunky, feisty young woman and was super glad that she is a fellow American and on our side.... Kyndra Rotunda is a very independent, highly intelligent, exceptionally patriotic, truly dedicated advocate of the rule of law and equally devoted to ensuring that it pertains not only to detainees but also to our American military personnel and their right to defend themselves in a combat or life-threatening situation.... I feel we are all fortunate that Captain Rotunda has taken the time to write *Honor Bound* so that her firsthand experiences can be shared with all who read these words, both to set the record straight and to make it clear to all that our American fighting men and women do conduct themselves in combat with honor and within the law and the Geneva Conventions."

—**Rear Admiral [Ret.] James J. Carey**, National Co-Chairman, The Flag & General Officers' Network

★ ★ ★

"Kyndra Rotunda has written a fascinating and important book that is both an enjoyable read and a source of valuable insider insight on a range of issues in the struggle against Al Qaeda. As a bright young Army Reserve JAG Captain, she served at Guantanamo during a key period as interrogation techniques were debated and changed, and was later recalled to serve in a top secret anti-terrorism unit. Her observations may surprise both critics and supporters of aggressive interrogation techniques. With accounts of espionage and heroism, this book is must reading for anyone interested in understanding what really happened in the treatment of detainees at Guantanamo."

—**Professor Robert F. Turner**, Co-Founder, Center for National Security Law, University of Virginia School of Law

★ ★ ★

"A thrilling account by a young American woman—an Army officer and a lawyer—who finds herself sent to Guantanamo Bay to confront America's enemies: prisoners from the war on terror. Kyndra Rotunda has written a must-read insider's account of what it was like to come face to face with Al Qaeda fighters in captivity. *Honor Bound: Inside the Guantanamo Trials* is an invaluable contribution to the literature on the war, and a compelling eyewitness account that shatters many myths about the controversial prison."

—**James L. Swanson**, *New York Times* bestselling author of *Manhunt: The 12-Day Chase for Lincoln's Killer*

HONOR BOUND

★ ★ ★

Honor Bound

★ ★ ★

HONOR BOUND

★ ★ ★

Inside the Guantanamo Trials

Kyndra Miller Rotunda

CAROLINA ACADEMIC PRESS
Durham, North Carolina

Library of Congress Cataloging-in-Publication Data

Rotunda, Kyndra Miller.
  Honor bound : inside the Guantanamo trials / by Kyndra Miller Rotunda.
    p. cm.
  Includes bibliographical references and index.
  ISBN 978-1-59460-512-3 (alk. paper)
  1. Detention of persons—United States. 2. War on Terrorism, 2001—-Law
and legislation—United States. 3. Civil rights—Government policy—United
States. 4. Due process of law—United States. 5. Military courts—United
States. 6. Prisoners of war—Legal status, laws, etc.—Cuba—Guantánamo
Bay Naval Base. 7. Detention of persons—Cuba—Guantánamo Bay Naval
Base. 8. Political prisoners—Government policy—Cuba—Guantánamo Bay
Naval Base. 9. Prisoners—Abuse of—Cuba—Guantánamo Bay Naval Base.
I. Title.

  KF9625.R68 2008
  341.6—dc22   2008010471

CAROLINA ACADEMIC PRESS
700 Kent Street
Durham, North Carolina 27701
Telephone (919) 489-7486
Fax (919) 493-5668
www.cap-press.com

To Ron

Contents

Foreword

HONOR BOUND came to life for me from the moment I opened the book. I was drawn into the scene "inside the compound" of the terrorist detention camp in Gitmo. Then U. S. Army JAG Corps Captain (lawyer) Kyndra Rotunda takes us from her law school days to her Army JAG Corps training through her pre-deployment training at Fort Benning, Georgia to her arrival in Cuba and her total involvement in the entire terrorist detainee operation there. I could see immediately that through this book, I was going to learn and sense and feel what was actually the situation with these prisoners in Gitmo, and not the standard assertions that our military treats horribly these people (who have made it clear they are committed to killing all Americans). The service men and women I know are honorable and honest and lawful military men and women. And that is exactly what this book demonstrates.

It was truly fascinating to learn that the circumstances and the adherence to the Geneva Convention that, with my military background, I was certain was the situation in Gitmo was, *in fact*, the situation in Gitmo and that the terrorists there were being treated and handled and managed with privileges well beyond what is required by the Geneva Convention. Captain Rotunda's on-the-scene experience with these terrorists finally gave me the facts and the situation and the truth of what was going on in these detainee facilities rather than the slanted versions of the situation that are propagandized daily by Al Qaeda. And how incredibly refreshing it was to finally learn the truth.

Captain (whom the Army recently promoted to Major as soon as she became eligible) Kyndra Rotunda, I learned, began life as a freckled-face girl from Wyoming who earned her law degree at the University of Wyoming and rather than choosing a life as a country lawyer joined the Army JAG Corps. She transitioned from peace to war on September 11, 2001 when Islamic terrorists murdered over 3,000 of our fellow Americans, and eventually found herself on duty in Guantanamo Bay, Cuba, where lawyers and Army commanders find themselves in the daily arm-wrestle as to whether the terrorists there are terrorist detainees or prisoners of war. When I met Kyndra, I quickly became an instant admirer of this spunky, feisty young woman and was super glad that she is a fellow American and on our side. Perhaps it's from some of the frontier history of Wyoming and her ancestral genes, but Kyndra Rotunda is a very independent, highly intelligent, exceptionally patriotic, truly dedicated advocate of the rule of law and equally devoted to ensuring that it pertains not only to detainees but also to our American military personnel and their right to defend themselves in a combat or life-threatening situation.

HONOR BOUND is an outstanding firsthand experience report of prisoner life behind the Gitmo prison wires and inside the interrogation booths, and from there to the inner workings of the first War Crimes prosecution team since World War II, and learning what went wrong with that effort. Through Captain Rotunda and her "been there, done that" experience, I was fascinated with her interactions with Private Jessica Lynch, World War II hero Senator Bob Dole, and Major General Miller. Just as I was stunned to learn that the USA hires translators (who have access to classified information) who are both vocal and obvious about their preference that the USA live under Sharia (Islamic) law. I am impressed with her commitment to fight for our American military combat troops' right to defend themselves when attacked—a situation that, at times, I have felt was perhaps being stood on its head as I read reports where it seemed clear to me that our troops were being forced into situations where they stood to lose their lives, and yet if they engaged the enemy or shot back or harmed them, they could be the subjects of investigation and possible courts-martial. I could not envision our country sending our sons and daughters into combat and life-threatening situations and then giving so much deference to our enemy. Kyndra Rotunda has taken on this issue, and thank God we have an American lawyer with her background, experience, and intellect to advocate for our troops.

We are all fortunate that Major Rotunda has taken the time to write HONOR BOUND so that her firsthand experiences can be shared with all who read these words, both to set the record straight and to make it clear that our American fighting men and women do conduct themselves in combat with honor and within the law and the Geneva Conventions. I am honored to have been given the opportunity to read HONOR BOUND before its publication, and to be able to share these thoughts and my own observations by providing this Foreword as my small part of this magnificent effort. If this book provides the actual facts of what goes on in America's treatment of terrorist detainees to just one single person, then it will have been, in my opinion, both successful in stating the truth and ensuring the accurate history of these events is available for future all generations. And if it encourages hundreds or thousands to rise up to demand that our troops be absolutely given the right to defend themselves every time their life is threatened, then it will have served a greater purpose that can make all Americans proud. I can say with certainty that HONOR BOUND has done these things for me, and that I will both now and forever be ever mindful that the need for eternal vigilance is perhaps as great as ever before as we are now forced to defend ourselves against this enemy without a country or a uniform, who publicly states that they intend to kill us all if we will but give them the opportunity to do so.

HONOR BOUND makes it clear to me that the words spoken long ago by another American Patriot are as true today as is this book which echoes them in this, the twenty-first century—"We must all hang together, or assuredly we shall all hang separately."

Or be beheaded.

Rear Admiral [Ret.] James J. Carey
National Co-Chairman
The Flag & General Officers' Network
www.flagandgeneralofficersnetwork.org

Preface

What follows is my personal story as a JAG Officer serving her country in the Global War on Terror. It begins on September 11th, 2001, when I worked at Walter Reed Army Medical Center in Washington, D.C. and watched out my office window in horror as helicopters hovered over the parking lot carrying Pentagon victims. In an instant, my world—our world—changed forever.

Through my eyes, you will see what I saw, hear what I heard, and learn what I learned. You will go through Marine Corps training in Quantico, Virginia and you'll learn a little bit about the fog of war. You'll also deploy with me to Guantanamo Bay, walk the prison blocks, and learn about radical Islamism. You'll go undercover to work with a team of elite terrorist hunters; and you'll see the inside story of the Guantanamo Trials where a team of prosecutors struggled against the odds to pursue justice, while facing ever-changing rules.

Through a series of intriguing vignettes, you'll meet interesting characters like Private Jessica Lynch, Chaplain James Yee, and General Miller. You will come to understand that we can't fight a war without lawyers.

You'll learn about the law of war, and in a few instances you'll see that America has over-lawyered this war. You'll learn the mistakes our government has made along the way, like paroling known terrorists back to the battlefield; changing the trial rules in the middle of trial; imposing rules that made it difficult for prosecutors to respond to defense counsel claims that deserved a response; and giving detainees more rights than the Geneva Conventions require.

I remain a JAG Officer (a Major) in the U.S. Army Reserves, and I hold a Top Secret Clearance. For this reason, I consulted with the Department of Defense to ensure that I could tell my story. It redacted classified information. What remains is a fairly intact telling of what happened.

Prosecutors, and other people I worked with, are legitimate terrorist targets. To protect their identity, I have not used their real names (except for those officials already in the public eye, like Private Lynch and Colonel Davis). I've identified a few people using just a random initial and I have blurred the faces of several photographs to protect the identity of the people involved. I hope this is not too distracting. Further, there are quotations throughout my book. Not all quotations are verbatim. They are my best recollection of what the particular person told me at the time. Where I've used direct, verbatim quotations, I've also included the source where the quotation derived.

And finally, my views and opinions are my own. I do not speak for the Department of Defense. This information is not classified. But it is the *untold* truth. Rest assured that everything in my book is true. I am not sufficiently imaginative to make up these incredible stories.

Acknowledgments

This book would never come to be without the gracious support and assistance of my family, friends and colleagues. I owe a particular debt of gratitude to my husband, best friend, and scholar, Ronald Rotunda for believing in me, and for encouraging me to pursue my book to the very end.

Thank you from the bottom of my heart to Irene Zion, Dr. John Peter Pham, and Professor Robert Turner, who read the book and offered helpful suggestions.

Thanks also to Bernadette Malone, John Thornton, and retired Rear Admiral James Carey.

Thank you especially to members of the army who reviewed my book for content and security classification. Colonel Swann, Colonel Davis, prosecutors at the Office of Military Prosecutions Team, and personnel at the Criminal Investigation Task Force were especially helpful.

HONOR BOUND

CHAPTER ONE

The Nightmare Begins,
September 11th, 2001

It was a pleasant September day in Washington, D.C. The sky was a beautiful shade of blue, and stretched on like a cloudless forever. I thought about home, miles away in Wyoming. Back home, on days like this one, children in overalls dot the banks of trickling rivers they call "cricks," and fishing poles rest lazily in their hands. I was far from "cowboy country" here in Washington, D.C. But, I was doing something with my life. I was an army lawyer ... an officer ... a "JAG."

Each branch of military service has its own lawyer corps, called the "Judge Advocate General's Corps." We "JAGs" are practicing lawyers. We're just like other lawyers in all respects. We've graduated from accredited law schools, and we've passed the bar exam.

Law school changes one's way of thinking. It can bring out the best and the worst in people. This highly competitive environment is an intellectual boot camp. But, unlike military boot camp, it lasts for three years instead of six weeks. It is challenging, but it makes us stronger, better and more confident.

> **JAG Fact**
>
> *Colonel William Tudor was the first Judge Advocate General of the Army. The Second Continental Congress selected him in 1775. During the Revolutionary War, he served along with 15 other JAG Officers, including Captain John Marshall, who later became the Chief Justice of the U.S. Supreme Court.*

JAG officers graduate from law school and pass the bar exam only to take an oath, put on a uniform, and go back to school. At JAG school, young lawyers learn how to be "soldier/lawyers" through a diverse and rigorous academic and military training curriculum. One day JAG recruits might learn to shine their boots and salute, and the next they'll learn how to try a military case. While the curriculum is diverse, one aspect is predictable. Most days begin with a run before sunrise at "0-dark-thirty."

But, that was all behind me now, and here I was, a JAG. Walking next to me was a young female soldier in a starched green dress uniform (called "Class As") that she had not worn since her basic training graduation. Her uniform ribbons were tacked neatly on her uniform's lapel and her hair rested at the nape of her neck in a bulky bun. It was just above her collar as army regulations require, and the sun reflected in her shiny shoes.

I wanted to do right by her. I wanted to be "on my game" today. My mind methodically went through the opening statement, including the theme, pauses in the right place, and the correct pronunciation of her medical condition that Uncle Sam said made her unfit for duty. She was going through an Army Physical Evaluation Board (or PEB). Sometimes the board separated deserving soldiers without benefits. The army would stamp SWOB (Separated Without Benefits) on their separation paperwork. The JAGs in my office called that "getting swabbed."

As we walked along together, I looked up to see a lieutenant colonel coming towards us. We were at Walter Reed Army Medical Center (WRAMC), the largest hospital in the Department of Defense, and home to many military doctors and nurses. I was a new captain in a sea of higher-ranking officers, and I was accustomed to saluting my seniors. The shimmering silver oak leaves on her shoulder boards were unmistakable. My client and I both snapped a crisp salute and said predictably in unison "good morning, ma'am."

I noticed that my client's hand lingered self-consciously for a moment at her beret. The army had recently changed the uniform policy and now required all soldiers to wear the coveted "beret," which was otherwise reserved for airborne rangers. It was supposed to set us apart from our sister services, make us more streamlined, and raise all soldiers to the elite level of the airborne rangers—as if wearing spurs makes one a cowboy.

The army considered its new beret a "symbol of excellence." Many soldiers didn't see it that way. They found the beret awkward, and preferred its predecessor, the field cap, which was essentially a camouflaged baseball cap with a bill to shade the sun and repel the rain. It was more practical than the fancy French styled beret, which was very high-maintenance. The fussy beret required its soldier to dunk it in (warm) water, shape it, mold it, and even *shave* it, before it was ready to grace its soldier's head. The beret is so difficult to wear correctly that the Army required soldiers to take classes—yes *classes*—to learn how to wear the new headgear correctly. The army trainer called it "donning the beret." In simpler terms, we learned to put on our hats.

It turns out that our collective beret wearing heads were in the sand. While our highest military leaders debated the laurels of the field cap versus the beret, our terrorist enemies laughed at our western vanity, and waited for the right time to strike a deadly blow, and bring America to its knees.

"So ma'am," my client said, clearing her throat as we approached the steps of the U.S. Army Physical Disability Agency for her medical board hearing, "Do you think we're ready?" I responded as I always did. "Yep. We're ready." Then

I gave her a few last minute pointers as we walked up the stairs of the Physical Disability Agency. "Give them a crisp salute, make eye contact, speak slowly and listen to my questions," I said as I glanced up at the second-floor windows that overlooked the entrance. Two of the board members were standing at these windows, holding their coffee cups and talking to each other. They watched my client as we walked up the steps of the Physical Disability Agency. One turned to the other and said something, while the other nodded and brought his coffee to his lips with a crooked smile. I tried to instill confidence in my client. But, the truth is, anything could happen. Not a single board member was a lawyer or a judge, and their results varied so widely that sometimes I wondered if they flipped a coin during deliberations. They were as fussy as the berets they wore.

We entered the waiting room and started going through paperwork. The army has a form for everything. We talked casually as I filled out the required forms. When we finished, I scrolled the date *September 11, 2001* in the date-block, gathered the documents, and left my client waiting in the room while I went to consult the board members.

Although the board members are supposed to remain impartial and objective until they hear all of the evidence, the pre-hearing consultations were helpful because I could sense where their apprehension lay. During these informal sessions, board members would pose questions about my client's case, or even banter a bit about details in a soldier's medical records that they planned to raise during the hearing. Overall, their candor made my job easier and increased the likelihood that my client would prevail.

Sometimes the board members pressured me to waive the soldier's hearing and just accept the army's earlier decision. Eventually, they stopped pressuring me when they learned that, unless there were extenuating circumstances where it benefitted my client to accept the earlier rating, I would go forward with the hearing. Soldiers have a right to be heard, and I was their advocate. My soldier client was my first and only priority.

A few weeks earlier, I had a heated disagreement with members of the medical board, and it had strained our collegial relationship. My client had traveled from his duty station in Germany, and all of his medical records were written in German. None of the members, nor I, nor even my client could speak or read German. I asked to have the documents translated into English, and amazingly, the board denied my request. They thought it was sufficient to translate the medical records *themselves* during the hearing using an online translation program though "Google." At first, I thought they were kidding. But they weren't. I protested, and a standoff ensued.

The board president ordered me to proceed, and I refused until they arranged to have the documents translated into English. Finally, they grudgingly granted my request for a delay. One board member (a lieutenant colonel) was angry with me for several days. I felt bad about that. He even made a "coupon" for a "one-time visit with Doctor Kevorkian" on his computer and gave it to me. I didn't know whether to be insulted or to consider it the Infantryman's way of smoothing things over. I preferred the later interpretation, and hung the certificate in my office next to my porcelain pit-bull miniature that reminded me to be tough in this man's Army.

Medical board hearings aren't supposed to be adversarial—but they are. Disagreement is inevitable, and the law requires that I act in my client's best interest. "Sir, you know I'm just doing my job," I said when he gave me the Kevorkian "coupon." "I know, captain, I know," he responded. Although we settled the disagreement, tensions still ran high in the boardroom. Board members who sit on medical boards are not lawyers. Usually they are fair and reasonable, but sometimes they stray from their calling, which is to afford soldiers due process. What makes matters worse is that the army assigns brand new JAG officers to represent troops before these physical evaluation boards. Many young lieutenants and captains are swayed, if not bullied, by members of the board.

It wasn't until 2007, when the plight of combat-wounded troops shined a light on the underbelly of the medical board process that the military decided to pay attention to what really goes on in the board room. A committee of distinguished leaders, including former Senator Bob Dole, has recently recommended changes to the PEB process that are designed to bring fair, consistent decisions.[1]

One time, I experienced Washington power first hand. I was a new JAG Lieutenant, preparing a vigorous challenge in a complicated case with volumes, and volumes of medical records. Board members were extremely skeptical about the case, and had already signaled their intentions to issue a low disability rating. I faced the harsh reality that we would lose. Until, one afternoon a well-respected, widely known lawyer-turned-politician reached for the phone in his Washington, D.C. office and dialed my number. I picked up the phone and the voice on the other end said, "Hello. This is Bob Dole." He pronounced his name like "Baaaab Dole."

We never know when acts of kindness will boomerang back to us. But, somehow, they do. Former Senator Bob Dole had a debt of kindness to repay from decades earlier, and I would witness this debt be squared. My client was the daughter of someone Bob Dole considered an angel. She—the mother—

---

1. Memo for Secretaries of the Military Departments, Policy and Procedural Directive-Type Memorandum (DTM) for the Disability Evaluation System (DES) Pilot Program, Nov. 21, 2007.

had been Senator Dole's occupational therapist when he was a young soldier injured in World War II. She saw him through his darkest days of recovery, which formed a bond between them greater than words can express. When he learned that her daughter, my client, was a disabled soldier, he wanted to help.

In the weeks before my client's hearing, Senator Dole was available any time of the day through his friendly receptionist, Betty. A trained lawyer, he wanted to do whatever he could, and this young lawyer was grateful for his esteemed interest.

On the day of my client's board hearing, the board members, and everyone else at the Physical Disability Agency stood taller than usual. They held the hearing in an elegantly furnished room on the first floor that was reminiscent of rooms at the U.S. Capitol, instead of the usual cramped upstairs office where they held all other medical board hearings. An American flag was prominently displayed in the background. Senator Dole attended the entire hearing, offered me helpful pointers during the breaks, and even waited with my client while the board members deliberated. He spent the better part of a full work day either carefully observing the hearing, or helping me behind the scenes.

After a long hearing, and an hour of deliberating, the board rendered a fair decision and agreed that my client had legitimate disabilities. They granted her a full, permanent medical disability retirement. We couldn't have asked for a better outcome.

My client was happy—and so was Senator Dole. Before he left, I snapped some pictures with him in front of the Physical Disability Agency. My favorite picture, and one that hangs in my office to this day, is a picture of all four: my client, her mother, Senator Dole, and me. It holds a prominent place in my office—and my heart. We presented a great case that day, and I witnessed a touching bond between Senator Dole and his angel that had only grown deeper with time. However, I can't help but wonder whether Senator Dole's interest in the case, and presence that day, influenced the board's final decision. Maybe his presence embarrassed the board into doing what they knew was right— awarding this young female officer the disability rating that she deserved and that they fought ardently against.

But, this day—September 11th, 2001—was different. There wouldn't be any witty exchange, or banter, and there wouldn't be any distinguished guests or visitors. On this day, the board wouldn't call a single witness, or even set eyes on my client. For on this day, the blue sky above Washington and New York would turn a hazy gray, and the world would change, forever.

I walked into the boardroom, paperwork in hand and said, "Good morning, gentlemen" just as I had done every morning. All three members of the medical board were huddled around a television screen "Shhhhh" they said, one of them motioning, as I entered. "What's going on?" I asked as I looked beyond them to the TV screen at images of the smoldering World Trade Tower against a cloudless, blue, New York sky. I gasped in disbelief. We all watched in silence. Words scrolled along the bottom of the screen informing us that two planes had struck the World Trade Towers, and some early speculators believed it was a terrorist attack. Terrorists? I thought. What terrorists?

Moments later a news announcer interrupted the Trade Tower coverage to report "... This just in ... we have reports about another crash at the Pentagon ... that's the Pentagon in Arlington, Virginia near Washington, D.C. ..." We were speechless. The Pentagon was only a few miles away from where we stood.

The phone rang, and someone on the other end ordered evacuation. The board president abruptly hung up the phone, looked at me, and sharply said, "We're evacuating. Get your client and leave the building at the closest exit." "Yes, sir," I said, with one foot already out the door.

My high heels clicked across the tile floor as I rushed to the waiting room, and flung open the door. My client was looking out the window, and humming to herself—ahh—the bliss of not knowing. I did my best to explain as we rushed toward the stairwell and out of the building together. We said good-bye at the doorway and went our separate ways. "Sergeant," I called as she walked away, "Be careful." She looked back and replied with a parting salute, "I will. You too, ma'am." I never forget a face. But, to this day, I cannot remember hers or a single detail of her case, not one detail.

I rushed across the street to the Judge Advocate General (JAG) Law Office, but nobody was there. Lawyers had left books open on their desks, and one secretary's computer was still on, displaying the flying windows screen saver. It was quiet, and I was alone. It was strange and surreal. I keyed into my office and just stood there for a moment, not knowing what to do. Then I stepped back into the hallway and called, without expecting a response, "Hello ... is anybody here?" One of my colleagues, another army lawyer, emerged from his office and said, "Everyone is gone. The enlisted soldiers are guarding the doors and directing people." "OK, but what about the colonel? Where is he?" I inquired. "He's advising the commander in the TOC," he said. "What's the TOC?" I replied, with the curiosity of a naive young officer. "The Tactical Operations Cell—TOC—you know—in case of emergencies. All of the leaders are down there." "Oh" I said, "OK, I guess that's good. But what about us? What are we supposed to do?" He replied, "They're looking for blood-donors so I'm heading to the main hospital to do that. No way am I going out there on the road. It is jammed up, and will be for hours." Then he walked away, with one hand in his trouser pocket.

I stepped back into my office, and was startled to see a helicopter just outside my window preparing to land. I felt like Alice through the looking glass— my world had changed. Medical troops and personnel erected a large triage tent, and were on standby for casualties to arrive. What I didn't know is that Walter Reed didn't just *receive* Pentagon victims on 9-11—it *went for them*. Within an hour after the Pentagon attack, Walter Reed sent two buses to the Pentagon with doctors, nurses, enlisted medical specialists, and medical supplies. Walter Reed's ambulances were the first two on scene at the Pentagon.[2] In what seemed like minutes the army responded.

In search of order and predictability, we humans hunt for meaning to explain events. We find comfort in believing that things happen for a reason, and that a higher, all-knowing power orchestrates it all. If there was ever an instance of a higher power preparing us for tragedy, it is Walter Reed. Only a few weeks earlier, on August 27th 2001, an electrical transformer caught fire at Walter Reed Army Medical Center, causing a four-day massive power-outage that affected the entire hospital. During that time, doctors and nurses worked around the clock stabilizing, and transporting patients to civilian hospitals in the D.C. area. It was practice for September 11th, and Walter Reed was ready. One nurse later recalled, "A lot of procedures that we used in the September 11th tragedy, we had just come out of this power loss where we had implemented a lot of what we did. We had good procedures in place that we had already just executed. It was really eerie."[3]

Everyone was off doing something to support the emergency—and I didn't know what to do. I thought, "Maybe lawyers are supposed to just get out of the way." I made another sweep around the office to see if anyone else was still there, but everyone was gone. "What in the world is going on? Have we really been attacked?" I thought to myself in disbelief. "Who is doing this to us?"

I suddenly remembered that my friend of several years, who was a U.S. Naval Academy graduate, had scheduled a meeting at the Pentagon today. I immediately felt sick to my stomach, and my heart raced as I dialed his number. I said to myself, "God, no, God, please no." I couldn't get through. Hoping I was mistaken about the date, I raced through the pages of my day planner searching for any annotation to calm my worst fear. My search was in vain. I continued furiously dialing his number on both the cell and land-line telephone, to no avail.

---

2. See history.amedd.army.mil/memoirs/soldiers/walterreed.pdf. The document summarizes compiled interviews with Colonel Michael A. Dunn, Lieutenant Colonel Edward Lucci, Major General Harold Timboe, Colonel Larry Bolton, Captain Daniel McGill, and Ms. Shannon Publicover.

3. NURSEWEEK, 145–146 (Sept. 17, 2001).

Finally, after what seemed an eternity, it rang and he picked up the line. "Where are you?" we each exclaimed to the other. He was safe, at home. He hadn't been at the Pentagon. Someone had rescheduled his meeting. I was relieved. The very quadrant where his meeting would have been held was attacked. Later, some of his colleagues recall racing out of the building, with fire and smoke on their heels.

Just as I hung up the phone, it rang. The voice on the other end said, "Captain Miller, you're still there." It was my supervisor. "We're going to need you and a few other attorneys to counsel military families about imminent death processing. Can you do that?" My mind raced: 'Imminent death … imminent death … oh yeah. Family members of gravely ill soldiers complete that paperwork, when death is certain, so the army can medically retire their loved one. If it is done before the soldier dies, her family receives additional benefits.' "Sure, sir. I can do that." "Take your pager," he clipped and we hung up.

I kneeled on the floor in front of my bookcase, and fumbled through binders of legal resources looking for materials about imminent death processing, so that I would be ready. I finally found what I was looking for in a red binder. It was only after finding it that I remembered specifically putting it in a red binder so it would be obvious and on-hand in an emergency. In the confusion of the moment, my careful planning proved to be in vain.

Hours later, sometime in the late afternoon, I left work and drove the four miles home to my Bethesda apartment building, the Topaz House. The streets were an eerie calm, interrupted only by intermittent piercing sirens, miles away. There were hardly any cars on the road, or people on the sidewalk. Some radio stations were still on the air, and covering the events as they unfolded. There was some speculation about a potential terrorist attack, and warnings to get off the roads and stay inside.

I pulled my Mazda Miata around the corner, and into the parking garage. I noticed all of the empty parking spaces, and considered it a sign that many of my neighbors were at their office buildings, still travelling home, or stranded somewhere in between. As I walked through the garage, passing one empty space after the other, I couldn't help but wonder if any of my neighbors left that morning for the Pentagon, and were among those trapped inside. I thought about them, and their families, and everyone in uniform.

As if on autopilot, I climbed the stairs from my parking garage, entered the lobby, and walked toward my mailbox while fumbling around in my bag for the mailbox key. Tenants gathered around the mailboxes, talking in disbelief about what had happened and asking questions that nobody could answer. "Is it terrorists … and are we at war?" One resident, whom I had never officially met, but often saw at the mailboxes, posed a perceptive question that would still be asked years later, "Is it a crime, or an attack? Is this war?" I just said, "I don't know any more than you do, but it sure feels like an attack." I went to my apartment and, without taking off my uniform, collapsed on the couch, turned on the television, and watched in horror, along with the rest of the world.

Later that night, and for the next several days, I received calls from old friends, family members, and law school classmates. Everyone who knew I was a soldier in Washington, D.C. called that week. I regretted that it took a tragedy to reignite old friendships.

Like many people, I didn't sleep well in the nights after September 11th. CNN aired around the clock coverage of Ground Zero, and my mind replayed the images over and over, long after I turned the TV off. People at work lingered around the water coolers and break rooms sharing what they had heard on the news or read on the Internet. It seemed like everyone had a story about a narrow escape, or about someone still trapped below the rubble.

There were a lot of stories ending with, "If only...." One such incident involved a prominent lawyer and Fox news commentator, Barbara Olson. She was the wife of the Solicitor General, Theodore Olson, and she perished on flight 77 when it crashed into the Pentagon. She was travelling to Los Angeles for a taping of Bill Maher's talk show, *Politically Incorrect*. She was supposed to leave on September 10th. But, she decided to take a later flight so that she could have breakfast with her husband, Ted, on his 61st birthday. When her plane was hi-jacked, she made two cell phone calls to her husband Ted asking, "What can I do?" If only she had left on schedule, a day earlier ... if only....

On the night of September 14th, I finally shut off the TV, and went to bed. After tossing and turning for what seemed like forever, my mind finally surrendered to fatigue, released the horrific images of billowing smoke and twisted steel, and allowed sleep to come.

Suddenly, my phone rang, and I immediately sat up in bed. The digital clock turned to 3:02, and I knocked a glass of water off the nightstand as my fingers fumbled in the dark to find the phone. I picked up the receiver with a racing heart, and thought, "here we go," sensing that the caller would ask me to counsel a victim of 9-11 about imminent death benefits.

I cleared a sleepy throat, brought the receiver to my ear and said, "Captain Miller here." The voice at the other end hesitated, and then said with an unidentifiable accent "Sorry, wrong number." "That's OK, goodnight," I said, and exhaled in relief as I hung up the phone. I turned on the light, cleaned up my water spill, and then went back to bed, where I watched the digital clock progress minute by minute from 3:20 until 6:00. I shut off the alarm before it rang, took a shower, and went back to work.

My call was a wrong number. But other JAGs in the Washington, D.C. area received calls to counsel victims' families. I remember hearing about the wife of a Pentagon colonel who refused to medically retire her husband, even after doctors said he wouldn't make it, and JAGs who told her about important benefits her family would lose otherwise. Her husband was suffering unimaginably. Raging fire from the explosion had severely burned 75% of his body. The wife protested, saying, "He might live; he's strong; he could pull out of this." She remained firm and would not sign the paperwork. I never learned for certain what happened to that colonel, but I've heard that she was right, and that he survived.

Weeks before 9-11, someone burglarized the military I.D. card office at Walter Reed and made off with the machine that makes military picture identification cards. These cards allow their holder access to every military installation in the U.S., and abroad. There were no investigatory leads. In the days after the attack, when we learned that terrorists operated clandestinely in the U.S., waiting for the right moment to strike and bring down our buildings, we wondered whether they held military identification cards. Gate guards were on high alert for suspicious vehicles and drivers, and most cars and drivers went through rigorous, daily inspections. I left earlier each day, to account for delay at the gate.

All Americans, and many people around the world, have similar stories about how they experienced 9-11. My neighbor holed up in her apartment with her cat, Zoë, for days, watching CNN coverage with continued disbelief. Others recount feelings of abandonment as they tried to find a way home from work in what seemed like Armageddon; still others recall uniformed soldiers and police officers barking commands to herd masses of people and enforce what seemed like martial law. We all experience and remember things differently.

I offer my personal vignette as a backdrop to my book. I am an army lawyer and I mistakenly believed on 9-11 that lawyers should get out of the way during wartime. The Army JAG Corps has a motto: "Soldiers First, Lawyers Always." My experiences have taken me to Marine Corps training in Quantico, to the detention camp at Guantanamo Bay, to Private Jessica Lynch's hospital room, to an assignment with an elite investigatory team hunting terrorists around the world, and finally to the Military Commission prosecution team, building our government's cases against terrorists. "Soldiers First, Lawyers Always" is much more than just a motto. This book is set in the framework of my personal experiences stemming from 9-11. It provides substantive, inside analysis of some of the most pressing legal issues facing our country, and the way forward for bringing terrorists to justice in the aftermath of 9-11.

The pages that follow recount what I saw, and what I heard, and what I learned in the days, months, and years following 9-11.

CHAPTER TWO

Getting My Boots Muddy

Months later, I stood looking out the same office window where I had seen the hovering helicopter on 9-11. My phone receiver was to my ear, and I was on hold. The JAG Captain's Assignment Officer came on the line: "Captain Miller, you must have made a decision about your next assignment. What will it be?" We had been doing a dance for months concerning my next assignment. I would suggest something, and he would counter with something else. Round and round we went.

In the army, negotiating a new assignment is like buying a car. I wanted the best deal possible, and he wanted to offer just enough to keep me in my beret. I opened the negotiations with good old-fashioned honesty by requesting what I really wanted—another assignment in Washington, D.C. There was silence on the other end of the phone. Then he flatly said "No. But, I can send you to Korea for a one year tour along the DMZ (Demilitarized Zone)." Our positions could not have been further apart.

Most JAGs prefer a tour in Washington, D.C. These plum assignments are the army's ace cards, but the army reserves them to entice young law school graduates into the JAG Corps and away from high paying law firms. The JAG dealt me an ace card earlier, when it sent me to Walter Reed for my first assignment, and was not about to put another on the table. Leaving me in Washington, D.C. would not benefit the JAG Corps. Further, it would lessen my promotion potential. The JAG Corps wants diverse lawyers, with some experience in all areas of law. Their experience is vast and wide, but not very deep—like an oil slick on water. It was time to "pay my dues" either by doing a "hardship" tour somewhere remote and primitive, or by taking a tour on a gigantic military post with thousands of troops and a busy JAG office. It was time to repay the army for a comfortable tour at in the largest, most prestigious military hospital in beautiful Washington, D.C. (The grounds of Walter Reed resemble an Ivy League college campus more than a military base.)

I had considered assignments at all geographic points around the globe, including Korea, North Carolina, Texas, and Germany. I understood that I must pay my dues, but I was not remotely interested in any of my assignment choices.

None of them seemed like the right fit for me. Finally, I made a counter-offer that I was sure he would accept. "Well, Sir," I said, "I've heard that we're holding prisoners of war in Guantanamo Bay. That is where I want to go. JAGs are everywhere; they must be in Cuba too. Send me there." After a long pause, he asked, "Guantanamo Bay? You want to deploy to Gitmo, Captain?" He said, "But, you are just a medical JAG. Sorry, but your boots just aren't muddy enough for Gitmo. I've given you a few choices, and Gitmo just isn't in your cards." That seemed odd, and inconsistent with his earlier claim. Why were my boots muddy enough for a tour along the Demilitarized Zone (DMZ) in Korea, but not for one along a similar, much safer, fence line in Cuba?

After several phone calls, and intervention from leaders in my office, one week later I was on a bumpy bus-ride headed to Quantico, Virginia, for intense field training with Navy doctors and the Marine Corps. I was going into the woods to play war. The Marine Corps calls the training "Kirkesner," which is the name of a made-up country engaged in a pretend war.

Quantico is a Marine Corps base south of Washington, D.C., with miles of densely wooded hills and swampy ravines. It is only a few miles from Washington, but its landscape is so different from the capital city that it might as well be on the moon.

Before we boarded the bus, the instructors barked orders and searched our bags for "contraband." They confiscated extra food and drinks, portable Walkmans (iPods didn't exist yet), cell phones, and any other "comfort items" that weren't on the list it had distributed to us a few days earlier. They even took breath mints and gum from the pockets of military doctors in training. I wanted the assignment in Cuba, and was determined to get my boots muddy one way or another. After all, how bad can Kirkesner really be? I had no idea what was in store for me.

Sleeping on the ground and playing war made for a hard week. The first night was the worst. It was July, 2002, and D.C. was experiencing a persistent heat wave. Temperatures soared above 100 degrees. While I was sitting under a tree near the firing range waiting for my turn to fire the M16, my head started to pound. "Push the fluids, captain" a marine said to me. I drank several canteens of water, but it didn't seem to help. My headache just got worse and worse as the day wore on. By dinnertime, my head pounded, I felt dizzy and it hurt to blink my eyes. My stomach was so upset that I couldn't eat. So, I skipped dinner and headed for the medical tent. On the way, I stopped to vomit in the trees. I tried not to splash my boots.

"Ahh, well come on in. We've been waiting for you—our first customer," the doctor said with a smile, looking up from his magazine. He had a mop of brown hair, a friendly face, and a good sense of humor. I used a footstool to climb on top of the medical cot, and then I collapsed. It felt as comfortable as a king sized bed. He started an IV, and gave me something for a migraine headache. I remember looking up at him in a nauseous, medicated fog, just before drifting off to sleep, and thinking that he resembled Hawkeye, my favorite character from the MASH television series.

Around 3 a.m., I woke up and was sick again. Hawkeye said, "How about we send you home in the morning?" I wanted to go home ... but I also wanted to stay. I remembered what the Assignment Officer had said about getting my boots muddy. Vomit wouldn't do. I also remembered the supportive words from my supervisor,[1] a square-jawed, salt and pepper haired Army JAG Colonel and Vietnam veteran, who had obvious reservations about sending a young female JAG to the woods with a bunch of marines. He told me before I boarded the bus to Quantico that there was no shame in coming home early. "It will be hot down there in Quantico, and it's no big deal if you come home early. If you need us, just give me a call and we'll come down there and pick you up." I must have looked pathetic, all loaded down with military gear, wearing a helmet that jostled around when I walked, and carrying a bag so big that I could fit inside. I was a real life Private Benjamin—and I knew it. Going home early would just reinforce my own insecurities about being a pipsqueak in the army. I wasn't willing to let that happen.

As I lay on that cot, I thought about the strong women in my family, especially my sister. At nineteen years old, she was a mom, plodding through college classes, and working nights as a prison guard. What she lacked in stature, she made up for in might. She had trekked the harshest mountain passes in Wyoming, set records at the Police Academy, and generally served as the "man of the house" when we were girls and my dad was away working on oil rigs. Her hard work eventually paid off. She earned her college degree, then her master's degree, and she became a state political appointee at the Department of Corrections. Along the way, she ran a half way house for male sex offenders, where she once talked an inmate out of igniting his gas-soaked body with a match. Nobody got anything over on her. She is a self-made woman and the best big sister anyone could have.

Within a few hours, I started feeling better. I don't know if it was because I willed myself to recover, or because my body was saturated with a cocktail of migraine medications and saline. Whatever the reason, I decided to stay, and finish the training. The doctor released me from the medical tent around 6 a.m.

---

1. Every JAG Office has a supervising lawyer who is in charge of the office. Ordinarily it is a full Colonel, or a Lieutenant Colonel. Their title is "Staff Judge Advocate" or "SJA."

I brushed my teeth next to a tree with water from a plastic canteen, ran a wet-wipe over my face, and returned to training, regretting that I was the first "training casualty." It wasn't my fault, but I felt ashamed. I knew from representing soldiers in medical hearings that the army calls its wounded "broke soldiers." Nobody wants to be a broke soldier.

Speaking of "broke," I almost broke my glasses that week when enemy marines attacked my squad (a group of about ten soldiers) with tear gas while we simulated patrol in a wooded area. I saw a soldier in front of me make the hand-sign for "gas" and I immediately closed my eyes, held my breath, and felt around on my hip for my gas mask, while counting the seconds in my head. We're trained to don our gas masks in nine seconds or less, to lessen gas or chemical exposure. In the dark and with a racing heart, I pulled-off my eyeglasses and threw them to the ground. With my other hand, I found the Velcro closure of my gas mask bag and ripped it open. I pulled out my mask and used both hands to shove it vigorously over my head. Then I checked the seal.

"I'm OK. I got a seal, I got a good seal," I thought, as I slowly opened my eyes and exhaled. I looked down to find my eyeglasses lying on the ground, less than an inch from the crushing sole of my boot. "Don't want to break these," I thought as I held them awkwardly in the palm of a gloved-hand. I was clumsy, but I met the nine-second requirement. The smoky green fog welling up around me couldn't get inside. As I walked through the fog, I could hear myself breathing in my mask, in and out, in and out. The sound had an eerie Darth Vader quality.

A few soldiers weren't as lucky. They couldn't seal their masks, and ran through the woods trying to escape the noxious fog with their gas masks in hand, tears streaming down their faces, and mucus running from their noses. One soldier, who couldn't get his gas mask on, threw it on the ground and took off running and cursing. These soldiers coughed and fought the urge to wipe their faces. Doing so would only make it worse, because tear gas fumes covered their gloves. I followed my group to a safe area where we were relieved to see a marine waiting to hose us down. Finally, we received the "all clear" hand sign and took off our heavy, plastic masks. My hair was wet and matted with sweat, and it felt good to breathe unfiltered air. I put on my eyeglasses and felt back to normal. As I gulped water from the hose like a thirsty animal, I overheard another soldier explain that U.S. troops often wore complete chemical suits, including rubber shoes, gloves, and restrictive gas masks, for days on end during the first Gulf War. I could not imagine it.

The training was chaotic, and it seemed like we were always on our bellies, taking cover from simulated incoming fire or doing the "low crawl" over rocks and dirt to find cover and return fire. Each night in my tent, I took off my boots and attended to my blisters. One cardinal rule of soldiering is to keep your feet clean and dry. Foot powder is like precious gold to a soldier in the field. After the second day of training, I pulled my socks down to look at the blisters, and found black and blue bruises over both of my calves and knees. I took down my trousers to examine my thighs, and they too bruised. I was a complete mess.

The next day in training a simulated grenade exploded near me and I heard another soldier holler, "Incoming!" I crouched down, and covered my helmet with both arms, but did not sprawl on my belly as the marines taught me to do. My legs hurt from the bruises, and I didn't want to make them worse. One of the trainers was near me, observing the exercise, and barked above the blasts, "Captain, you are dead! Mortar just went through your helmet! When we say get down, we mean get down!" Nobody could cut corners at Kirkesner.

I remembered his command later that night when we set out to form a perimeter around our camp. We were supposed to find a spot with some trees and brush for cover, dig a hole, lie there with our weapons pointed out, and watch for the enemy. It was dark. I found a spot, dug my hole, and crammed my body into the earth. It was cool, and damp. I tried not to think about the critters that made their home in the wet earth beneath me, and I tried to ignore the sensation that they were crawling all over me. It was so quiet. Just then, I heard twigs crack under the sole of a soldier's boot. I couldn't see him, but I could sense him. He was right in front of me. I wanted to call out to him, but I didn't know if he was friend or foe. I held my breath, and let him pass.

Then it was quiet ... so quiet. I strained to hear anyone. But, I could not. I could not hear, or see anything. After what seemed like forever, I reached one arm out to the right and whispered softly, "Is anybody there?" but nobody answered. I laid there, breathing, watching the darkness, and waiting, for what seemed like hours. I wondered what time it was.

Then I heard somebody's wristwatch go "beep-beep." Seconds later, shots erupted all around me. Later, the marines lectured our platoon about the dangers of wearing digital watches into combat. The soldier with the beeping watch gave away our position. (The upside is that it cut the exercise short. Otherwise, we could have been out there all night, facing off against our enemy, who was facing off against us, in blind silence.)

The rest of the week was more of the same: running, taking cover, returning fire, learning to exit tactical vehicles, and learning to operate a satellite radio (which is a giant, heavy contraption that the radio operator hauls around on his back). By the end of the week, I was exhausted.

"Stand tall," I thought to myself during an awards ceremony. I looked down at my five-foot shadow cast along the dusty field outside of Combat Town, an urban warfare-training site hidden in the dense woods around Quantico, Virginia. I focused on the American flag as another officer carried it to the front of formation. I shifted my weight from one foot to the other, trying to be inconspicuous. The sling on my M16 was digging into my shoulder and the barrel rested at the back of my knee. That's not how it is supposed to fit, but most soldiers are taller. I recalled the army JAG Corps motto that I first heard several years earlier when I was a law student intern, "The Pen is Mightier than the Sword." I was proud to be an army lawyer—but glad that I did not make a living in the field.

The trainers called our squad leader to the front of the formation. Our squad of ten had earned another ribbon for outstanding soldiering. We had performed heroically in the combat town, and we were the only squad to find the downed pilot.

The combat town exercise was near the end of the training. It was the final exercise and we were supposed to apply all of the skills we learned that week. They hauled us by the truckload to a dusty, abandoned "town" that consisted of empty concrete buildings. In the woods outside of combat town, we painted our faces with camouflage paint and looked over crude maps of the town. We planned our strategy for "clearing" the town of our enemies while we loaded our weapons and our pockets with ammunition. Our squad leader called us into a tight circle and briefed us about the suspected location of the dummy. He put an "X" on the map to mark the spot.

The trainers warned, "Keep your head about you. If you see the sign for gas, reach for your masks and get them on. Remember, you get nine seconds and that is it—only nine seconds to save yourselves if the enemy attacks with gas." I gulped and practiced ripping open the Velcro closure on my gas mask. I hoped the enemy would not use gas. Then, we attacked.

We lined up outside of the first building and followed our lead soldier, who gave us the sign to enter. We went from building to building, encountering "enemies" hiding inside. They shot at us, and we shot back. Soldiers called "hooah" in a guttural yell, green smoke welled up around us, and grenades exploded, punctuated by the "tut-tut-tut" sound of our weapons. We went from one building the next; sweat rolled down my face and stung my eyes. My heard pounded wildly. Somewhere in combat town, fantasy and reality collided and I found myself transported to a street somewhere in Baghdad. The training became real, my instincts took over, and I felt real fear and a real desire to survive. Soldiers either fight or flee. This time, I fought.

"Captain," the trainer called to me, "Your turn to take the lead." I was hoping we would finish the exercise before they called on me. But I wasn't so fortunate. I ran to the front of the line and assumed leadership, telling myself it would all be over soon. I signaled to my troops that we should enter the building. I heard the familiar "tut-tut-tut" of a soldier's weapon. There was more yelling and more smoke.

We went up the stairs with our backs to the wall. Soldiers in the front pointed their weapons up the stairs, those in the middle pointed their weapons out, and those in the back of the line pointed their weapons down the stairs. We worked as a unit, guarding our fellow soldiers and ourselves. We went from one room to the next, sweeping the area, clearing the building, and killing the enemy. "All clear," I would yell as we left one room and went to the next.

Just then, an enemy soldier hiding in a closet pointed the barrel of his weapon at me. I was in his sites. I turned, and with an angry yawp, I aimed my weapon at him and pulled the trigger. In a real situation, I would probably be dead. He surprised me. In an instant, he was there. I was his prey. It was a kill or be killed situation.

My squad[2] made it to the furthest room in the building, and there in the middle of the room was the 180-pound "downed-pilot" that we were supposed to rescue. We found him, and it was our duty to get him out safely. Another soldier and I rushed to the pilot, and my companion yelled, "Get a litter, let's get him out of here."

Somebody brought a litter (a stretcher with handles at both ends so that two soldiers can carry an injured soldier). We rolled the dummy onto it and hauled him out of the building. I didn't anticipate that it would be so heavy. To simulate combat, the military designs realistic dummies that are around six feet tall and weigh about 180 pounds. I struggled, but together we managed to lift the litter and shuffle to the door. At the doorway, I looked outside and didn't see the enemy. Then I hollered in a voice louder than I knew existed inside of me, "Go! Let's go!"

We ran, hauling the litter between us as shots fired and smoke filled the air. Another soldier saw me struggling and ran to help with the front of the litter. Together we ran toward the wood line. My feet were heavy, and my equipment bounced. I wanted to run further, faster, lighter. But I couldn't go any faster. I struggled. We grunted and yelled as we ran through the rocks and the ruts, and the smoke and the fog to the wood line. I tripped and almost fell, but caught my balance and kept going.

My ill-fitting Kevlar helmet bounced around on my head and against my neck as I struggled to carry the litter. "Oh man," I thought, "this seems so real ... just get to the trees." I held tight to my end of the litter and ran as fast as my heavy legs would carry me. A few troops stood at the wood line motioning and scream-

---

2. About ten soldiers compose a squad, with one person in charge, called the "squad leader."

ing to us, "Come on! Hurry it up! Come on! You can do it!" Then I heard the words, "Bring him home! Bring him home!" I ran harder and faster.

To me, it was real. I was in Iraq, the enemy was firing at us, and I was using every bit of my strength to save myself and rescue the pilot. "Go, go, go!" I said repeatedly to myself. We made it to the wood-line and I collapsed. Someone said, "Good job, soldiers," as the doctors went to work administering CPR on the wounded (dummy) aviator.

I felt hot, sticky, and dehydrated. Major With, another JAG officer who worked in my office at Walter Reed and who had finagled my spot at the training, emerged from the smoke-filled combat town with smiling eyes and her camera in hand. I didn't even know she was there. She exclaimed, "Captain Miller, I can't believe your squad found the pilot! I've got it on camera, I got the picture." I looked up, adjusted my Kevlar helmet and said sarcastically, "Kind of a miracle, huh?" "Take the Kevlar off," she said, patting me on the back. "Oh yeah," I replied, tugging at the frayed chinstrap.

I felt a little overwhelmed, and I was embarrassed about it. I put my head down, and I felt tears welling up in my eyes. I took a deep breath and I told myself, "It wasn't real. It wasn't real. This is all just a game."

I looked up at Major With. She looked good—freshly showered—and I envied her. I wanted to jump into her Suburban and ride away from here—back to reality in D.C. I was tired of playing war games. It was a little too real.

> **JAG Fact**
>
> *The Army Commissioned Officer Ranks begin with the lowest rank of Second Lieutenant (O–1). The next level is First Lieutenant (O–2), then Captain (O–3), then Major (O–4), then Lieutenant Colonel (O–5), Colonel (O–6) and then there are four levels of General Officers.*

I admired Major With. She was a young Army JAG officer who had deployed all over the world, including a tour in Haiti. Service ribbons galore adorned her uniform. It was the most ribbons I had ever seen on one uniform. I respected her service and leadership. She is what we call in the army, "Hooah." She was a major, but she had more "field experience" than do most colonels. As a captain, she had deployed to Haiti and participated in "Uphold Democracy."[3] Soldiers respect that kind of

---

3. Frederick L. Borch, Judge Advocates in Combat, at 254, (Office of the Judge Advocate General and Center of Military History United States Army, 2001), featuring Major (then Captain) With and including a picture of her at Nos Petits Freres et Soeurs, a Haitian orphanage, in February 1995. The text states, "On the last day of March 1995, as Uphold Democracy ended, Captain With remained in Port-au-Prince—the only judge advocate with the Multinational Force to exchange her battle dress uniform cap for a blue beret."

experience, because it comes the hard way, with sweat and sacrifice. You can't learn to be a soldier inside a classroom.

Major With had traveled from the JAG office at Walter Reed in Washington, D.C. all the way to Quantico for a day of training, just to be supportive. Before I went to Kirkesner, she taught me to stuff a duffle bag and made sure my first aid kit was in order. "Don't forget your hundred-mile-an-hour tape," she told me, referring to duct tape. In Major With I found a friend and a mentor.

I had struggled all week. I had stomped through a muddy swamp at night, lost and tapping on a compass I thought was broken; underwent two embarrassing tick retractions; and dangled on the wrong side of a wall, while the others continued. Thankfully, my "battle buddy" realized I wasn't with them and turned back. He found me with one foot over the wall, struggling to pull myself over. He reached down, grabbed the front of my t-shirt, and lifted me over the wall like puppy dangling from its mother's mouth.

Later that night, after going through the chow line, I spotted my battle buddy sitting on a dirty tree stump, balancing his dinner plate on his knee. "Hey, thanks for helping me with the obstacle course. Getting over that wall is much harder than it looks." "No problem," he said with a shrug. "Someone said you're a JAG lawyer, is that right?" "Yep. That's right." I said, as I swept the ground with the sole of my combat boot for a place to sit down. "Well, what are ya' doin' out here with us?" he asked. "Oh, it's a long story, but basically I want to deploy to Guantanamo Bay so I'm here to prove that I can ... well ... handle it," I said. "Oh, I see ... you'll be fine," he said. His comment was generous, considering that he had hauled me over a brick wall only hours before.

Then we each pushed the food around on our plates in silence, until he asked, "So, what's the deal with those people the military is holding in Guantanamo Bay anyway?" I responded, "Well, I've heard that the military has built a real brick and mortar prison with cells in Guantanamo Bay. So they're moving all of the detainees from the chain-link cells where they've been holding them the last few months to the new facilities." "A real prison, huh? Sounds like the military is planning to keep them for a while." "Yep. Probably so," I said. "It has been a long time since the United States has held prisoners of war, but according to the Geneva Conventions, which are the rules that parties must follow during a war, the military can hold them until the war is over." "That could be a while," he said. "Yep. Sure could," I responded, taking a drink from my canteen.

I went on, "A few months ago the president declared that detainees in Guantanamo Bay are not POWs. He requires the military to treat them 'humanely' and in a manner 'consistent with principles of the Geneva Conventions.'[4] "So," he asked, "does that mean that the military can do whatever it wants to the detainees? Can they treat detainees like the Viet Cong treated our soldiers during Vietnam?" "Nope," I said. I reached for a stick that was nearby and drew two horizontal, parallel lines in the dirt. "This line on the bottom represents the humane standard. Soldiers can't do anything to a detainee that falls below this line. That means they can't torture detainees. They can't starve them or deny them water, or beat them, or do other sadistic things. The United States must treat the detainees humanely."

Then, I pointed to the second line, above the first. "This line represents the way the United States, and other signatories to the Geneva Conventions, must treat POWs. If humane treatment is the floor, then this line represents the ceiling. (But you can always go above the ceiling and give POWs more rights.) Under the Geneva Conventions, POWs receive a lot of rights and privileges. For example, the countries detaining POWs must allow them to work and must even pay them in Swiss Francs. There is even a worker's compensation program, so that POWs receive pensions if they are injured or sick and unable to work. The detaining power must provide a camp canteen for POWs, which is a convenient store where they can buy things. POWs are only required to provide their name, rank and serial number. The detaining power can't even selectively reward POWs who voluntarily provide helpful intelligence."

He responded, "I saw on TV a few weeks ago that some detainees like Big Mac Hamburgers from McDonald's. Are you saying that soldiers could not use hamburgers to entice detainees to talk if we call the detainees POWs?" "That's exactly what I'm saying." I went on with the analogy. "The United States can give detainees some Geneva Convention privileges and withhold others that interfere with military necessity." I waved the stick over the two parallel lines, and continued. "Anything between these two lines is permissible. The military could even grant more rights than POWs receive—but it can never go below this bottom line and treat detainees inhumanely." "Seems fair to me," he said "especially with Bin Laden still on the loose." But, what does it mean to treat somebody humanely? Where does humane treatment end and torture begin? These are questions we two soldiers could not answer in the Quantico woods, and questions that the United States has yet to answer.

---

4. Memorandum from Secretary of Defense Donald Rumsfeld to the Chairman of the Joint Chiefs of Staff, 19 January 2002, classified Secret. The Military declassified the memo and released it per DoD General Council Memo. It and other documents released by DoD are available at http://www.defenselink.mil/releases/2004/nr20040622-0930.html.

Without a clear definition of "torture" it means nothing when the United States claims it doesn't torture detainees. What is torture? Is sleep deprivation torture? Is it torture to deny Muslim detainees time to pray? Is it torture to require a detainee to stand for a few hours at a time? And what about more extreme measures, like water-boarding (a tactic that simulates drowning)? Where does torture start? Even after the inhumane acts at Abu Ghraib, the United States still failed to define torture.

In fact, as late as January 2007, leading JAG officers described the anti-torture "standard" to soldiers by using the golden rule, e.g., "If you wouldn't want it done to your buddy, then don't do it to somebody else." But that is hardly a clear standard because it is entirely subjective. Eventually, the U.S. government criticized a few soldiers for supposedly mistreating detainees in Guantanamo Bay. This mistreatment included a female interrogator sitting briefly on a detainee's lap and putting her hands through his hair. What U.S. soldier would think such a measure is torture?

Then there was silence. I threw my stick behind a rock, and he picked at a callous on his thumb. "I was an Army Ranger, so I've been in the field a lot. Would you like some more pointers?" he asked. "Sure would," I said. "As you have probably observed, I need all the help I can get." Then he told me many useful things about working in the field, including how to "get down" without getting so many bruises (a skill I still cannot master). He concluded by saying "And finally, don't wear underwear under your uniform." That statement caught my attention. "Did you say *no underwear*?" I asked, emphasizing each syllable. "Yep. They're bacteria traps. Just keep clean with wet wipes and dry with baby powder." I thought it was disgusting, but said "interesting" and popped a lime-flavored Skittle into my mouth.

> **JAG Fact**
>
> *"Army Rangers" complete an intense and competitive course at Fort Benning, Georgia. If they finish the course, they wear an insignia on their uniform called a "Ranger Tab" and call themselves "Rangers." Rangers are part of the Army's "Special Forces." Their mission includes reconnaissance, unconventional warfare, and counterterrorism. They often deploy around the world to teach military and paramilitary forces of foreign countries.*

Then we said goodnight and lugged our M16s back to our tents. I lay on the ground in my sleeping bag and thought about our conversation. I wondered if soldiers really know what it means to treat detainees humanely. Maybe the military has drafted some guidelines. Surely, I thought, when I get to Guantanamo Bay, I'll learn more about these issues. I wondered if I would come face to face with detainees and I wondered what they would think of me. I wondered how they would react to a female soldier. I tried to imagine what it must be like to be a woman in a Muslim country, where women have almost no rights and the law regards them as little more than property. I could not imagine it. Sleep came easily that night.

The next morning, standing in formation, only minutes from the comfort of an air-conditioned bus, I was grateful for the experience, but glad to be going home. I looked down at my boots—and they were muddy. I chuckled to myself, "I sure hope that assignments officer makes good on his promise."

The training in Quantico was my first and only intensive field training experience in the army. For me, it put the "Soldier" in the "Soldiers First, Lawyers Always" JAG Corps motto.

Aside from gaining immense respect for field soldiers, I learned some important lessons that week. Sometimes the road is bumpy; sometimes we must take a detour to get where we really want to go; and occasionally we need a stronger soldier to pull us over the wall.

This is in Combat Town at Quantico. I am the one in the middle, running from one building to the next through green, simulated grenade smoke.

Here I am at Quantico about to enter "City Hall," where we thought the enemy was hiding.

I am on the left front of the litter, carrying the downed pilot to safety. Ours was the only team to find the downed pilot during the Combat Town exercise.

We three soldiers struggle to move the downed pilot to safety. The pilot dummy weighed approximately 180 pounds. The soldier in the background returned fire for us.

This is a picture of Major Catherine With, the Deputy Staff Judge Advocate at Walter Reed Army Medical Center, who arranged my training in Quantico and came to observe the combat town exercise. In Major With I found a friend and mentor. Someone once described Major With as having "an extra scoop of hooah."

Lawyers from Walter Reed's JAG Office pose at Quantico with Combat Town and tactical vehicles in the background. Left to Right, Captain Jason Barocas, Major Catherine With, Captain Kyndra Miller (Rotunda), and Captain Andrew Tobman. Captains Barocas and Tobman attended training at Quantico, too. They were assigned to a different squad.

CHAPTER THREE

Young JAGs Go Head to Head

It was a pleasant August afternoon and fall was already settling in to the hills and tree-lined roads along Interstate 66, just outside Washington, D.C. I drove with the convertible top down past the Manassas Civil War Battlefield toward Charlottesville, Virginia, tapping the steering wheel to the beat of my favorite country tunes, with the autumn wind whipping. I was on my way to the army JAG School, which shares a campus with the University of Virginia Law School. It is an accredited law school and the only accredited law school within the Department of Defense. For that reason, JAG officers from all branches of the military take courses at the army JAG School.

> **JAG Fact**
>
> *Army JAGs existed since 1775, but the Army did not offer specialized training for them until February 1942 — the beginning of World War II. At first, the JAG school was temporary and changed location several times. In 1951, the Army decided on a permanent JAG School. At first, it shared facilities with the University of Virginia School of Law. In 1975, the school moved to its own facility next door.*

I pulled into the circle drive of the JAG school. The American flag was at full mast, waving her colors. I had been there many times before. After graduating from law school and passing the bar exam, JAG officers begin their army career by studying military law for several months at the U.S. Army JAG School, where more experienced officers affectionately call them "Baby JAGs." The army calls this required training the "JAG Officer Basic Course" and it lasts about four months. During that training, the army assigned us each to a squad of ten other JAGs. I was in the "Fourth Squad," where I was the only female. We named ourselves the "Fighting Fourth," although most of our "fighting" occurred in a classroom. Eventually, the army JAG School changed its course curriculum to entail more field training in order to prepare new JAGs for wartime realities and the likelihood of deployment. It added an additional two months of officer training, which includes at least six weeks at a deployed location. The army's new robust training requirements may help air force JAG recruitment.

Aside from the JAG Officer Basic Course, the school offers various refresher courses throughout the year that JAGs can attend. This time, I was on my way to the Law of War class. My boots were muddy, but now I had to learn the Law of War so that I would be useful in Guantanamo Bay.

Beginning in the early days of the Afghanistan War, news reporters and pundits resurrected terms like "Prisoners of War" and "Rules of Engagement" without clearly grasping their meaning, or understanding their origin. No one source contains the full body of laws that govern war, but many exist in treaties, or other

> **JAG Fact**
>
> *Law of War principles include:*
> *Military Necessity*
> *Humanity*
> *Proportionality*
> *Distinction*

agreements between nations. Some of the "rules" aren't written down anywhere. They're just basic standards that are generally accepted around the world. These unwritten rules we call "customary international law."

Laws of War govern when a nation can use force against another and what restraints apply to waging war. During war, soldiers must adhere to four basic principles. They are military necessity, humanity, proportionality, and distinction.[1] These rules minimize civilian deaths.

The doctrine of military necessity helps soldiers decide what targets they can attack. Appropriate targets are those that offer a definite military advantage, such as enemy tanks, terrorist training camps, or weapon factories. Innocent civilians in shopping malls and children at school are not appropriate targets. U.S. troops follow this rule, but our terrorist enemies do not. Instead, they send suicide bombers to where civilians are gathered.

The principle of humanity governs the type of weapons soldiers can use. Soldiers cannot use "arms, projectiles or materials calculated to cause unnecessary suffering."[2] Soldiers must use their issued weapons as the army trains them to do. The United States follows this rule. Our terrorist enemies do not. They often fill suicide vests with BBs, shards of glass, and even razor blades that gruesomely maim and kill their victims.

The third law of war principle is proportionality. Soldiers weigh loss of life and property damage against military advantage before they attack. The United States

---

1. Army Field Manual No. 27-10, *The Law of Land and Warfare*, Department of the Army, Washington, D.C. 18 July 1956 (amended on 15 July 1976). See paragraph 3 for the four basic principles.

2. The Hague Convention IV, Convention Respecting the Laws and Customs of War on Land, 18 October 1997, art. 23(e). See also Army Field Manual No. 27-10 *The Law of Land and Warfare*, Department of the Army, Washington, D.C. 18 July 1965 (amended on 15 July 1976).

will not kill many people only to gain a slight military advantage. The U.S. follows this principle, and our terrorist enemies do not. They seek to kill innocent civilians and "infidels" without a clearly defined military advantage. Instead, they kill in order to die a martyr and earn seventy-two virgins in their after-life.

Under the principle of distinction, soldiers must distinguish the enemy from civilians. The U.S. does not attack civilians, and our terrorist enemies do. Terrorist bury explosive devices that detonate indiscriminately when a person steps on them or a car rolls over them. Terrorists use this method, but U.S. soldiers do not.

Terrorists also use booby-traps that violate distinction principles because they kill or injure anyone who disturbs these otherwise harmless-appearing objects, like a dead bodies or even children's toys. In one incident, during the current war in Iraq, U.S. Marines approached what they believed was an injured Iraqi in Fallujah. As they approached to help him, his booby-trapped body exploded, killing one Marine and seriously injuring others.[3]

The Laws of War protect certain items against attack, including ambulances, medical helicopters and medical planes. Military forces paint "Red Cross" or "Red Crescent" symbols on these protected items to keep the enemy from attacking. U.S. soldiers follow this rule. Our terrorist enemies do not. They hide their weapons in mosques and hospitals, and take advantage of law-abiding U.S. soldiers. Under the rule, an otherwise protected place loses protection if it is misused. Therefore, when terrorists fire on soldiers from mosques under the law, soldiers can return fire, though they often don't. One commander of the 101st Airborne Division explained that it was "difficult to continue to target the enemy" that hid in the mosque, and came out to fire on U.S. troops. Though attacked from inside mosques, the commander explained that part of the mission was "protecting the most holy site here in the Middle East. We, and all my soldiers are very, very sensitive to the fact that this is an extremely sensitive site."[4]

The Law of War also governs treatment of wounded and captured soldiers. A significant stepping-stone in the Law of War occurred in 1859, when the sight of thousands of injured and dying soldiers on the battlefield at Solferino, Italy, so disturbed Swiss executive Henry Dunant that he summoned local residents to help the victims. He later published a book recounting the atrocities, and urging countries to adopt an international agreement designating how opposing sides should treat battlefield victims. From there, he established the

---

3. The O'Reilly Factor, *The True Story about the Fight in Fallujah*, Nov. 16, 2004. Available at http://www.foxnews.com/story/0,2933,138722,00.

4. *On Patrol with the 101st Airborne*, CNN Live on Location, Apr. 1, 2003. Available at http://transcripts.cnn.com/TRANSCRIPTS/0304/lol.04.html.

"International Committee for Relief to the Wounded," which eventually became the "International Committee of the Red Cross (ICRC)." (The Red Cross Organization that helps with disaster relief and sponsors blood drives is not the same organization as the International Committee for the Red Cross, though the two are often confused).

Under Dunant, The International Committee for Relief to the Wounded drafted a treaty entitled the "Geneva Convention for the Amelioration of the Condition of the Wounded in Armies in the Field." In 1864, the Swiss Government convened a conference in Geneva, and twelve governments adopted the convention.

After the atrocities of World War II, Geneva hosted another conference, and after months of deliberation, participating nations adopted the Four Geneva Conventions of 1949. Each Convention protects a different category of people. The first addresses wounded and sick members of the armed forces; the second addresses wounded, sick, and shipwrecked members of the armed forces at sea; the third protects prisoners of war; and the fourth protects civilians in times of war. Essentially, the Geneva Conventions set forth guidelines for treating certain categories of people on the battlefield, and the International Committee of the Red Cross (ICRC) works to ensure that countries follow these conventions.

I enjoyed all of the lectures that week at the Law of War Course. However, the most interesting and relevant lecture was one by an ICRC delegate. The JAG Corps invited her to teach a block of instruction at the Law of War Course, and to answer questions about the ICRC.

She moved slowly to the front of the classroom, maneuvering her pregnant belly through the aisles and down the steps of the amphitheater style classroom. A soldier walked behind her distributing small booklets entitled "Getting to know the ICRC." On the cover was a large color photograph of a waving ICRC flag, and an African child in the foreground. Using the booklet as a prop, she explained that ICRC delegates visit more than 100,000 detainees every year in over fifty countries around the globe.

She told stories about her personal experiences assisting detainees held by their captors in deplorable, diseased, and often isolated prisons around the world. With a French sounding accent she explained, "Sometimes there is nothing we can do. We can only encourage captors to follow the Geneva Conventions and treat prisoners humanely. We're less concerned about the countries who work with us, because usually they intend to abide by the conventions. Those countries who lock us out and deny prisoners an opportunity to meet with us are usually the greatest human rights violators."

At the end of her lecture, a student asked whether the ICRC was in Guantanamo Bay and if the camp complied with the Geneva Conventions. She responded along the lines of, "Yes, we do have delegates that travel to Guantanamo

Bay regularly. However, our conversations with every country that holds detainees are completely confidential, so I cannot share any details with this group. However, we are working very closely with the United States and generally maintain a very good and productive working relationship." (Later, the ICRC violated its own confidentiality rules by alleging that conditions at the detention camp in Guantanamo Bay were "tantamount to torture.")

ICRC delegates are committed to international humanitarian work that often takes them to dangerous and remote countries around the world. Occasionally, they are caught in the fray, captured, and even killed. Indisputably, their mission is a noble one. However, one can't help but speculate about their silence during the Vietnam War. Vietnam War veterans, who languished for years in Vietnamese prisons and fell victim to brutal torture from the Vietnamese, wonder, "Where was the ICRC back then?" Why did the ICRC remain on the sidelines when Vietnam committed flagrant human rights abuses against captured U.S. troops? The ICRC has never explained why it was silent while U.S. soldiers suffered at the hands of a brutal enemy in the jungles of Vietnam. It seems to pretend that the Vietnam War never happened.

These lectures, the war in Afghanistan, and the U.S. detention camp in Guantanamo Bay provided fodder for scintillating conversations among the students that carried over from class to dinner discussions. "I just don't see why the Geneva Conventions don't apply to the Taliban," an officer said, reaching across the dinner table for the breadbasket. "The country of Afghanistan signed the Geneva Conventions, just like the United States. Why does President Bush get to decide that they're not POWs?" The one-year anniversary of September 11th was a few weeks away, and already young JAG Officers were planting seeds for larger debates in the classrooms and taverns around Charlottesville.

Another square-jawed officer responded, "The analysis doesn't stop there. The Geneva Conventions say that only combatants who wear distinctive uniforms, carry their arms openly, and follow the laws of war can be POWs. Terrorists do the opposite. They operate in the shadows, and dress like civilians. They violate every Law of War rule. They fight from mosques and target innocent civilians. Our soldiers wear their uniforms like bulls-eyes and follow the Laws of War. Terrorists shouldn't benefit by their willful disregard for the Rules of Law."

The two officers continued the debate, and others around the table joined in the discussion that lasted late into the evening. The debate was colorful. Officers bolstered their arguments with hypothetical scenarios and quotations from the Geneva Conventions uttered over foamy mugs of beer. We hadn't reached a consensus that night when the server brought our change and put the closed sign in the window. Many issues we raised around that table would eventually reach the United States Supreme Court, and justices would discuss them around a much different kind of table.

In a nutshell, the Supreme Court would ultimately decide that the United States can hold detainees in Guantanamo Bay until the end of the war. It also said that detainees *who are United States citizens* should receive a "status hearing" where a "competent tribunal" would decide whether they are enemy combatants. The Supreme Court said the purpose of this hearing is to ensure that the U.S. doesn't mistakenly capture and hold the errant tourist or embedded journalist. The Supreme Court decisions were narrow. That is, only U.S. citizen detainees were entitled to such a hearing. But, the United States military went one step further by giving every detainee held in Guantanamo Bay (Taliban and Al Qaeda[5] alike) a status hearing to determine whether each is an enemy combatant.

---

5. I use the term "Al Qaeda" throughout the book. There are many different spellings when we translate the Arabic alphabet into Latin, including "Al Qaida." I am using the spelling most often used by the print media, but all are acceptable spellings. In instances where a source that I cite uses a different spelling, I have left the quote intact, using whatever spelling the original authority used.

This is a picture of me with some JAG School classmates during the JAG Officer Basic Course. We were in the Fourth Squad, so we called ourselves the "Fighting Fourth," which is why we held up four fingers. I was the only female in my squad.

CHAPTER FOUR

"Follow Me" to Fort Benning

After training with the Marines in Quantico, Virginia, and learning about the Laws of War at the JAG School, my muddy boots were ready to hit the ground in Guantanamo Bay. I had resumed working at Walter Reed Army Medical Center, in Washington, D.C. while I waited for the army's written "orders" directing me to deploy.

Anyone who has been in the army knows about waiting on orders. The army expression "hurry up and wait" definitely applies when it comes to orders assigning a soldier from one place to another. A story circulates around the army (maybe it is apocryphal) about a soldier during the Vietnam War whom the army told to return home and await orders. He did that, and called the army several times when the orders never arrived. Weeks turned into months, and months turned into years. He continued contacting the army, and each time they told him to "wait on orders." He waited, and waited.

Finally, while waiting, he reached retirement eligibility and submitted his application for retirement. The army protested, on grounds that he never served, and only waited. Ultimately, the military granted him retirement because he followed orders. He did what the army had told him to do—await further orders. We all secretly hope the army will repeat that mistake, and eventually it will.

But, not this time. After waiting for several weeks, the orders finally came. However, they specified that I should travel to another army post, Fort Benning, Georgia, for more field training before continuing on to Guantanamo Bay. Fort Benning is located near Columbus, Georgia, and it is where most U.S. soldiers received basic training before deploying during World War II. Today it is the largest U.S. Army post dedicated to training soldiers, and home of the army's Infantry (foot soldier) School. The school's motto is "Follow Me." That is because effective leaders usually lead their troops from the front.

I underwent another week of soldier training in the woods of Fort Benning at a military camp called the "Continental United States Replacement Center" or "CRC." The CRC trains soldiers to deploy to overseas combat mission and accounts for them when they return from deployment. The camp is a dynamic mixture of soldiers getting ready to leave the U.S. for combat and those who just returned.

For some, it is a purgatory, and stands between soldiers and home. I met one of these soldiers over dinner at the chow hall. While scanning the small, crowded cafeteria for a place to sit down he called, "Ma'am, there's a spot here," and motioned to an empty seat at his table. I thanked him, and sat down. "It's always like this around dinner time," he said.

Then he looked down at my plate, "So, looks like you're giving the apple pie a try. Well, there is an ice-cream machine over there and you can make it à la mode. I think it tastes better that way." With a chuckle, I said, "you sure seem to know a lot about this chow hall. How long have you been here at the CRC?" He explained that he had been at the CRC for many days. He had returned from a deployment overseas and was waiting to catch a flight home to Boston. "I'm real anxious to get back home. I've got a baby boy I've never seen and I sure can't wait to hold the little guy." Then he pulled a picture of a wrinkled baby from his wallet and handed it across the table for me to see. "They're a little slow around here. I can't complain though, I'm just glad to be back on American soil. I'll talk to them again tomorrow about getting me home. I sure hope they hurry it up." I studied his expression. He had honest eyes.

Every day he rolled out of his bunk, and asked the trainers if today he would fly home to Boston. Each day their response was the same, "maybe tomorrow," and he retreated to the day room to play pool, flip through out-dated magazines, and wait for the army to send him home. "You know how the army is ma'am," he said, "hurry up and wait." The army is so notorious for unnecessary delay that every soldier around the globe has heard the expression "hurry up and wait." The CRC trainers were over-extended, and focused on getting soldiers ready to deploy. But it was unfortunate that this poor soldier couldn't get home. After traveling across the world, the army waylaid him in Georgia, only a short plane ride away from Boston.

For the next several days, I trained alongside all of the other soldiers. We qualified on the 9mm pistol, updated our wills, learned about death benefits, updated our shots, and received our uniforms and protective chemical masks at the Central Issuing Facility, otherwise known as CIF. (The army uses acronyms for everything.)

It turns out that the Army does not make the jungle boot in my size. Jungle boots are combat boots made of breathable, water resistant canvas. The military designs these boots for hot, humid, jungle conditions. They are both cool and durable. The assistant behind the counter handed me a boot three sizes too big. It was so huge that I could practically climb inside and live there. "Next," he shouted after handing me the giant boot. "Sir," I said, "This boot is way too big." "Smallest one we've got, captain," he retorted, wiping his sweat-dripped forehead with a handkerchief, "Keep the line moving." "OK. Well, no thanks," I said, and left the boots on the counter.

One early morning with our shot records in hand, we crowded into a bus before sunrise for a trip to the medical clinic. I hoped my deployment wouldn't require the "peanut butter shot," a thick mixture injected in the largest muscle (i.e., one's bottom). I've heard that even the toughest soldiers have trouble sitting for days afterwards. Midway through the line a sergeant handed me a slip of paper, with checked boxes for the shots I would need. I noticed, with relief, that he hadn't marked the box next to the peanut butter shot.

We marched through the line getting one shot after the other. Then we all waited in an over-crowded seating area to make sure nobody had a bad reaction. Some soldiers slept in their chairs while they waited. To pass the time, I read Senator McCain's book about being a POW during Vietnam that I had bought on an outing to the Army Exchange.

> **JAG Fact**
> *Every military installation is like a small city. "Exchanges" are discount stores, and "Commissaries" are grocery stores.*

While in the middle of a chapter, I couldn't help but overhear the young soldier next to me, complaining about having had over a dozen shots. He claimed that this was his second round in one month of the same shots, because he had forgotten his shot record at home. Since he had no proof, the army required him to have them all over again. I asked why he didn't refuse the shots and insist on time to prove he'd already had them. According to him, the nurse said he could either take the shots and deploy on time; or wait for the record and deploy later with the next group. He didn't want to deploy late, "Ma'am, they're 'spectin' me over there. I can't tell the commander I forgot my shot record and that's why I'm late. No way. I just took 'em again. But, ooooeeee, did it hurt!"

I didn't tell him about a client I once represented who was disabled from something called "nerve demyelization." His symptoms were like MS, and his doctor suspected the cause was "over-vaccination." I didn't want to scare the young soldier. Besides, he'd already had the shots. I went back to my book and hoped he would be OK.

We stayed in run-down, World War II barracks with concrete floors and about eight metal bunk beds to a room. There was one bathroom down the hall, without stall doors or shower curtains. It was no place for a modest person.

There weren't a lot of women deploying, so I only had one roommate, Munira. Weeks before she had been a hairdresser in New York City, after moving to the United States from Uzbekistan. She had responded to a radio add recruiting native linguists. Within in a few weeks she landed a job with a prominent defense contractor, and tripled her salary. Her pay-grade was equivalent to a lieutenant colonel. She liked to ask people, "What are you? I'm a lieutenant colonel." She was on her way to Afghanistan to be an interpreter. She also knew a lot about cosmetics, and was quick to point out the wrinkles on my forehead and to offer an elixir that she guaranteed would make them vanish. (It didn't work).

Across the hall from our room was another JAG officer, Major B. Although Fort Benning was only a temporary home, she transformed her dreary, concrete barracks room into a cozy, welcoming abode. Pictures of her family and of her chocolate lab, Dakota, decorated her nightstand. On her bunk were a colorful throw blanket and a pillow from home. A copy of the Geneva Conventions and a travel journal rested on top. "You're reading the Geneva Conventions, Ma'am?" I asked. Coincidentally, Major B. was also deploying to Guantanamo Bay.

This wasn't her first deployment. A few years before, when she was a captain, Major B. had deployed to Bosnia, where she was a claims officer. During a conflict, if the U.S. damages civilian objects, it reimburses the owners. JAGs often remain behind after the conflict to investigate and settle these claims. Major B. told a story about a Bosnian farmer she encountered who was a "frequent filer." He continued filing claims with the JAG office, alleging that U.S. soldiers had destroyed his livestock. Day after day, he came to the claims office with more dead livestock as evidence. He brought chickens, goats, and sheep. Each day he brought more livestock, but his stories about their cause of death became weaker and weaker. Eventually, a JAG investigation revealed that he was intentionally killing his own livestock because the claims settlement offered by the U.S. military was more than he could get on the depressed open market.

In between training events, I palled around with my new Uzbek friend. We ate in the chow-hall together and sometimes sat outside at a rickety picnic table passing the time. I taught her how to wear a uniform, and she told me about Uzbekistan. Across the road from the female barracks were the male barracks. There were several other linguists from various middle-eastern countries, also new "translator" recruits. I noticed that they seemed to watch her a lot. It made me uncomfortable.

One evening Munira was outside at the picnic table with the male soldier I had met earlier that week in the chow hall, who was still trying to get home to Boston. He was teaching her how to pack her military duffle bag to maximize the space. It is amazing how much can fit inside an army duffle bag when soldiers utilize every quarter-inch. One Afghani linguist, who had eyed her all week, aggressively approached Munira from across the road, yelling and scolding her as he moved closer. There was a heated exchange in their native language with hand waving and finger pointing, and then the man turned and angrily walked away. Munira explained that he was upset because she was married to an Afghani man, yet she was having a male soldier help with her duffle bag. He also criticized her for wearing revealing clothes all week. Culturally, her marriage to an Afghani permitted, in fact, *required* other men to keep a watchful eye on her when she was away from her husband. It was July in Georgia, and Munira dressed as every other woman did—shorts and t-shirts. "Why don't they bother me?" I asked. "You're an American, and you're not married to an Afghani," she said. "They forgive you." I found it strange that the U.S. had recruited translators with such radical ideas—translators who seemed to prefer Sharia law. I wondered how extensive their background checks were.

Our last day of training Munira and I hugged and exchanged contact information. We had become good friends in a short time, and she had helped to pass the days at Fort Benning. We promised to keep in touch, wished each other luck, and boarded different busses going in different directions. I never heard from Munira again.

Munira in our room at Fort Benning.

Munira and me at the Fort Benning CONUS replacement Center. In the background are the barracks where we stayed.

CHAPTER FIVE

Guantanamo Bound, "It Don't Gitmo Better!"

The plane dipped this way and that. I thought about Munira as I looked out the window. A sheet of turquoise blue water lapped against the island's shores in mesmerizing rhythm. As we descended toward the island of Cuba, spots of green interrupted white sand. As we drew closer, the images came into focus and I realized the green dots were giant cactus plants. They covered the island. "Where are the toucans and the palm trees?" I wondered to myself. Then I said to the freckled-face soldier across the aisle from me, "It looks like a desert." He replied with a clever grin, "That's 'cause it is a desert. You must be a first-timer to Guantanamo Bay, the island where it don't Gitmo better." Soldiers refer to Guantanamo Bay as "Gitmo" and the military abbreviation is "GTMO."

Guantanamo Bay is located on the southeast "hook" of Cuba, about 400 air miles (a two-hour plane ride) from Miami, Florida. It takes so long to get there because the plane cannot fly over Cuban airspace, so it must fly around the island. Also, since the U.S. has started holding detainees on the island of Cuba, it restricts access to the island and only a few flights go in and out of Gitmo each week. Troops travelling to Gitmo must first fly to Florida, then spend the night and catch an early morning military flight to the island. Getting from the U.S. to Cuba takes at least two days.

Cuba is a small island surrounded by a hostile power, with surveillance towers always observing all aspects of the base. (The Navy operates Guantanamo Bay and calls it a "base." Army installations, like Walter Reed Army Hospital and Fort Benning, are called "posts.")

In 1903, the United States leased approximately 45 square miles of water and land from Cuba in Guantanamo Bay as a station to refuel its ships. It is about the size of Manhattan Island.[1] The original lease payment was $2,000.00 per year in gold coins. In 1934, Cuba and the U.S. amended its lease so the U.S. could

---

1. J.A. Sierra, historyofcuba.com, *Notes on Guantanamo Bay*, available at www.historyofcuba.com/history/funfacts/guantan.htm.

pay in dollars instead of gold coins. The value was $4,085.00. At that time, the parties added a restrictive termination clause to the lease, which is still in effect to this day. Under that clause, no one party can terminate the lease. It can only end if both Cuba and the U.S. jointly decide to end it or if the U.S. abandons its base there.[2]

Originally, sailors could cross through Gitmo's gates and into the Cuban towns for drinking, entertainment, and whatever else sailors do when they're not working. That changed in 1959, after Cuban rebels kidnapped 29 Marines and held them hostage in the hills of Cuba for twenty-two days. Eventually, the rebels released them. The marines survived, but

> **JAG Fact**
>
> *The military calls army installations "posts." Naval installations it calls "bases." Guantanamo Bay is operated by the Navy, so it is a "naval base."*

the U.S. had learned an important lesson about its Cuban neighbors and didn't want another incident. The U.S. military responded by closing its base and making Cuban land strictly off-limits to its sailors and marines. The U.S. fenced its sailors in and the Cubans out.[3] Fidel Castro planted a ring of cactus plants just outside the naval base, to discourage his people from seeking refuge there.[4] The U.S. erected a fence of barbed wire and Castro erected a fence of barbed cacti.

Fidel Castro resents the U.S. presence in Cuba, and since 1959, the Cuban government protests U.S. presence by refusing to cash the lease checks. However, the United States, ever an honest tenant, continues to send its lease check each year. The lease payment, though not accepted by Castro, makes clear that the U.S. has not abandoned the base, and fully intends to stay. In a 1971 speech, Castro claimed "that base is there just to humiliate Cuba; just like a knife stuck in the heart of Cuba's dignity and sovereignty."[5]

The plane made a bumpy landing, and we sat on the tarmac for what seemed like an eternity. When we stepped off the plane, armed security officers told us to put our bags on the ground in front of us and line up. We stood there as military police officers walked down the line with giant, sniffing dogs, and metal detecting wands. They asked questions, critically reviewed our travel orders, and examined everything we came with. Security was tight. I understood that

---

2. M.E. Murphy, Rear Admiral, U.S. Navy, The History of Guantanamo Bay, 1494–1964, available at www.nsgtmo.navy.mil/htmpgs/gtmohistory.htm.

3. M.E. Murphy, Rear Admiral, U.S. Navy, The History of Guantanamo Bay, 1494–1964, available at www.nsgtmo.navy.mil/htmpgs/gtmohistory.htm.

4. Associated Press, *Brief History of Guantanamo Bay*, 28 December 2001, available at www.foxnews.com/story/0,2933,41744,00.html.

5. J.S. Sierra, historyofcuba.com, *Notes on Guantanamo Bay*, available at www.historyofcuba.com/history/funfacts/guantan.htm.

the dogs were necessary. Since seeing my niece mauled by a (supposedly harmless) dog years earlier, I was skeptical of big dogs. I held still while the dog sniffed me up and down and nuzzled through my bags. I didn't like the intrusion, but I understood the reason for it.

After a long ferry ride from one side of the island to another, I finally reached the last leg of my journey. An air force JAG officer with a friendly demeanor and a soothing voice walked up to me and said, "Are you Captain Miller?" "Yes," I said, "how did you know?" He replied, "The boss told me to look for a redhead. My name is Carl. I'll take you to your quarters so you can check in, and then we'll go to the office to meet the boss, Lieutenant Colonel Beaver." "Sounds good" I replied, "but what about Major B? She's another JAG I met at Fort Benning. Aren't you expecting her today, too?" Carl answered, "Don't worry about that, she's with another task force. They'll send someone for her." I thought that seemed strange. "There is more than one task force on this tiny island?" I said. Carl responded, "It's complicated. I'll explain in the van."

A "task force" is a temporary military organization created for a particular purpose (or "mission"). They are often "joint" which means that the military assigns personnel from all branches of service to work in the task force. At the Guantanamo Bay Naval Base were two joint tasks forces: JTF 160, and JTF 170. The job of JTF 160 was to run the detention prison camp. JTF 170 was responsible to extract intelligence from the detainees. Therefore, soldiers called JTF 160 the "detention mission" and JTF 170 the "intelligence mission."

> **JAG Fact**
>
> *Military personnel often refer to joint task forces as "purple environments" because if one mixed brown, blue, and green (the color of all service uniforms) together, the result would be purple. This leads to terms like "purple justice," which is a form of discipline that includes aspects of each service.*

Major B. worked for JTF 160, and I worked for JTF 170. "Doesn't it get confusing with two JAG offices on such a small island? Whose opinion trumps when the two JAG offices have different opinions about the law?" I asked Carl as we drove away from the ferry dock. He responded, "You hit the nail on the head. General Bacchus, who is the general in charge JTF 160 (detention mission) doesn't get along with General Dunlavey, who is in charge of JTF 170 (intelligence mission.) It can be frustrating. Our boss, Lieutenant Colonel Beaver, ends up in the middle a lot. What can she do? They're generals. Rumors circulate that eventually the Pentagon will merge these two task forces. Until then, just follow Lieutenant Colonel Beaver's lead." To this young officer, it seemed like there was too much brass on this small island.

Carl drove the van along a dirt roadway and then pulled onto the main road, with one narrow lane going in each direction. "Guantanamo Bay is like a very small town. There isn't a lot to do when we're not working," he said. Then he pointed to an outdoor movie theater that shows recent movies twice each night, free of charge. "That's what most people do in the evening."

The "downtown" section of the Guantanamo Bay Naval Base hints of small-town America. It has a local store called the Navy Exchange where shoppers can buy everything from highly pasteurized milk that lasts for months to designer perfume. The currency is, of course, American dollars. There is no sales tax. For those longing for a taste of America, McDonald's is conveniently located and offers the same menu as that offered in typical U.S. McDonald restaurants. "Sometimes the buns are stale, though," he said.

"Over there, just beyond the hill, is a dive shop. They rent scuba diving equipment and snorkel gear, too," he said pointing to his left. "The naval base offers scuba diving classes, but it takes time to get certified, so most people assigned to the task forces don't do that." Then his foot lightly touched the breaks, and he said, "Looks like an iguana wants to cross. They're endangered, so we just let them cross." A large, brownish iguana that looked like a small dragon lumbered across the road in front of our car. Then it stopped for a rest in the middle of the road. Carl laid on the horn, which got the iguana moving again. Many iguanas live in Guantanamo Bay. The naval base posts signs asking people not to feed them, but people do it anyway.

Guantanamo is home to lots of exotic creatures, including roosters, turkey vultures, banana rats, and even boa constrictors. Later I learned that a boa constrictor once made his home in our backyard. The naval base personnel had to move him out.

There are many spiders, too, including tarantulas, which look very deadly but aren't, and brown recluse spiders that look harmless but can be deadly. Brown recluse spiders bit a few soldiers, who became so ill that the military medically evacuated them back to the United States for emergency medical care. Their venom causes the victim's skin to turn black and die, much like a deadly flesh-eating bacteria. Untreated bites can kill victims in a matter of days.

"Does anyone live in those homes?" I asked, about a neighborhood of run-down houses with overgrown weeds and brush. "Not now. Navy families used to live there, but they've been vacant for years. Things at the naval base were slowing down until the task force came." In 1995, two large tenants (the Fleet Training Group and the Shore Intermediate Maintenance activity) relocated to other ports, and Guantanamo Bay downsized.[6]

---

6. Historical Information about Guantanamo Bay Cuba comes from M.E. Murphy, Rear Admiral, U.S Navy, *The History of Guantanamo Bay 1494–1964* available at www.ngs-gtmo.navy.mil/htmpgs/gtmohistory.htm.

We passed by a large school for children of navy base personnel. The grade school and the high school occupied one building, together. The children had pushed colored paper cups through the chain-link fence to spell "USA."

He signaled for a right turn, and pulled into a housing division called Winward Loop, which would be my neighborhood for the next six months. The houses had sand-colored stucco, and they all looked alike. While trying to cart my heavy bags through the front door, a tiny lizard with a curly-Q tail darted from his shady refuge and startled me. Eventually, we would learn to live peacefully together.

I hauled my bags up the stairs, and passed another soldier who was hauling her bags down. She was finishing her tour and I was starting mine. She seemed happy to leave, which concerned me a little about what lay ahead for me. Our home was sparsely furnished, and had two bedrooms with four beds, and one and one-half bathrooms. It was modest, but clean, and nicer than I expected.

The next morning, I car-pooled with several other soldiers to the office. The office was in a long building that used to be a day-care center. On the way inside, I saw several soldiers sitting on abandoned playground equipment, smoking cigarettes. It seemed incongruous.

> **JAG Fact**
>
> *Ever JAG Office has a lead JAG who is in charge. It is usually a Lieutenant Colonel, or a Colonel. That Officer is the "Staff Judge Advocate" or "SJA." Most also have a "Deputy Staff Judge Advocate" or "Deputy SJA." They are the second in charge.*

The JAG officers and their support staff were in one big room with desks lined up along the wall. The staff judge advocate (or SJA, the leading JAG officer), was Lieutenant Colonel Diane Beaver, and she sat behind her desk at the front of the room, hollering to a legal assistant across the room about a problem with her computer. "Hi, captain, come in," she said, and sized me up with her eyes. She had a reputation within the Army JAG Corps as a tough boss. Nobody wanted to get on her bad side.

She rose from her desk chair and firmly shook my hand. She was tall, with a solid, square build, clipped blond hair, and a no-nonsense attitude. Lieutenant Colonel Beaver began her career in the army as an enlisted military police officer, then worked her way up the ranks, went to law school, and became a JAG officer. She advanced by proving her worth and paying her dues, and she expected her officers to do the same. She never offered gratuitous compliments and was quick to correct her troops. She set high standards for herself and others. Lieutenant Colonel Beaver was skeptical, direct, and commanded respect. Later, an air force sergeant would explain, "She believes in tough love. She's hard as nails, but she'll do anything for her people."

During the first week I and other island newcomers attended a briefing where the JTF 170 Commanding General cautioned us that we were being "collected on" at all times, and to watch what we said and did. He pointed out that the island was teaming with foreign defense contractors and construction workers who did not have a clearance. A few local Cubans with work permits enter Guantanamo Bay from the small town on the Cuban side of the border. Each morning they pass through the gate to work on the installation, and each night they return through the gate and back to communist Cuba.

We were directed to carefully guard what we said over the telephone, shred documents that contained any personal information, and exercise discretion in our e-mail communications back home to family members. "Don't make your loved ones targets," he warned. I wondered if his remarks were true—until that evening when I called home and heard an unmistakable "click" on the telephone. Countless "clicking" off and on the line occurred each time I made a long-distance phone call. I don't know exactly who was listening in on my conversations home, but there were at least three of us on the line each time I called.

Soldiers don't make many phone calls from Guantanamo Bay. Cell phones do not work, and the local long-distance service is extremely expensive. Some soldiers had *AT&T Caribbean Calling Cards*, sold at only a few locations in Florida, which offered the best long-distance rate.

Those assigned to Guantanamo Bay, even for short tours, have an immediate sense of being cut off from the rest of the world because communication to and from the island is so restricted. On top of the expensive phone service, there are no daily American newspapers available in Guantanamo Bay.

The mail is slow, too. Mail and packages come on a giant barge every few months. For hours before it docks you can see the heavy barge lumbering along in the waters off the Guantanamo Bay coast. When the barge finally docks, muscular workers unload thousands of pounds of mail and supplies. When the barge comes in, soldiers call it *Barge Days*, and distribute packages from home. Empty store shelves are finally re-stocked, and everyone stands a little taller. Soldiers holler down the hall to one another, "The barge is here; she's docking right now!" That fall, during *Barge Days*, I received my August birthday greetings, just in time for Halloween.

A view of Guantanamo Bay from one of its many hills.

Pictures of the naval base at Guantanamo Bay. Bottom right picture is the security check-point that separates the military base from the rest of Cuba. This photograph is located at www.defenselink.mil.

The Navy Commissary and Exchange at Guantanamo Bay where everybody shops.

CHAPTER SIX

A 9-Eyed Critter and
a Trip to the Camp

Early one morning, soon after I arrived at Gitmo, I rolled over in my bunk, pulled the covers over my head, and tried to savor the last few minutes of sleep before the alarm would echo through our dark, little room. Just then, rising over the quiet hills of Gitmo I heard an echoing "c-caw, c-caw" as the island roosters called to the rising sun. I sleepily rolled out of bed and shuffled to the shower.

The water trickled down my tired face and I tried to rouse myself. I've never been a morning person. Just as I lathered my palms with the Dial soap bar, I spied a dark spot on the shower's wall that looked like a mini Hershey's chocolate bar. I didn't have my glasses on, so I squinted through the trickling water and tried to focus on the little brown dot. Just then, it moved. It was alive! I stood there naked and screaming at a huge brown spider that was on the move. My mind immediately flashed to pictures of brown recluse spiders and their bite victims that had circulated on our office computers only the day before. Somewhere amid the flailing and screaming, I found the composure to chuck the soap bar, grab my shampoo bottle and squish the trespasser.

As soon as I arrived at the office, I went to the housing manager to report my unpleasant brown recluse incident and ask the army to exterminate our house. The sergeant taking my report listened carefully with his hand under his chin and then asked, "Ma'am, did the spider have nine eyes? That is one way to know whether the spider was indeed a brown recluse." "Yes," I said, with confidence, nodding affirmatively, "Absolutely, sergeant, there were most definitely nine eyes on that creature." Just then, Lieutenant Colonel Beaver walked by with a knowing smile and said, "Sounds like Captain Miller knows what she wants. Better exterminate, sergeant." He agreed.

Honestly, I have no idea how many eyes the spider had; or if it had any eyes at all. How could I possibly know that? Only a fool would get close enough to find out. But, I wanted full on execution of *any and all* multi-legged critters living in our house, and I wasn't about to lose my case over uncertainty about the number of eyes it had.

Later that day I sat at my computer among several other JAG officers and our paralegals. Each was clicking away on their computers, reading e-mail, and working on various projects. Another officer broke the silence; "listen to this," she said and then read portions of a letter that one detainee had written to his family in a far away country. Not surprisingly, the army reviews detainee mail. The detainee's letter included poetic verses about the nice weather, and the beautiful sunsets over Guantanamo Bay. He closed the letter by saying something like, "Wish you were here!" He can't be serious, I thought to myself. Maybe he was writing in code. Later I heard about a detainee who the army offered to release. But, when it informed the detainee, he said, "No thanks. The weather will be nicer in my country next spring. I'll wait until then."

Just then, a defense contractor with round glasses and a bushy beard stepped into the office. "Knock, knock," he said. I had met him earlier that week in a newcomer's briefing. He walked toward my desk, "I'm on my way to the detention camp. I've got time to give you a tour, if you want one." I accepted the offer. I was curious to see the detention camp, especially after hearing one detainee's views of life at the camp.

It took us about twenty minutes to drive to the detention camp in his rental car. I was surprised that a rental car agency exists on Guantanamo Bay. However, getting around requires a car, because although the island is sparsely populated, it sprawls along for miles. Guantanamo is home to countless jalopies from the 1980s. They are barely operable and probably wouldn't pass even the most liberal safety and emissions inspections. The mechanical deficiencies may stem from the fact that they drive a lot of miles, but never at a speed exceeding 25 miles per hour. "We call these run-down cars Gitmo Specials," he explained. Some people say that Gitmo is a "legal black hole," but drive 30 miles per hour and you will get a ticket. So much for the theory that there is no law on Guantanamo Bay.

In the summer of 2002, approximately a month before I arrived at Gitmo, the U.S. military closed the temporary holding cells at Camp X-Ray, and evacuated detainees to much more comfortable and spacious living quarters on a different part of the island.

Even years later the news media still airs pictures of the older, more primitive camp X-Ray, which was a series of large, fenced cells that the media calls "cages." The U.S. only held detainees at Camp X-Ray for a few brief months, while contractors worked quickly building a permanent prison camp. Once finished, the U.S. quickly relocated the detainees to the new camp, called Camp Delta, and that is where detainees remain to this day. The general public wrongly believes that Camp X-Ray is still used. By now, 2008, Camp X-Ray is barely recognizable. It is overgrown with weeds, and banana rats have taken up residence there. One must look carefully to see what remains of Camp X-Ray.

We pulled into the gravel parking lot and parked next to a large trailer just outside the gates of the camp. "What is this trailer for?" I asked. "That's the ICRC (International Committee of the Red Cross) trailer. They come to Guantanamo Bay a lot, and pick up mail to send to detainees' families around the world. They're in and out of the camp several times a day, so that's probably why the trailer is this close to the camp." He explained. "That's good," I said, and thought about what the ICRC delegate said during her lecture at the JAG school. Ordinarily, countries that open their camps to the ICRC delegates have nothing to hide. Human rights abuses generally occur in closed camps that exclude the ICRC.

A tall chain-link fence topped with rows of barbed wire and spirals of razor wire surrounded the camp. There were two giant locking gates, and two security checkpoints to enter the camp. Inside the camp were more fences and wire surrounding long, narrow buildings—the cellblocks. We passed through several security checkpoints. At one, the guard handed me strips of silver duct tape, and suggested I "sanitize" my uniforms. Soldiers cover their names and ranks to avoid sharing identifying information with detainees. I followed the advice, and covered my uniform with strips of shiny duct tape.

A guard escorted us to one of the cellblocks. The cells were spacious, and each had an elevated bed, and a Muslim style, ground level toilet. Orange metal in a crosshatched pattern separated cells, so detainees could see and talk to their neighbors on both sides and across the aisle.

We walked in silence. Some came to the doors of their cells and eyed us as we walked down the block. Others averted their eyes, and still others were occupied sleeping, or reading. One hollered to me in English, "doctor, doctor." He had seen the medical patch, indicating that I worked at a military hospital, on my sleeve and assumed I was a doctor. I had not covered the patch. I looked at the detainee, and shook my head no. But, I made a mental note of his request. Did he need a doctor? I remembered the Geneva Convention rule requiring the detaining power (in this case, the U.S.) to provide prisoners of war (POWs) with appropriate medical care. Under the rule, the U.S. prison camp must have an "adequate infirmary where prisoners of war may have the attention they require." It goes on to state that prisoners of war have the right to "present themselves to the medical authorities for examinations." The U.S. must bear the expenses of maintaining the POWs "in good health."[1]

---

1. Third Geneva Convention, Relative to the Treatment of Prisoners of War, 12 August 1949, article 30.

"What's that smell?" I asked. A very distinctive odor became stronger as we walked down the block. "Prayer oil," the guard said. "The U.S. military issues prayer oil, prayer beads, and a copy of the Holy Quran to every detainee. It also paints a black arrow in each cell pointing to Mecca so detainees can pray. Five times a day the loudspeaker plays the call to prayer. We don't disturb the detainees during those times," he explained.

We reached the end of the block, which opened into a large courtyard. I stepped outside. There were several recreation areas, and detainees were walking and running around the yards. Some were kicking and throwing small, foam soccer balls.

One detainee looked up and made eye contact with me. There wasn't any particular emotion in his eyes. It was just a blank look—like a glance that stuck for a moment. Most detainees refuse eye contact with women, so it was a bit unusual.

Off to one side were several metal shower stalls. Two male soldiers were standing near the shower stalls while a detainee showered. One of them called to the shower, "Okay, you have a few more minutes, and then it is time to come out."

I noticed a female guard sitting on the steps. She looked bored, if even a little defeated. She said to me, "I can't escort them to the shower. We used to be able to do that, but it *offends* them." Eventually the U.S. military made the rule stricter, by prohibiting female guards from walking beyond a designated point in the cellblock when a detainee was outside in the shower area, lest she catch a glimpse of him. The victors adhered to the cultural mores of the vanquished. Our government engaged in gender discrimination to appease the detainees.

Later, I learned about a female interrogator whose detainee would not look at her. He refused to acknowledge her existence because she was a woman. He would talk to the men, but he would not talk to her. In frustration, she crouched on the ground in front of him, where he directed his gaze, and yelled up at him while pounding her chest in frustration, "I exist! I am right here in front of you. In my country, men look women in the eye. I am an American and I am your interrogator, and I want you to look me in the eye!" He ignored her. The army criticized her for failing to adhere to the detainee's cultural mores. "They don't look women in the eye. Stop making him uncomfortable" her supervisor said. Years later, interrogators still used this as an example of what *not* to do. To please our radical enemies, the U.S. government allows detainees to disrespect their female interrogators. This only sends the incorrect, and dangerous, message that they are right, and that we are wrong.

We walked back through the cellblock to leave. I was a little concerned about the detainee who called out and thought I was a doctor. Maybe he needed medical attention. I mentioned this to the guard at the other end of the block. She explained that detainees could request to see a doctor and go to the field hospital any time. Soldiers have "sick call" in the army where they can report to any military medical clinic between certain hours in the morning and a doctor will see them the same day. The detention camp had instituted a similar practice in Guantanamo Bay for detainees. "Where is the hospital?" I asked. She pointed several buildings over, outside some of the inner gates. She said, "You can go over there if you want to ma'am. Just show them your ID."

I was curious, so I went to check out the hospital. It had several large examination areas, and state of the art medical equipment. At this clinic, military doctors issued detainees prosthetic limbs. Many detainees from the war-torn Afghanistan countryside were victims of landmines. Military eye doctors fitted them for prescription eyeglasses, if they needed them. Most were able to see clearly for the first times in their lives. Military dentists scraped lifetimes of tartar from detainees' decaying mouths and filled their cavities.

Army and naval doctors treated detainees at great risk to themselves. Some detainees even physically attacked their treating doctors. One slashed his doctor when the doctor was trying to save his life. This led some physicians to wear body armor in the treatment room.[2]

Aside from detainees who physically and intentionally lashed out at their captors, some carried highly infectious diseases that put physicians and soldiers at risk. Many detainees tested positive for tuberculosis and hepatitis. The army isolated detainees with known infectious diseases by assigning them to a cellblock away from healthy detainees. It also required infected detainees to wear medical masks. Their caregivers also wore masks and gloves. (The Third Geneva Convention regarding POWs allows for medical isolation.)

Several months after I visited the medical clinic, the military flew a heart specialist and specialized surgical equipment to Guantanamo Bay to perform heart surgery on a detainee who had a congenital heart defect. The defect was not combat related, and the U.S. did not cause his condition. But it saved his life.

2. Richard Miniter, *Deadly Kindness*, N.Y. Post, 15 Sept. 2006. Available at http://www.nypost.com/seven/09152006/postopinion/opedcolumnists/a_deadly_kindness_opedcolumnists_richard_miniter.htm?page=0.

By 2006, prison accommodations were even better. Camp Four, which the military designed after an Indiana prison,[3] houses the most compliant and co-operative detainees. Detainees live in open bays, with forty per building. Detainees eat their meals outside together around picnic tables and serve themselves in home-style fashion from large, communal pots. Camp Four offers both soccer fields and basketball courts. The U.S. government offers a selection of basketball shoes for detainees upon request.

Even Camp Five, the most restrictive camp for the least compliant detainees, conforms to U.S. prison standards and offers an exercise room. Early in 2006, the Department of Defense ordered all new aerobic equipment for the detainee exercise room.[4]

The United States spends $95 million dollars each year to operate JTF-GTMO, and maintain superior prison conditions for the detainees held there.[5] The prison conditions at Guantanamo Bay far exceed those of other countries, and some Belgian officials observe that conditions at Guantanamo Bay are much better than those in a typical Belgian prison. A Belgian law enforcement official described the facilities at Guantanamo Bay as a "model prison where people are better treated than in Belgian prisons."[6] The President of the Belgian Senate commented that the cells in Gitmo were larger than those in Belgian prisons.[7]

In fact, in 2005 the U.S. Supreme Court unanimously (all 9 justices) *approved* significantly harsher prison conditions in an Ohio super-max prison, where prisoners remain in complete isolation twenty-four hours a day, with virtually no contact with the outside world, and sleep on floor mats under a light that is on all of the time.[8]

According to the court, in the Ohio prison, every aspect of an inmate's life is "controlled and monitored." The cells measure 7 by 14 feet, and inmates are required to be inside their cells for 23 hours a day, except for the one hour a day that inmates may leave their cells to recreate in "one or two indoor recreation cells." The court said that incarceration here is "synonymous with extreme isolation." The cells are essentially solid metal and configured to prevent conversation, communication or interaction with the other inmates.

---

3. Statement by Department of Defense, Deputy Secretary of Defense, Detainee Policy Representative, to students at George Mason University School of Law, public forum, 16 February 2006.

4. *Id.*

5. *Id.*

6. Chicago Daily Law Bulletin, 4 April 2006.

7. *Id.*

8. *Wilkinson v. Austin*, 545 U.S. 209 (2005).

Inmates eat all meals alone, and visits are rare and, when they do happen, occur through glass walls. The court commented, "It is fair to say OSP [Ohio State Penitentiary] inmates are deprived of almost any environmental or sensory stimuli and of almost all human contact." What's more, inmates go there for an indefinite term. Inmates lose their parole eligibility while in OSP, and there's no telling how long a prisoner with a life term will be in OSP once assigned there.

In this instance, Ohio treats its prisoners more harshly that the military treats detainees in Guantanamo Bay. Further, Ohio assigns inmates there with very little procedural protections (fewer protections than detainees held in Gitmo receive). In Gitmo, detainees may call witnesses at their hearing. In Ohio, they may not. But, the ICRC, human rights groups, and even the U.S. Supreme Court don't seem to mind. Nobody objects to the way Ohio holds these U.S. prisoners. But, for some reason, many people demand better prison conditions for suspected terrorists in Gitmo.

When evaluating conditions at Gitmo, it is important to keep the matter in perspective by understanding what we do with U.S. citizens, and what our Supreme Court allows in U.S. prisons.

Shower facilities that detainees use in Guantanamo Bay. Official DOD Picture, available at www.defenselink.mil.

A forty-eight person detention block in Guantanamo Bay, Cuba. DoD photo by Staff Sergeant Stephen Lewald.

An individual cell in Guantanamo Bay with bunk, toilet, and sink (L). A detention camp in Guantanamo Bay where soldiers live in groups. Religious items displayed on the bunk (R). DoD photo by Staff Sergeant Stephen Lewald.

A detainee exercise yard in Guantanamo Bay. Sun shades are drawn in this photo. DoD photo by Staff Sergeant Stephen Lewald.

The detainee hospital ward at the prison camp in Guantanamo Bay. The military released this photo at www.defenselink.mil.

While assigned to Guantanamo Bay, the soldiers responsible for securing the area invited officers to accompany them on a live patrol through the Gitmo hills. I was the only officer who accepted the invitation. Afterwards we took this picture. Later I received an award for this patrol. I'm smiling in this photo because the patrol was over.

CHAPTER SEVEN

Commemorating September 11th, 2002

" ... The people who died on 9/11/2001 were not innocent ... my group will shake up the U.S. and countries who follow the U.S."[1]

—Guantanamo Bay Detainee

It was exactly one year after the terrorist attacks on America, and here I was sharing a small Caribbean Island with over 800 detained terrorist enemies.[2] We soldiers stood quietly in a military formation for a ceremony recognizing our fallen fellow Americans.

As we saluted our flag and remembered our fallen, an eerie sound hung in the air over the Guantanamo Bay prison camp. It was the call to Muslim prayer, which the U.S. military base broadcast over loud speakers with over 800 detainees singing the call in unison. I thought about detainees who claimed "to pray every day against the United States,"[3] and I thought about the prayers of those who perished on September 11th.

That day was a solemn one. Even the chow-hall line was quiet as soldiers went through the motions in a disconnected way, reflecting on the events of the previous year, and remembering the horrible attack on our shores.

---

1. JTF GTMO Information on Detainees, 4 March 2005, released by JTF GTMO, available at http://www.jtfgtmo.southcom.mil/.

2. The number of detainees held in Gitmo has fluctuated drastically. At its height, the numbers exceeded 800. The U.S. military has released many detainees over the years, bringing the numbers down to only a few hundred. It releases more every day, so the numbers continue to drop.

3. JTF GTMO Information on Detainees, 4 March 2005, released by JTF GTMO, Guantanamo Bay, available at http://www.jtfgtmo.southcom.mil/.

CHAPTER EIGHT

The U.S. Exceeds the Geneva Conventions and Gets Burned

" … If people say that there is mistreatment in Cuba with the detainees, those type speaking are wrong; they treat us like a Muslim not a detainee."[1]
—Guantanamo Bay Detainee

People criticize the U.S. for supposedly failing to adhere to the Geneva Conventions. In many ways, the U.S. military affords *greater*, not *fewer*, rights than the Geneva Conventions require. This is particularly true in the realm of religious accommodation.

Under the Geneva Conventions, detaining powers only must afford detainees the right to practice their religion and attend religious services.[2] The Convention conditions this right on detainees complying with disciplinary rules. The Convention also explains that relief societies like the Salvation Army or the Red Cross, and specifically the ICRC, may provide prisoners with religious items like Bibles and prayer books. Prisoners can also receive "articles of a religious character" through the mail.[3] The Geneva Conventions *do not require* a detaining power to provide religious articles to its prisoners.[4]

No law or treaty, including the Geneva Conventions, *obligates* the U.S. to provide religious articles to the detainees. However, the U.S. military does it anyway. In Guantanamo Bay, the U.S military spends millions of dollars to provide

1. JTF GTMO Information on Detainees, 4 March 2005, available at http://www.jtfgtmo.southcom.mil/.

2. Third Geneva Convention, Relative to the Treatment of Prisoners of War, 12 August 1949, article 34.

3. Third Geneva Convention, Relative to the Treatment of Prisoners of War, 12 August 1949, article 72.

4. Jean S. Pictet and Jean de Preux, COMMENTARY TO THE THIRD GENEVA CONVENTION, RELATIVE TO THE TREATMENT OF PRISONERS OF WAR, 12 AUGUST 1949, comments to article 34, International Committee of the Red Cross, 1960.

each detainee with a Quran (the Islamic Bible), a prayer cap, prayer beads, and prayer oil "as part of their basic-issued items." It even distributes traditional Islamic prayer rugs to those who are the best-behaved."[5] Another U.S. run detention camp in Iraq hosted a mural painting contest for the detainees and awarded large editions of the Quran to the first and second prizewinners.[6] The U.S. government purchases Qurans to give detainees with tax payers' dollars.

Aside from providing religious items, the U.S. military paints arrows pointing to Mecca in each detainee's cell so detainees can pray in the right direction, and it broadcasts the Islamic call to prayer over loud-speakers five times each day. It assigns U.S. Muslim chaplains (there are approximately 14 in the military)[7] to Guantanamo Bay who ensure that camp commanders follow the rules of Islam and fully accommodate detainees. Following advice from these chaplains, the U.S. acknowledges Islamic holidays by providing special meals that include imported seasonal fruits and nuts.

The first year, at the end of Ramadan (the holiest time of year for Muslims), the U.S. military even contemplated sacrificing a goat for the detainees. Ultimately, it decided not to do that to avoid upsetting animal rights group, such as PETA. But in November 2006, the U.S. hosted two holiday meals on two consecutive days, because detainees could not agree on the appropriate day to celebrate. To avoid conflict, the U.S. Military honored both days and paid for two celebrations.

The United States is deeply committed to protecting religious freedoms and ensuring individual liberties, so it is not surprising that it exceeds the Geneva Convention requirements for religious accommodation. However, in a war our enemies call a "religious war," where radical Islamists use their religion to justify brutally beheading innocent civilians, is it smart to exceed the Geneva Conventions?

In at least one incident, in Camp Bucca, Iraq, detainees turned our generosity on us.[8] Few people know about this incident, because the military kept

---

5. Donna Miles American, *Joint Task Force Respects Detainees' Religious Practices*, AMERICAN FORCES PRESS SERVICES, June 29, 2005.

6. Sergeant Lynne Steely, *Abu Ghraib Detainees Enter Art Contest*, MPRA QUARTERLY, Winter 2005, p. 18.

7. In 1993 the U.S. Military had no Muslim Chaplains to minister to its 3,150 Muslims. Since that time, the number of Muslims in the U.S. military has increased and the military allows Muslim Chaplains. One month after September 11th, 2001, there were more than 4,000 Muslims in uniform and 14 Islamic chaplains ministering to them. Laurie Goldstein, *A Nation Challenged: The Clergy; Military Clerics Balance Arms and Allah*, N.Y. TIMES, October 7, 2001 Section 1B.

8. Steve Fainaru and Anthony Shadid, *In Iraq Jail, Resistance Goes Underground*, WASHINGTON POST FOREIGN SERVICE, Aug. 24, 2005 at A 01.

it quiet, and when the story finally broke it was only reported in one newspaper, the Washington Post, and only for one day. Camp Bucca is home of another U.S.-run detention camp, located in Southern Iraq just a few miles from the Kuwait border. The U.S. accommodated detainees even more at Camp Bucca than in Guantanamo Bay. Detainees lived in tan-colored tents, or air-conditioned huts with approximately 20 people per unit. They were free to roam into the courtyards or stay inside. Most detainees remained inside during the day, supposedly passing time devoted to religious lessons organized by the inmates. Inside the confines of the prison, the U.S. military erected a tent for detainees to practice their religion. However, the U.S. military only allowed detainees inside the makeshift mosque. The commander ordered the soldiers in charge of the camp not to go into the tent. It was *specifically off-limits* to U.S. personnel.[9]

In fact, detainees weren't devoting all of their time to religious studies. For months more than 600 detainees worked in shifts, undetected, digging an escape tunnel that continued under the camp and led to a concealed trench, just outside the gates. They dug at night, and then gradually distributed the tunnel dirt over the soccer-field during the day, one bag at a time. Interestingly, satellite imagery revealed fresh dirt covering the area, but the U.S. overlooked its significance. Additionally, soldiers reported loose floorboards in several areas of the camp, and small piles of dirt, as if the ground was rising beneath them, and noted that the showers and portable toilets were clogging, but didn't grasp the significance of these telling clues.

Detainees fortified the tunnel walls with a paste they made from water and milk provided by the U.S. military in their rations. Remarkably, at the last minute, before what would have been one of the largest prison-breaks from any U.S. run facility in history,[10] one of the detainees lost his gumption and reported the plan to security guards on March 24, 2005. Using bulldozers, the guards leveled areas of the camp, destroying the tunnel underneath.

Days after U.S. forces destroyed the tunnel, Camp Bucca suffered another blow from its inmates when a violent riot erupted. Inside the "off-limits"

---

9. For information about the Camp Bucca tunnel and riot, see Steve Fairnau and Anthony Shadid, *In Iraq Jail, Resistance Goes Underground*, WASHINGTON POST FOREIGN SERVICE, WASHINGTON POST, Aug. 24, 2005 at A 01.

10. Comment by Colonel James B. Brown, Commander of the 18th MP Brigade that oversaw the three detention facilities in Iraq. Specifically he said, "The escape would have been one of the largest from any U.S.-run facility in history." Steve Fairnau and Anthony Shadid, In *Iraq Jail, Resistance Goes Underground*, WASHINGTON POST FOREIGN SERVICE, WASHINGTON POST, Aug. 24, 2005, at A 01.

mosque prisoners had created a primitive but effective weapons cache, where they had stashed concrete-shards dug from the concrete around tent poles and bombs made from feces, socks, and flammable hand-sanitizer. For four days, the prisoners rioted. They didn't kill any U.S. soldiers, but their impressive aim seriously injured several, including one officer who was hit in the eye by a chunk of cinderblock, fracturing his cheek in three places and breaking his teeth. One soldier called the violence "absolutely incredible," due to the number of rocks and sheer accuracy.

The detainees managed to hold-off U.S. forces for days. The United States finally called for backup. A Black Hawk helicopter arrived at the scene, and hundreds of soldiers encircled the compound. Eventually, the detainees gave-up their efforts, and the U.S. restored order at its Camp Bucca.

The United States foolishly excluded guards from an area where prisoners congregated privately, and invited this disastrous situation. It exceeded what the Geneva Conventions require and had its kindness turned against it.

Commentary to the Geneva Conventions explains that the POWs should have an "adequate" place to practice their religion, but the detaining power can use the place for other purposes, too. It is not required to set aside a place devoted exclusively to religious practices. Therefore, under the Geneva Conventions, it would be sufficient if the tent were both a mosque and a dining facility, or served some other dual purpose. The conventions do not even contemplate a situation where the detention camp commanders only allow its prisoners, and no others, access to certain locations. Indeed, doing so invites disaster.

The Geneva Conventions say that POWs must follow the military disciplinary routine of their captors in order to preserve their right to religious latitude. This is similar to the standard applied in U.S. prisons. In *O'Lone v. Estate of Shabazz*,[11] the Supreme Court said that prison officials could impinge on prisoners' right to exercise their religion for reasons related to legitimate prison management. The court upheld a regulation regarding prisoner work duties that precluded Muslim prisoners from attending religious services on Friday afternoons, as their faith required.[12]

However, despite the disaster at Camp Bucca and the relatively modest requirements of the Geneva Conventions for religious accommodation, the United States continues to exceed these requirements, and put soldiers at risk.

---

11. *O'Lone v. Estate of Shabazz*, 482 U.S. 342, 107 S.Ct. 2400, 96 L.Ed.2d 282 (1987), on remand 829 F.2d 32 (3d Cir.1987).

12. Rotunda and Nowak, Treatise on Constitutional Law, Vol. 5 §21.6, fn. 25, (Thompson West, 3d ed. 1999).

In June, 2005 (three months after the Camp Bucca riot), senior officials testified before Congress and explained that at Guantanamo Bay religious practices are incorporated into nearly "every aspect of camp life."[13] Nobody who testified mentioned Camp Bucca.

Army Command Sergeant Major Anthony Mendez explained that during the "call to prayer" the U.S. guarantees Guantanamo Bay detainees 20 minutes of "uninterrupted time."[14] Despite the debacle in Camp Bucca, Sergeant Major Mendez made clear that certain items remain "off-limits" to guards in Guantanamo Bay. He stated, "The rule of thumb for the guards is that you will not touch the Qu'ran ... that's the bottom line."[15] The U.S. military did not mention the Camp Bucca debacle, and kept the American public in the dark. It still allows "off limits" policies that put soldiers at risk and invite disaster.

The United States accommodates the religious practices of the detainees more than any other country has done in previous wars. For instance, Nazi war criminals held at Nuremberg in the aftermath of World War II could only celebrate Christmas and New Year's Day by attending religious services. The prison warden specifically disallowed other festivities, like special meals and gift exchanges.[16] However, despite its efforts to accommodate Muslim detainees during this war, critics roundly allege that the U.S. violates the Geneva Conventions. Oddly, the U.S. does not refute the allegations. I do not know why.

At the prison camp in Gitmo, the U.S. exceeds the Geneva Conventions in other ways, too. One day I was standing at the file cabinet in the back of our hut when the door burst open and I heard heavy boots on the wooden floor and a soldier exclaiming, "Captain Miller, you in here, Ma'am?" I called to him that I was in the back of the hut, and in a few moments a soldier in a dusty uniform wearing a "camel back" (a backpack that holds water with a long rubber straw running from the pack to the soldier's collar) stood before me. He said, angrily, "What am I supposed to do when detainees throw urine on me and spit in my face?" He then explained that he was a prison guard and that detainees repeatedly assaulted him. "I'm sick of it," he said. "They spit at me and throw everything you can imagine on me!" He was especially upset because one of them spat in his eye. "What will the army do for me when I find out later that I've contracted some disease from the de-

---

13. Donna Miles, *Joint Task Force Respects Detainees Religious Practices*, Department of Defense, American Forces Press Service, June 29, 2005.

14. *Id.*, quoting Army Command Sgt. Major Anthony Mendez.

15. *Id.*, also quoting Mendez.

16. Joseph E. Persico, Nuremberg, Infamy on Trial 185 (Penguin Books 1995). See this source for general information about the Nuremberg trials and defendants.

tainee?" He wanted to "document" the incident. He filed an incident report, but wanted to know what would happen if, eventually, he was attacked or permanently injured by a detainee. I explained the physical disability process—because frankly—that is the only remedy he would have. Under the law, soldiers cannot sue the military.[17]

The reason that detainees continue behaving badly is because the army does not have a disciplinary system to hold them accountable for crimes they commit while detained. That's right—there is no disciplinary system in Gitmo. Every U.S. prison has a disciplinary system to maintain order. Otherwise, our prison guards would be at a high risk for injury or even death.

The Geneva Conventions recognize that maintaining order in a prison camp is very important. The Third Geneva Convention (relative to the treatment of prisoners of war) devotes an entire chapter to camp discipline. Article 39, Chapter 6, entitled "Discipline," states, "The prime purpose of measures of discipline is to ensure that the prisoner of war remains in the hands of the Detaining power, so that he can neither do harm to that Power within the camp, nor by escaping be enabled to take up arms again. It must not be forgotten that his life has been spared only on condition that he is no longer a danger to the enemy." It goes on to state that it is "essential for the implementation of the Convention that prisoners of war should be subject to military discipline." Under the Geneva Conventions, detainees are even required to salute the detaining powers. But that never happens in Guantanamo Bay. Detainees do not salute their captors.

Articles 82 through 98 discuss disciplinary systems within POW camps. It states "A prisoner of war shall be subject to the laws, regulations and orders in force in the armed forces of the Detaining Power; the Detaining Power shall be justified in taking judicial or disciplinary measures in respect to any offense committed by a prisoner of war against such laws, regulations and orders." Therefore, under the Geneva Convention, the U.S. should bring detainees to trial and sentence them for their crimes committed against U.S. prison guards in Gitmo. Under the convention, the U.S. could apply several different disciplinary sanctions including fines, discontinuance of privileges, fatigue duties, and confinement.[18] But, that doesn't happen in Gitmo. There is no disciplinary system in Gitmo, and the U.S. does not hold detainees accountable for their crimes and offenses. For this reason, the problems continue and U.S. prison guards are at risk.

---

17. *Feres v. U.S.*, 340 U.S. 135 (1950).

18. Third Geneva Convention Relative to the Treatment of Prisoners of War, 12 August 1949, article 89.

A Holy Quran hangs in a surgical mask at Gitmo. Prison guards cannot touch the Qurans. The military released this photo (photographer unnamed) at www.defenselink.mil.

CHAPTER NINE

Major General Miller
Shakes Up Gitmo

As Carl indicated months earlier when he picked me up at the ferry dock, internal struggles between the two task forces were brewing. The commander of JTF 160 (detention mission) believed that detainees were POWs; and the commander of JTF 170 (intelligence mission) didn't. This conflict was impossible to reconcile. Soldiers in charge of running the prison camp believed one thing, and those in charge of interrogations quite another. This led to heated ideological battles that eroded morale.

Lieutenant Colonel Beaver, the Staff Judge Advocate for JTF 170 (where I was assigned) often retreated to our office after these exchanges, frustrated by the insistence of JTF 160 that detainees were POWs. "Can't they read?" she would say with irritation. "These people are terrorists. They don't follow the law of war, and they don't wear uniforms. The President has made that clear." She was referring to a January, 2002 directive signed by Secretary Rumsfeld stating that members of Al Qaeda and the Taliban were not prisoners of war.[1]

The legal advisor for JTF 160, Major B., would retort, "but we're to treat them *humanely* and *in a manner consistent with* the Geneva Conventions." Both were correct. But, what does it mean to treat detainees *in a manner consistent with* the Geneva Conventions? Moreover, if the two commanders disagree, who decides? The two sides just could not agree—and so round and round they went.

Finally, in November 2002, the Pentagon threw a towel into the ring and ended the battling between JTF 160 and JTF 170. It merged the two task forces, into one, JTF-GTMO. The legal advisor for JTF 170, Lieutenant Colonel Beaver (my superior) stayed and our office assumed all legal functions of JTF 160, which the Pentagon dissolved. After only being at Guantanamo Bay for a few months, Major B. went home.

---

1. Memorandum from Secretary of Defense Donald Rumsfeld to Chairman of the Joint Chiefs of Staff, January 19, 2002.

I became the "Joint Detention Operations Group JAG" or "J-DOG JAG." My responsibilities included providing legal advice to the Camp Commander and working with ICRC delegates. I moved from the main JAG office up on the hill to a small, dusty, plywood hut near the Detention Camp in an area called Camp America. I was among soldiers, where I am happiest.

Simultaneously with the JTF merger, Major General Geoffrey Miller, an active duty army general, replaced Major General Dunlavey, an army reservist and Pennsylvania judge, as the JTF-GTMO Commander. We speculated that the Pentagon, sensing growing world-wide curiosity about the camp in Guantanamo Bay, wanted an active duty general at the helm. Major General Miller's reputation preceded him. He was coming to us from Korea, and rumor had it that he was a no-nonsense officer who led from the front.

I saw Major General Miller for the first time when he stepped in front of the formation and assumed command. He was confident and friendly. He offered a few words of encouragement and then dismissed the formation. Within the first few days, he toured the detention camp, and talked to the soldiers. When it came time for lunch, he was troubled to learn that soldiers working at the detention camp did not have a chow-hall and were forced to eat outside on rickety picnic tables or while sitting in the dirt. He ordered supply personnel to find a dining tent, with air conditioning, and put it up. "Just get it done," he commanded.

Supply personnel made flurries of phone calls on and off the island to meet his demand. Frustrations ran high, as he inquired about the progress every few hours. Soldiers made the mission within only a few days, and finally guards at the detention camp had a cool place, close to the detention camp, where they could sit down and enjoy a civilized meal. This tent eventually became a permanent facility called the "Sea-side Galley." Service members regard it as the best place in Guantanamo Bay to get a good meal.

Major General Miller was concerned about morale. While the leadership had fought its internal JTF160-170 battle, soldiers at all ranks felt the effects of a mis-aligned command, and tensions ran high. Some soldiers had worked for weeks without a day off. Many were tired, homesick, and had low morale. Realizing that well-rested soldiers make better decisions, Major General Miller revised the work schedules and increased recreation time for soldiers. He also restored Sunday as a day of rest for all unnecessary personnel. Finally, I was able to go to church in civilian clothes, without rushing back to work. The U.S. military accommodated the detainee's religious practices, and it only seemed fair that soldiers should have time to worship, too. At church, Navy Chaplain Bush (a woman), whose fiancé deployed to Afghanistan while we were in Gitmo, led us in prayer and song. We prayed for the troops and the detainees, too.

Every unit has a call that soldiers recite when saluting one another. They range from "One Team, One Fight" to simply "Go Airborne." Saluting shows respect to senior officers, and the cadence reiterates the mission and increases esprit de corps. The detention camp at Guantanamo Bay had been in operation for over a year, but before Major General Miller assumed command, it was an island of divided loyalties and waning morale. Major General Miller announced that the new "slogan" at Gitmo would be (for the saluting soldier) "Honor Bound" and (for the responding saluting soldier) "To Defend Freedom." It would remind us that we were an important part of the War on Terror. He expected us to act honorably and in the name of freedom. We were then—and are forever—"Honor Bound."

"Captain Miller," my supervisor called as she entered our Gitmo JAG office, where we sat in front of computers reading the daily news-clips about life outside the island, "are you up to speed on Rules of Engagement?" "I think so ma'am—but why?" I asked. She explained that Major General Miller had queried on-duty soldiers about the rules of engagement during his tour of the camp and was disappointed at their responses. "Seems our soldiers are confused about when they can fire their weapons" she said. "The General wants to launch a massive Rules of Engagement training effort, and he wants the JAG Office to lead the effort. Can I count on you?" "Yes ma'am, I can put some training together."

It seems that high-level squabbling over the larger mission had overshadowed important training aspects of the day-to-day mission, and soldier confusion about the basic rules of engagement had gone undetected. The high rate of personnel turnover aggravated the problem. New soldiers and units were constantly rotating through JTF GTMO, and they all came with different backgrounds and slightly different training. Some of them were active-duty soldiers deployed from their home units; others were active guardsmen—part-time soldiers who left their civilian positions to assume military duties full-time; and yet others were "individual augmentees" who requested individual deployment and came from different active duty stations. Some of them had deployed through Fort Dix, New Jersey. Others had deployed through the CRC at Fort Benning, Georgia (as I did); while still others had come directly from their home units without specific training. Some of them were prison guards in their civilian capacity, and others had civilian jobs in vastly different areas, such as accounting or teaching, and were only military policemen in the army reserves.

Given the diverse personnel, it is not surprising that training varied from soldier to soldier. However, what Major General Miller discerned that others before him had not, is that soldiers must all receive the same instruction. To this end, I and another JAG officer, Lieutenant Colonel C., went to work preparing a lecture to cover basic rules of engagement, and the rules that applied specifically to Guantanamo Bay. We included concrete, realistic scenarios to make sure every soldier understood. At General Miller's direction, we even created a written test. Each soldier was required to pass the exam, or repeat the training. This Rules of Engagement training became one of several blocks of required instruction, and soldiers received refresher training approximately every three weeks.

Major General Miller did not leave us to our own devices. He reviewed the briefing slides, and met with us personally to discuss them. Although it was uncharacteristic of a General Officer to be so involved in coordinating training, I never doubted that Major General Miller trusted our legal expertise. It signaled that he wanted clear standards, and assurance that every soldier from the lowest-ranking soldier to the general himself knew and understood the Rules of Engagement.

He didn't waste time. General Miller wanted the training up and running right away. In fact, we spent Thanksgiving Day that year perfecting our presentation. "We're at war," I told myself. When we finished our work, we went to the base grade school, where they were hosting a Thanksgiving dinner for the troops. There was plenty of turkey and pumpkin pie.

Then, instead of flopping on the couch as I usually did after a big Thanksgiving meal, Lieutenant Colonel C. (who had helped with the presentation) and I went back to our hut in Camp America. I aimed to keep my mind on work and off the homesick feeling in the pit of my stomach. I couldn't stop thinking about my family back home in Wyoming around a plentiful Thanksgiving table.

Just then I heard Lieutenant Colonel C. say into the phone, "Hi guys, it's Daddy!" I left the hut to give him privacy. Lieutenant Colonel C. was such a devoted father. Some officers decorated their workspaces with military accolades and pictures of their buddies. Lieutenant Colonel C. decorated his cubicle with finger-painted works of art, and pictures of his smiling children. On our long drives around the island, he talked a lot about his family. One of his children was having trouble in school, and another was rebelling and being "a little naughty." Lieutenant Colonel C. often stayed at the office late to call home and do math homework over the phone with his son.

Some soldiers took advantage of Lieutenant Colonel C. because he was so nice. Some said he was *too* nice. He was tall, blue-eyed, and gentle, and seemed uncomfortable when junior soldiers saluted him. He saluted back, with a crooked smile and a shrug. His body language seemed to say, "Gee, you don't *really* have to salute me."

We shared a car and spent a lot of time together commuting to and from work. Occasionally, we made up an excuse to get away from our dusty little hut. We didn't miss a meal, and often chatted about last week's news over waterlogged peas in the chow hall. Although he significantly out-ranked me, Lieutenant Colonel C. made sure that I had the car at least as often as he did. It was very considerate of him. Some senior officers allocated cars to themselves, and junior officers car-pooled or hitched rides.

I appreciated his gentle leadership and intellectual insight. Although he was quiet, he analyzed things carefully and didn't easily bend his view of the law to appease others. One evening over dinner, while making a trail through his mashed-potatoes with a fork, he said, "I think it is permissible to use dogs for security, but I think the handlers should be careful. I hear they can get a little aggressive while detainees are in processing at the camp. I don't think it is right to torment detainees just to torment them." He was right, and years later, the U.S. military would prosecute dog-handlers and specifically forbid using them to torment detainees. Lieutenant Colonel C., in his quiet way, saw and predicted the dog problem before anyone else. (Personally, I never observed dog-handlers misuse dogs or threaten detainees with the dogs. But, only senior JAG officers attended detainee in-processing. I never attended.) He was a good lawyer and a good man.

I enjoyed working with Lieutenant Colonel C., and creating training materials to teach soldiers the Rules of Engagement. We both took great care to satisfy Major General Miller's request.

Eventually, the media attacked Major General Miller for supposed harsh interrogation techniques permitted at Guantanamo Bay. From my perspective, Major General Miller brought stability and consistency to JTF-GTMO. Assuming a difficult and fragmented mission, he made his expectations clear and improved morale in short order. Overall, I found him to be fair-minded and reasonable.

CHAPTER TEN

The Two Faces of the International Committee of the Red Cross

Like most days in Guantanamo Bay, it was hot. I had just finished teaching a class about the Rules of Engagement to a group of fifty soldiers in a billowing white tent. Upright fans made the temperature bearable. Usually all of the soldiers passed the exam, but this time one soldier missed one question too many. I excused the others, and asked him to stay behind to discuss his exam.

The exam question asked whether guards at a vehicle checkpoint could fire their weapons at a car that failed to stop, did not heed verbal orders to halt, and sped toward the detention camp. I explained, "You never lose the right to defend yourself or others. A speeding car racing towards the detention camp is a weapon, and you would be justified in using deadly force. In this scenario, the gate guards did everything they could to stop the car, including verbal orders to halt."

I found it odd that most soldiers who got questions wrong failed to understand the right of self-defense. They seemed tentative about firing their weapon, even when it was fully justified. Some were afraid the army would prosecute them if they made a mistake in the heat of the moment. Eventually I included a giant slide in the presentation with bold red letters stating, "You Always Have the Right of Self Defense!" I found it amazing that some soldiers didn't realize that.

What I didn't know then, is that eventually the military would change its policy regarding self-defense. In 2005, whirling from a rash of criticism from CNN about civilian deaths, the military changed the Rules of Engagement. The change allowed commanders to deny—yes *deny*—soldiers the right to defend themselves.[1] Now, nearly every time a soldier fires her weapon, the military conducts an investigation into whether the firing was legitimate. Senior lawyers at the Judge Advocate General School claim the reason for the change is to ap-

---

1. Kyndra Rotunda, *Denying Self Defense to GI's in Iraq*, Christian Science Monitor, March 2, 2007, at p. 9.

pease CNN! One even said that soldiers could face *courts martial* for firing their weapons (even in self defense). The change remains controversial.

Just then I looked at my watch, and cut our conversation short. "Let's continue this later, I have a meeting." I gathered up the Powerpoint equipment, and hauled it back to the plywood hut we called an office. The phone was ringing as I struggled through the door. I barely picked it up in time. "Captain Miller, JAG Office," I said, resting the receiver on one shoulder, and the computer bag on the other.

"Captain, Ma'am, this is Sergeant Strong. Did you forget the ICRC meeting." "Nope, my class ran long. Sorry, I'm on my way." "All right, I'll let 'em know. Mercy Buckets to ya Ma'am!" he said and hung up.

Sergeant Strong was an enlisted airman who worked in the JAG office. He was from Tennessee, and spoke with a deep, southern accent. One time when he brought something to my desk, I thanked him in French, saying "merci beaucoup." He adapted that to "Mercy Buckets," which caught on. Eventually it evolved, and we replaced "thank you" with one simple word—"buckets."

After a drive that seemed to last forever, I raced up the steps of "The Pink Palace," a big, run-down building on the other side of the island. I have no idea why soldiers call it a pink palace, because it is not pink on the outside or the inside. Probably somebody called it that, and the name stuck. I glanced at my watch. I was very late.

"Terribly sorry I am late," I breathlessly said as I walked through the door. Sergeant Strong had sent another JAG officer in the mean time. I took my place at the table, next to the commander of the detention camp. I was near the air conditioner, which felt so good. The air conditioner on our vehicle was on the fritz, yet again. I put my feet as close to the air conditioner as I could. I was wearing thick, black combat boots designed for cooler weather. Maybe I should have accepted the giant jungle boots at the Fort Benning CIF. They were way too big, but at least they would be cool. (Incidentally, detainees wear shorts and flip-flops because the Geneva Conventions require the U.S. to provide climate-appropriate clothing to POWs.)

Across the table were two delegates from the International Committee of the Red Cross (ICRC). These meetings with the camp commander occurred every week and always lasted about an hour. The ICRC also had regular meetings with Major General Miller. Usually I attended both meetings.

I liked working with the ICRC. They are exceptionally diplomatic, well spoken, and genuinely committed to improving the conditions of those imprisoned around the world. One of them, Daniel Cavolli, was the most elegant diplomat I have ever encountered. Despite the oppressive heat, he always looked professional, and delicately chose his words without sacrificing content. Daniel spoke many languages, and English was not his native tongue.

He began "Once again, thank you very much for meeting with us today to discuss a few matters about the detention camp." Although we met regularly, he never failed to start and end by graciously thanking the commander. Because the U.S. maintains that detainees in Gitmo are not POWs, it could simply refuse to meet with the ICRC and deny them access to the camp. However, the U.S. learned early on that working with the ICRC is mutually beneficial, and the right thing to do.

"Today we request the U.S. military to issue a bucket for detainees with prosthetic limbs, so they have a place to put their limbs when they are not using them." The detention camp Commander agreed that their request was reasonable. We then proceeded to other matters. ICRC delegates were concerned that U.S. translators were taking too long to translate some letters, and it reported that a new gate guard would not let them in the camp. The commander acknowledged their concerns, one after the other, and assured them that each would be addressed. He didn't always grant every request. But he granted many, and always followed through.

All of the meetings that I attended were very collegial. The ICRC worked cooperatively with the U.S. for several years at Guantanamo Bay and the U.S. followed their suggestions. A few years later, after a history of cordial relations, the ICRC suddenly alleged that conditions at Guantanamo Bay were "tantamount to torture." It is a strange allegation, because nobody knows what it really means. They stopped short of claiming that the U.S. government actually tortured detainees, and cushioned their statement by calling U.S. actions "tantamount to torture."

Not only is the allegation vague, it is completely inconsistent with claims they raised in Guantanamo Bay when I worked with them. If they believed that the conditions were so deplorable, why did they raise menial issues like speeding up the mail and purchasing checker board games for detainees? Why did they ask for more candy Skittles and softer soccer balls for the detainees, if they really believed detainees were being tortured on their watch? And especially, why did they use the media to air their grievances? Why didn't they tell the camp commander and me? I was surprised at these allegations and disappointed that they violated their *own rule* ensuring confidential communications. The ICRC cast its confidentiality policy aside to attack — of all countries — the United States.

The ICRC has been vociferously criticized for its "political" role in the War on Terror. The committee is supposed to communicate (confidentially) with leaders of the detention camp. But some believe that it has become a political, ideological organization aimed at attacking the United States, and that the ICRC has used our taxpayer dollars to advance their agenda (in 2002, the

U.S. provided over 25% of the ICRC's $665 million field operations budget).[2] The Wall Street Journal states, "Once upon a time, the International Committee of the Red Cross was a humanitarian outfit doing the Lord's work to reduce the horrors of war. So it is a special tragedy to see that it has increasingly become an ideological organization unable to distinguish between good guys and bad."[3]

The ICRC draws some criticism for purporting to interpret the Geneva Conventions, but relying on provisions that the U.S. has *never approved*. The ICRC passes off as law provisions that the U.S., and many countries around the world, have never agreed to, such as the Protocol 1.[4] In 1977, something called the "Diplomatic Conference on the Reaffirmation and Development of International and Humanitarian Law Applicable in Armed Conflicts" wrote two new treaties. In the first (called Protocol 1), it changed rules that apply to POWs by extending POW protections to people who otherwise did not qualify.[5]

But the U.S. did not agree to Protocol 1. It would not ratify this protocol, and never intended it to bind the U.S. The U.S. never intended to give POW protections to detainees who don't meet the definition of a POW. Instead, it intended to follow the Third Geneva Convention, which only gives POW protections to people who qualify, e.g., combatants who wear uniforms and follow the laws of war. Otherwise, what is to stop all of the world's militaries from going underground and adopting terrorist tactics?

Some argue that the U.S. should adhere to Protocol 1 because the ICRC (and I suppose the terrorists who don't wear uniforms) want it to do so. Some believe a legitimate argument exists that Protocol 1 is what we call "customary international law," which would require all countries to follow it, even those who did not sign or ratify it. This customary international law argument derives from the fact that 150 countries have ratified Protocol 1.[6] But, whether a particular provision is so widely accepted that it becomes customary international law and thereby binds the world, is up for debate. Furthermore, it is compelling

---

2. See http://www.genevabriefingbook.com/chapters/icrc.pdf.

3. *Red Double Crossed Again*, WALL STREET JOURNAL, December 2, 2004 at A12.

4. *Red Double Crossed Again*, The WALL STREET JOURNAL, December 2, 2004 at A 12, *citing*, Final Report of the Independent Panel to Review DoD Operations, August 2004 at 85–90.

5. For a brief discussion of The Geneva Conventions and Protocol 1, *see* GREGORY E. MAGGS, TERRORISM AND THE LAW, at App. C, 585–587 (Thompson West) (2005).

6. *See* GREGORY E. MAGGS, TERRORISM AND THE LAW, at App. C, 586, *stating*, "Over 150 nations have ratified these protocols, but the United States has not. A disputed issue is whether these additional protocols have become part of customary international law and as such may bind the United States." (Thompson/West Publishing) (2005).

that countries experienced with terrorism either refused to ratify the protocol (Israel), or ratified it with extensive reservations (the United Kingdom).

When the U.S. gives to terrorists (those that do not wear uniforms, hide their weapons, target civilians, etc.) all the privileges it gives to uniformed soldiers, it takes away any incentive for the terrorists to comply with the law of war. That endangers civilians. And, there is the policy question of whether the U.S. should give all the privileges of POWs to people who do not obey the laws of war, who do not wear uniforms, who do not carry their weapons openly, and who target women and children. The purpose of the Geneva Conventions that require soldiers to obey the laws of war is to protect civilians. The uniform is like a bulls-eye. It tells the soldier to shoot enemy soldiers and not civilians.

When I worked closely with the ICRC in Guantanamo Bay, it was before the ICRC resorted to publicly attacking the U.S., and before it resorted to arguing that the law was not settled. At that time, the U.S. did all it could to meet the ICRC's demands, and relationships were cordial. For instance, at the end of this particular ICRC meeting, we all shook hands. One of them asked me, "Will you be able to come to our BBQ tomorrow night? It will be at the Windmill Beach, and we'll have lots of food and drink." "Sounds fun," I said, "I'll definitely try to make it." Then I gathered my things and left.

Back at Camp America, I drove past one plywood hut after the other. "Where's the darned JAG office?" I thought to myself. They all looked alike, and were packed closely together. I had not been working at the camp office for very long, and occasionally I had trouble finding it.

I decided to stop for a map at the hut that handled administrative matters. I walked up the plywood steps and into the hut. It was very cramped inside with filing cabinets, too many workstations, and document-covered bulletin boards.

"Do you have a map of the camp?" I asked. A sergeant sent me to an office in the back corner of the hut, where I asked the same question. Another captain opened a locked file cabinet and handed me a hand-drawn map detailing where all of the huts are located. "Make sure to mark FOUO at the top of that map, and keep it 'close hold,'" he said. The acronym FOUO means "for official use only" and the expression "close hold" means that soldiers should guard the document, and not display it in open public. I borrowed a red pen from his Army logo mug and wrote FOUO at the top of the map.

The captain explained that Army Special Forces had found a photocopy of a similar, hand-drawn map of the camp in a remote cave somewhere in the hills of Afghanistan during a routine raid. Somehow, the map had made its way, with the aid of some nefarious person, from Cuba to Afghanistan and potentially into the hands of our enemies. Armed with this information, I started to realize the even supposedly secure locations aren't secure, and seemingly disinterested workers aren't necessarily disinterested. I folded the map, and put it in the top pocket of my uniform, where it remained until I learned where everything was located. Then I shredded it.

I do not know who handed the map of Guantanamo Bay to our enemies, or even if that story is true. However, I do know that some soldiers were suspicious of others working at Guantanamo Bay.

Rumors circulated that security guards confiscated the journal of a contract worker while she attempted to board a plane leaving Guantanamo Bay. They questioned her, and finally she surrendered the journals so that she could board the plane and travel home. After that, several soldiers who were keeping private journals decided to shred them to avoid any problems, or even the appearance of impropriety.

The way that some Muslims behaved raised suspicions. One Muslim airman insisted that he had a duty to minister to the detainees—his "Muslim Brothers." His claim was bizarre, because he was not a chaplain, but just happened to be a Muslim airman assigned to Guantanamo Bay in some other capacity. He became friendly with the detainees and began lingering around their cells and having private conversations, when he was supposed to be working. When asked about these conversations, he insisted that he was a religious leader and that his conversations with detainees were "privileged." Despite warnings and direct orders to stop, he persisted. Eventually Major General Miller punished the airman by reducing him in rank, taking away pay, and ordering him to leave Gitmo.

Soon after the airman left, Muslim Chaplain James Yee arrived in Guantanamo Bay. Yee is a Chinese-American West Point Graduate and was born into a Lutheran family. While in college, he became interested in Islam and eventually traveled to Damascus, Syria, to attend a traditional Islamic school. There he studied Arabic and Islam for four years.[7]

When he came to Guantanamo Bay, he was one of only fourteen Muslim chaplains serving in all of the military, and one of only eight in the army. In the months after September 11th, he was recognized for his efforts to educate people about Islam and stated that the attacks on the World Trade Center and Pentagon were "clearly un-Islamic."[8]

For a short while, my office in Guantanamo Bay was down the hall from Chaplain Yee's office. One afternoon he stopped by to chat, and the conversa-

---

7. Laura Goldstein, *A National Challenged: The Clergy: Military Clerics Balance Arms and Allah*, N.Y. TIMES, Oct. 7, 2001, section B1.

8. *Muslim Chaplains' Role Unique, Growing*, THE ATLANTA CONSTITUTION, Oct 14, 2001, 10A.

tion turned to a few questions he had about the extent of his role and whether his conversations with detainees were "privileged" the way they would be with soldiers. He asked me to review some web sites that he claimed supported his view. I didn't think his conversations with detainees were privileged, but he insisted that they were. I referred him to my supervisor, the Staff Judge Advocate, Lieutenant Colonel Diane Beaver. Chaplain Yee then met with Lieutenant Colonel Beaver who clearly explained that the Muslim chaplain's role at JTF GTMO was primarily to advise the *Commander*, not to provide religious counsel to *detainees*.

He apparently did not like her answer, because he seemed to ignore it. Many times after that, I observed Chaplain Yee brief new coming soldiers to Gitmo. His presentation intimated that his job was to minister to the detainees. One time a JAG colleague who attended Yee's briefing turned to me and whispered, "Yee doesn't seem to get it. Guess he needs another chat with Beaver." Lieutenant Colonel Beaver was extremely direct—and there is no way that Yee could have misunderstood her earlier directive.

Months later, after I had returned home from Guantanamo Bay, I heard on my car's radio that the military police had arrested Chaplain Yee, whom it suspected of espionage. Eventually the prosecutors added adultery charges. But ultimately, the Army dropped all charges against Chaplain Yee.

I do not know whether the charges against Chaplain Yee were legitimate, or whether the negative experience with the previous Muslim airman fueled hysteria and suspicion. Yee allegedly left Guantanamo Bay with drawings and documents related to certain detainees and their interrogators. A Guantanamo Bay investigator tipped off Florida customs officials, who later testified that the documents were "of interest to national security." At first, the government indicated that it would charge Yee with espionage. But instead it only charged him with lesser accounts of mishandling classified documents and other "Mickey Mouse" crimes like adultery and having pornography on a government computer. Finally, it dropped all of these charges too.[9]

I suppose it is possible, but it seems odd that Chaplain Yee would "accidentally" pack sensitive documents in his luggage and leave Gitmo. In a camp where detainees have threatened to hunt down and slaughter interrogators and their families, the military carefully safeguards its documents. Was Yee part of a greater plan to target U.S. interrogators and their families? Was he attempting to aid the enemy—his Muslim brothers? If not, why would Yee leave Guantanamo Bay with this information? And what exactly were the documents? We

---

9. Laura Parker, *The Ordeal of Chaplain Yee*, USA TODAY, May 16, 2004.

don't know because the government hasn't told us. Instead, it dropped all of the charges and then sealed the records to protect national security.

The government first alleged that Yee committed the most serious crime of espionage and then later dropped all charges against Yee after he spent weeks in solitary confinement. Perhaps the government overreacted. Or, perhaps the case against Yee was solid but holding a public trial would have revealed classified information and put others at risk. Nobody really knows. But, one thing is for sure: after September 11th, the U.S. must balance precious Constitutional liberties against national security. Americans cannot simultaneously enjoy perfect freedom and perfect national security. It cannot target suspects based on their religion, but it cannot ignore suspicious activity by Muslims in the armed forces.

CHAPTER ELEVEN

Interrogation Techniques

I heard the screen door of our house open and shut. "Hey, I'm in here," I called from the kitchen, assuming it was one of my roommates. Lauren, who was an interrogator at the Office of Naval Intelligence, stepped into the kitchen with her hat in hand. "What's all this?" she said, when she saw me rifling through a large cardboard box. "Can you believe this care package from home?" I said, pulling one item after the other from the box and placing it on the counter. This was the first of many generous care packages from the JAG office at Walter Reed.

"Take whatever you want," I said. Together we inventoried packages of candy, CDs, disposable cameras, travel size toiletries, wet-wipes, fashion magazines, calling cards, stamps … and even a miniature Christmas tree for the upcoming holiday season.

"I had a great day in the booth with my guy," she said, holding a stick of deodorant in one hand, and licorice ropes in the other. (Interrogators refer to rooms in a trailer where they interviewed detainees as the "booth," and the detainee they interview as "my guy.") "Why, what happened?" I asked. "He finally trusts me. Today he dropped his cover story, and told me a story that actually makes sense," she said. "I don't know how you interrogate detainees all day," I said.

Earlier in the week, I had observed some interrogations through mirrored glass. During a break, one detainee (who believed he was alone) saw his reflection in the mirror and watched himself wiggle his nose. Then he opened his mouth for a long look inside. He also tried smoothing his hair with cuffed hands. It was strange. He had no idea I was watching him from the other side. Being inside a mirror offers an unusual vantage point.

Most interrogations were long and tedious. Interrogators asked the same questions for hours, and detainees gave long, trailing answers. The interrogator would say something like, "Tell me what happened from the beginning," and the detainee would respond, "My grandfather was born in a village next to a grove …" and on and on it would go.

Lauren then explained that interrogating detainees is difficult, because Al Qaeda trains its recruits in counter-interrogation techniques. Detainees know how to steer the conversation away from the question asked. Sometimes they lie, just to test the interrogator. "You must study their file front to back before confronting the detainee," she said. Later I heard about a detainee who became frustrated with his interrogator and demanded "a better interrogator who knows what he's doing and won't waste my time." She also explained that building rapport with the detainee is the best way to obtain information. "If they like you, they'll talk," she said.

Lauren's observations were similar to what I had heard from others. Some interrogators shared tea with the detainees, or brought them sandwiches from Subway or French fries from McDonalds. From what I gathered, gentle interrogation approaches were the most effective.

But, some interrogators became frustrated when they were unable to extract intelligence from particular detainees. Usable intelligence gathered at Guantanamo Bay began to decline as the months passed by. Hoping to jump-start the interrogations, the officer in charge of interrogations, Lieutenant Colonel P., drafted a list of more aggressive techniques. They were organized in three distinct categories and each category proposed increasingly more aggressive techniques. He asked Lieutenant Colonel Beaver in the JAG office for a legal opinion.

Category I techniques encompassed the "direct approach" and recommended enticing detainees with things like cookies and cigarettes. Categories II and III were considerably more aggressive. Category II permitted "stress positions," like requiring the detainee to stand for four hours at a time and switching the detainee from hot meals to cold meals, called MREs (Meals Ready to Eat). Soldiers eat MREs in the field. I ate them at Quantico while training with the Marines. Category III techniques included tactics like using a wet towel to simulate suffocation (called waterboarding); and mild physical contact such as grabbing, poking, and lightly pushing the detainee.[1]

Lieutenant Colonel Beaver issued a memorandum of law, explaining that the United States had taken reservations on several International Conventions defining cruel, inhumane, or degrading treatment. Instead, the United States agreed only to be bound to the United States Constitution prohibition against cruel and unusual punishment. Therefore, the Eighth Amendment to the United States Constitution, prohibiting "cruel and unusual punishment" and cases interpreting that provision, should govern.

The Eighth Amendment cases make it clear that inflicting unnecessary, wanton pain and suffering constitutes cruel and unusual punishment. One case, *Ortiz*

---

1. Memorandum for Commander, Joint Task Force 170 from Jerald Phifer, Lieutenant Colonel, Director, J2, 11 October 202. The original document was classified secret/noforn. It was declassified by the Secretary of Defense on June 21, 2004 and released. It can be viewed at www.defenselink.mil/releases/2004/nr20040622-0930.html.

v. Gramajo,[2] involved a nun (and a U.S. citizen) who was kidnapped, beaten, and raped by Guatemalan military personnel when she was in Guatemala engaged in missionary work. The court decided it was torture under the Torture Victim Protective Act of 1991. But, the case did not provide a bright-line rule defining where legitimate interrogation methods stopped, and torture started.

The cases were not clear about what constitutes torture. Even if there was a "bright line" soldiers must abide by the Uniform Code of Military Justice (UCMJ), which makes assault and battery illegal. For these reasons, the memorandum backed away from fully endorsing category II and III techniques. It suggested additional legal review and consultation with other experts, including medical, behavioral science, and intelligence personnel.[3]

While Lieutenant Colonel Beaver expressed some skepticism, the Department of Defense (DoD) did not back away from category II and III techniques. Instead, it decided that soldiers can commit assault and battery, even though it is a crime under the law. It suggested that soldiers would receive immunity for their criminal acts. The DoD did not rely on the memo drafted by LTC Beaver in Gitmo. Instead, it relied on another legal opinion drafted by the Department of Justice Office of Legal Counsel, which the media later dubbed the "Torture Memo."

Oddly, the date on that memo is August 1, 2002—at least one month *before* interrogators posed the question to the Gitmo JAG office. Either the right hand was not talking to the left, or several offices simultaneously addressed the same question by design. It is difficult to say for certain what happened, but the Gitmo JAG Office memo couldn't have been considered in drafting the infamous "torture memo," since it was finalized long before JTF Gitmo put pen to paper. If the government had considered Lieutenant Colonel Beaver's recommendation for greater scrutiny, perhaps things would have worked out differently.

---

2. *Ortiz v. Gramajo*, 886 F.Supp. 162 (D. Mass. 1995).

3. Memorandum for Commander, Joint Task Force 170 from Diane E. Beaver, Staff Judge Advocate, 11 October 2002. Also available at www.defenselink.mil/releases/2004/nr20040622-0930.html.

CHAPTER TWELVE

The Justice Department Back-Peddles on Torture

The Torture Memo, which was drafted by the Department of Justice, Office of Legal Counsel that the administration accepted, narrowly defined torture as severe physical pain of the type that accompanies death or organ failure. Legal experts and politicians criticized the memo for inviting harsh interrogations techniques and for suggesting that the president could authorize illegal torture during an ongoing war. It even discussed defenses that soldiers could raise for violating the law, which raised questions about whether the U.S. truly intended to comply with laws prohibiting torture.

The Torture Memo was controversial. The Department of Justice, Office of Legal Counsel revoked it eighteen months after releasing it and replaced it with a tailored version.

The new version concurred that "torture" usually refers to extreme, intentional conduct (such as cutting off fingers, removing fingernails, and administering electric shocks to the testicles). It broadened the definition by acknowledging that "severe physical suffering" may also constitute torture, but backed away from defining the term.

The new memorandum was silent on the issue of whether the president had authority to permit illegal torture, and it did not discuss defenses that soldiers accused of torture could raise.

The new memorandum lacked the bravado of the original, and raised more questions than it answered. What constitutes severe physical suffering? Who decides?

Most people agree that the U.S. should not torture detainees—but nobody can agree about the definition of torture. For example, if the U.S. were to capture Osama Bin Laden, and learn that another September 11th were about to occur somewhere in the world, what would be the outer limits of our interrogation abilities? In these instances, when a time bomb is ticking and we believe that lives are at stake, how far can interrogators go to discover the location of the bomb? We just don't know.

Prominent Harvard Law Professor Alan Dershowitz, maintains that non-lethal torture tactics are permissible in some cases—such as the ticking-bomb scenario introduced above—when we know that a terrorist has information that could thwart a terrorist attack that is about to occur. Dershowitz opines that inserting a sterilized needle under one's fingernails to produce unbearable pain without possible death is permissible and argues, "The simple cost-benefit analysis for employing such non-lethal torture seems overwhelming: it is surely better to inflict non-lethal pain to prevent an act of terrorism than to permit a large number of innocent victims to die."[1]

On the other hand, what if the extreme pain causes the victim to have a heart attack and die? Then there is death. Death may always result. And, what if the victim does not really know the location of the ticking bomb? The ticking time bomb hypothetical is inherently imperfect because it assumes what we cannot know. It assumes that the person being interrogated *actually knows* the information sought. In the real world, we can never be sure. If the detainee doesn't tell us, is it because he doesn't know, or because we haven't inflicted enough pain? And how much pain is too much?

The only country to admit using violent and coercive interrogation tactics against terrorists is Israel.[2] This isn't surprising, considering that Israel is a popular terrorist target and "the only functional democracy in its neighborhood."[3] In 1987, due to allegations that the agency responsible for counterterrorism and security (known popularly as Shin Bet), had abused and tortured suspects, Israel established a commission to investigate Shin Bet interrogation tactics.[4] It discovered instances where suspected terrorists in Israeli custody had been tortured and it revealed that interrogators are in a catch-22. On one hand, they are bound to use legitimate interrogation tactics to extract information. On the other, the government pressures them to get information and thwart terrorist attacks.[5]

These findings led Israel to adopt specific interrogation guidelines that allowed interrogators to apply certain "moderate" and "nonviolent physical pressure" to extract information from suspects when the information could save lives.[6]

---

1. ALAN M. DERSHOWITZ, WHY TERRORISM WORKS: UNDERSTANDING THE THREAT, RESPONDING TO THE CHALLENGE, 143–144 (2002).

2. John Peter Pham, *Torture Democracy and the War on Terrorism*, THE LONG TERM VIEW: J. OF THE MASS. SCHOOL OF LAW, Vol. 6 no. 4, Spring 2006 at 9.

3. *Id.*

4. John Peter Pham, *Torture Democracy and the War on Terrorism*, THE LONG TERM VIEW: J. OF THE MASS. SCHOOL OF LAW, Vol. 6 no. 4, Spring 2006 at 10.

5. *Id.*

6. *Id.*

Approved methods included shaking prisoners, depriving them of sleep, placing them in stress positions including sitting on a low, uncomfortable stool, hooded, hands tied behind the back, with blaring loud music. Other positions include painfully stretching the prisoner, or requiring him to crouch like a frog.[7] However, in 1999, the Israeli Supreme Court, after acknowledging that the tactics had successfully thwarted numerous terrorist attacks, nonetheless invalidated them because the tactics violated human dignity and liberty.[8]

Israel is the only country in the world that has attempted to publicly confront, define, and codify torture.[9] In 2005, the U.S. Congress passed the Detainee Treatment Act, often referred to as the "McCain Amendment." However, as Cardozo Law Professor Gail Miller points out in the January 2006 addendum to her book entitled "Defining Torture," the legislation does *not* prohibit, or *even define* torture.[10] Professor Miller observes, "Indeed, it does not even use the word torture."[11]

Instead, it broadly guarantees, "No individual in the custody or under physical control of the United States Government shall be subject to cruel, inhuman, or degrading treatment or punishment." It uses the definition of "cruel and unusual punishment" as conduct that violates the 5th, 8th and 14th Amendments to the U.S. Constitution—which is nothing new. Senator McCain, himself, has acknowledged that fact. He stated, "The second part of this amendment really shouldn't be objectionable to anyone since I'm actually not proposing anything new. The prohibition against cruel,

> **JAG Fact**
>
> *The U.S. Constitution's **5th Amendment** protects against double jeopardy (being tried twice for the same crime), being called as witnesses against oneself (asserting that right is often called "pleading the fifth") depriving one of life, liberty or property without due process, and taking private property for public use without just compensation.*
>
> *The **8th Amendment** prohibits excessive fines and prohibits cruel and unusual punishment.*
>
> *The **14th Amendment** (among other things) guarantees that the state may not deprive a person of life, liberty or property without due process of law and it cannot discriminate (deny the equal protection of the laws).*

---

7. John Peter Pham, *Torture Democracy and the War on Terrorism*, THE LONG TERM VIEW: J. OF THE MASS. SCHOOL OF LAW, Vol. 6 no. 4, Spring 2006 at 11.

8. *Id.* at 11–12.

9. John Peter Pham, *Torture Democracy and the War on Terrorism*, THE LONG TERM VIEW: J. OF THE MASS. SCHOOL OF LAW, Vol. 6 no. 4, Spring 2006 at 12.

10. GAIL H. MILLER, DEFINING TORTURE, January 2006 addendum (Floersheimer Center for Constitutional Democracy, Benjamin Cardozo School of Law) (2005).

11. GAIL H. MILLER, DEFINING TORTURE, January 2006 addendum (Floersheimer Center for Constitutional Democracy, Benjamin Cardozo School of Law) (2005).

inhumane and degrading treatment has been a longstanding principle in both law and policy in the United States."[12] (One wonders why the Bush Administration opposed the law, at least at first).

The media often refers to Guantanamo Bay as the *Gulag of our Time* because of interrogation tactics that interrogators supposedly used on detainees. (Gulag is a term used for Soviet forced labor camps created in 1919 where the Soviets starved, mistreated, and forced their prisoners to work exhaustingly long hours in remote areas of Siberia. Hundreds of thousands died). Major General Miller, former Commander of JTF-GTMO, has also been criticized for bringing tactics used at Guantanamo Bay to Abu Ghraib, where shocking instances of abuse occurred. Supposedly, Guantanamo's tactics migrated to other places and precipitated widespread abuse, and death of detainees at Abu Ghraib in a few instances.

However, in May 2004 Secretary of Defense Donald Rumsfeld appointed an independent committee headed by Vice Admiral Albert Church to investigate interrogation operations within the Department of Defense. The results, often called *The Church Report*, indicate that abuse happened not *more*, but *less often* at Guantanamo Bay where Major General Miller published clear (albeit controversial) guidelines. The investigation revealed that in Guantanamo Bay, unlike in Iraq and Afghanistan, the commander disseminated interrogation policies and most interrogators followed them. The report found that "close compliance with interrogation policy was due to a number of factors, including strict command over-sight and effective leadership...."[13] When the two task forces merged into one, interrogators and military police worked closely together collecting valuable intelligence without detainee abuse. About Guantanamo Bay, *The Church Report* concluded, "In our view, it is a model that should be considered for use in other interrogation operations in the Global War on Terrorism."[14]

Overall, the Church Report investigators found 71 total cases of abuse occurring in Afghanistan, Guantanamo Bay, and Iraq (including 6 deaths).[15] Only 20 of those 71 cases were in any way related to interrogations.[16] The most common detainee abuse was "straightforward physical abuse, such as slapping, punching and kicking."[17]

---

12. Senator John McCain, Statement on Detainee Amendments, October 5, 2005, *available at* http://mccain.senate.gov.

13. *The Church Report*, Unclassified Executive Summary, at 9. The unclassified report is available at http://www.defenselink.mil/news/Mar2005/d20050310exe.pdf.

14. *The Church Report*, Unclassified Executive Summary, at 10.

15. *The Church Report*, Unclassified Executive Summary at 2.

16. *The Church Report*, Unclassified Executive Summary at 2.

17. *The Church Report*, Unclassified Executive Summary at 15.

In Guantanamo Bay, where there had been over 24,000 interrogation sessions, the investigators found *only three* cases of substantiated interrogation-related abuse. Two of those involved female interrogators who "touched and spoke to detainees in a sexually suggestive manner...."[18] (For instance, one time a female interrogator sat briefly on a detainees lap and put her arms around his neck.) In all three cases, the army disciplined the interrogators.[19]

These few instances of abuse at Guantanamo Bay pale in comparison, both in type and severity to abuse that occurred in Afghanistan and Iraq. For instance, in Afghanistan one army lieutenant colonel, who worked with the Defense Intelligence Agency, participated in a fighting campaign where the U.S. detained an entire village for four days to "conduct screening operations." During these operations, the lieutenant colonel punched, kicked, grabbed, and choked numerous villagers. The army disciplined him too, and suspended him from participating in any operations involving detainees.[20] In another incident that occurred on August 20, 2003, a lieutenant colonel serving in Iraq and questioning an Iraqi detainee "fired his weapon near the detainee's head in an effort to elicit information regarding a plot to assassinate U.S. service members."[21] The Army disciplined him and relieved him of command although his tactic secured useful information. This former lieutenant colonel is now running for U.S. Congress.[22]

Interrogators at Guantanamo Bay attempted to codify interrogation tactics, to distinguish permissible measures from those considered "torture." While it drew criticism, facts revealed in the *Church Report* indicate that substantially few instances of abuse occurred at Guantanamo Bay—fewer than at other detention facility in Iraq and Afghanistan.

While the reasons are many, *The Church Report* credited the limited instances of abuse at Guantanamo Bay to clear guidelines and sound leadership. This makes clear that codifying interrogation tactics (even if some are controversial) leads to *less*, not *more* abuse.

The Church Report also made clear that Guantanamo Bay tactics could not have "migrated" to Afghanistan. The panel discovered that, for an unknown reason, commanders in Afghanistan and Iraq received no guidance about inter-

---

18. *The Church Report*, Unclassified Executive Summary, at 14.
19. *The Church Report*, Unclassified Executive Summary, at 14.
20. *The Church Report*, Unclassified Executive Summary, at 14.
21. *The Church Report*, Unclassified Executive Summary, at 16.
22. Gina Cavallaro, *Army O–5, relieved of duty, runs for Congress*, THE NAVY TIMES, January 5, 2008.

rogation tactics. In fact, the panel noted "we cannot be sure how the number and severity of abuses would have been curtailed had there been early and consistent guidance from higher levels."[23] That is, the committee determined that Gitmo tactics did not migrate to Afghanistan. If they had, perhaps some of the abuses at Abu Ghraib wouldn't have happened.

Despite *The Church Report*, some FBI Investigators have reported seeing detainees shackled to the ground, and mistreated by interrogators at Gitmo. I suppose it is possible that some abuses occurred, and it is even possible that they occurred without the chain of command, or the JAG office, knowing about them. But, I didn't see, or hear about, any torture at Gitmo.

In Gitmo, I worked briefly with psychologists and psychiatrists who assisted interrogators. They were part of the "behavioral consultation team" (the acronym is BSCT, pronounced like "biscuit"). They observed detainees during their interrogations for "deception signs," which are subtle movements and body gestures that people make when they are lying. The "biscuits" carefully watched detainees and then consulted with interrogators when they perceived that the detainee was lying. This seems harmless. Indeed, U.S. law enforcement officers use similar tactics every day on American criminal suspects. What grade school teacher or parent hasn't detected a child's lie this way?

Is that torture? The International Committee of the Red Cross says yes. It said these tactics were "tantamount to torture" and called on the U.S. to ban them. Some said this tactic violated the Hippocratic Oath, an ethical vow that doctors take. In one portion of that classical oath, doctors vow, "keep them [the sick] from harm and injustice."

> **JAG Fact**
>
> The Church Report *supports my recollection of the "BSCT" role in Gitmo.*
>
> *It states, "It is a growing trend in the Global War on Terror for Behavioral science personnel to work with and support interrogators. These personnel observe interrogations, assess detainee behavior and motivations, review interrogation techniques, and offer advice to interrogators. This support can be effective in helping interrogators collect intelligence from detainees; however, it must be done within proper limits. We found that behavioral science personnel were not involved in detainee medical care (thus avoiding any inherent conflict between caring for detainees and crafting interrogation strategies), nor were they permitted access to detainee medical records for purposes of developing interrogation strategies."—*
>
> The Church Report *at 19–20.*

---

23. *The Church Report*, Unclassified Executive Summary at 3.

Eventually the army disbanded its "biscuits." Instead of fighting the criticism waged by the ICRC, the army accepted the falsity and decided to interrogate suspected terrorists with one arm tied behind its back.[24]

The United States is the most advanced country in the world and an ardent supporter of human rights and liberties. Our mission in Iraq is fostering democracy in an oppressed country that wants to be free. Saddam Hussein tortured and oppressed his own people, and lived in marble palaces while his people starved and suffered. When U.S. soldiers entered Baghdad, cheering crowds hungry for hope met them and cheered them on. On arrival in Baghdad, one marine recalls, "I had an Iraqi citizen come up to me. She was female. She opened her mouth and she had no tongue. She was pointing at the statue of Saddam Hussein. There were people with no fingers, waving at the statue of Saddam, telling us he tortured them. People were showing us scars on their backs."[25]

We are liberators—not torturers. We deplore leaders like Saddam Hussein, who reign through fear and oppression. In this war, some soldiers have forgotten that and have gone astray. And when they do, JAG Officers prosecute them, and the military punishes them. What happened at Abu Ghraib had nothing to do with interrogation tactics. *The Church Report* concluded, "none of the pictured abuses at Abu Ghraib bear any resemblance to approved policies at any level, in any theater."[26]

By March 2006, the U.S. military had tried and sentenced over ten soldiers for mistreating detainees. The military sentenced Specialist Charles Garner, the supposed ringleader of abusers at Abu Ghraib, to a ten-year prison sentence and a dishonorable discharge.

A military jury found Private First Class Lynndie England, who posed for sadistic pictures with detainees at Abu Ghraib, guilty of maltreatment, indecent acts, and conspiracy and sentenced her to three years in prison and a dishonorable discharge. They are but a few—and they do not define the whole.

---

24. Kyndra Rotunda, *Hollywood Interrogates al Qaeda*, THE WALL STREET JOURNAL, April 18, 2007 at A16.

25. *In Their Own Words*, THE WASHINGTON POST, Sunday March 19, 2006, *quoting* Lance Corporal Daniel Finn. (The article quotes 100 veterans of the Iraq War after returning home).

26. *The Church Report*, Unclassified Executive Summary at 3.

CHAPTER THIRTEEN

A Soldier Comes Home,
No Room at the Inn

It was March. I was finally going home. I packed my duffle bags and waved goodbye as the ferry pulled away from the dock. I was excited to go home, but sad to leave. The military has a way of reuniting people. I hoped that someday I would serve with these officers again.

JAG Fact

Packed in my bag was a framed plaque that my marine friends gave me the night before I left. It is a common Marine saying, and they replaced the word "weapon" with the word "JAG." It is entitled, "This is My JAG" and it reads as follows:

This is my JAG. There are many like her, but this one is mine.

My JAG is my best friend. She is my life. I must listen to my JAG as I must master my life. My JAG without me is useless.

Without my JAG, I am useless. I must keep my JAG true.

I must listen to my JAG better than my enemy who is trying to kill me. I must listen to be JAG before my enemy shoots me.

I will ...

My JAG and myself know what counts in this war is not the rounds we fire, the noise of our burst, or the smoke we make. We know that it is the R.O.E. [Rules of Engagement] and hits that count.

We will hit ...

My JAG is human, even as I, because she is my life. Thus, I will learn from my JAG as my sister.

I will learn her weaknesses, her strengths, her education, her training and her expertise. I will guard her against the ravages of weather and damage as I will ever guard my legs, my arms, my eyes and my heart against damage.

I will keep my JAG clean and ready.

We will become part of each other.

We will ...

Before God, I swear this creed. My JAG and myself are the defenders of my country. We are the masters of our enemy. We are the saviors of my career.

So be it, until victory is America's and there is no enemy, but peace.

After a long day of ferry rides, plane rides, bus rides, one taxi ride, and countless hours of waiting for each, I arrived back at Fort Benning Georgia. I was tired and longed for sleep. The Army required me to go back to Fort Benning before it would send me home. I deployed from there, so it wanted me to go back to Fort Benning on the way home to be counted.

The cab wound along the narrow road, nestled in the woods of Fort Benning. Eventually it rolled to a stop at the Conus Replacement Center (CRC). It was like déjà vu. I was right back where I started, only a changed person by all of my experiences in Guantanamo Bay.

I lugged my bags from the cab, and just as I was paying the driver, someone called to me from the building nearby, waving his arms, "No room, ma'am," he said. I asked the driver to wait, while I investigated. "What do you mean no room?" I asked a soldier, as I walked toward him. "There's so many people deploying right now, and we're plum full." He suggested that I try the Bachelor Officer Quarters (BOQ), which is like a hotel for officers on Fort Benning.

I thanked him and got back in the cab. As we drove back down the road toward Fort Benning, I had a sinking feeling that it would be a while before my head found a pillow. I was right.

There weren't any rooms available at the BOQ, so the receptionist there told me about a building across the street where soldiers were staying. "You'll need your sleeping bag," she called after me, as I lugged my bags out the door. It was ironic that I deployed with a sleeping bag that I didn't unroll, until this night, back home at Fort Benning.

I had an uneasy feeling as I walked in the dark toward a building that looked abandoned. At one time, it was probably soldier barracks, but now it was empty and run down. The old, splintered front door was standing wide open. I thought it was strange, particularly since it was near midnight.

I pulled my bags over crumbling concrete steps and dragged them behind me, into the building. I didn't see anybody. "Hello," I called looking left and right down an empty hallway. A male's voice responded from somewhere, and echoed through the empty corridor, "Females upstairs!" I hollered "thank you" to the anonymous voice, and made my way up a dark stairway.

At the top, I heard the rhythmic sound of dripping water, and looked up to see an unmarked restroom with a sign taped to the door that said "BYOTP." I interpreted this to mean, "Bring your own toilet paper." "Great," I thought, and started looking for a room.

Some rooms didn't have doors and others didn't have light fixtures. Finally, I found a room with both. However, the door didn't close all the way, and there wasn't a doorknob or lock. Anxious to lie down, I thought, "It'll do," and flung my bags to the floor. It felt good to put them down. I shook my arms and hands before perching them on my hips and scanning the room from one side to the other. Every wall was filthy, and a layer of dust covered the tile floor. Aside from the grime, it was completely empty except for a lonely, crumpled Twinkie wrapper in one corner, next to a twisted wire hanger.

I unrolled my sleeping bag, turned off the light, and tried to rest. But I couldn't sleep. It was quiet—too quiet. I felt completely exposed and alone in this run down room with a door that didn't lock. I was cold, too. Georgia seemed frigid compared to Guantanamo Bay. Finally, shivering and unable to sleep, I rolled up my sleeping bag, and went looking for somewhere else to spend the night.

It was Friday night, so I managed to get a cab without too much trouble. I shared the ride with two soldiers about to deploy to Iraq. They were looking for a good time. When the driver pulled up to a crowded bar one soldier reached in his wallet. I said to them, "Don't worry about the cab fare, it's on me." It was the least I could do for two soldiers going off to war. They thanked me, and the cab driver pulled away. I turned to watch them disappear into the smoke filled bar and quietly said a prayer, "Lord, look after them." I still wonder what became of those young troops.

We went to several hotels, and each turned me away. There was no room at the inns. I couldn't understand why. "What's going on this week-end that is causing all of the hotels to be completely booked?" I asked the cab driver, as we encountered one "No-Vacancy" sign after the next. He explained that every Friday night was like that around Fort Benning. Drill sergeants let soldiers leave post for the weekend, so they pool their money and get hotel rooms where they can escape watchful eyes.

"In that case," I said, "Go to a nice hotel that soldiers can't afford." He took me to a very nice hotel, and it had a vacancy. I said goodnight, went upstairs, and finally found the pillow I'd been searching for. It had been a long day, and sleep came easily.

The next morning was Saturday and I woke up thinking I was still in Gitmo. When the sun peaked through the curtains, I acknowledged it, and then rolled over and slept some more. Finally, I put my feet on the floor, feeling refreshed and relieved to be home. It had been months since I had slept in a room without a roommate, or taken a shower without someone else waiting. It was glorious, quiet, and relaxing. I was grateful for the smallest things.

I put the Do Not Disturb sign on the door, called for room service, and ate in front of the television. I wondered if every soldier coming home feels the same way—ahhh, the good ole' U.S.A. After breakfast, I called my family, and had a long conversation, without a third party listening in.

Then I called the Conus Replacement Center at Fort Benning to find out what I should do next. The soldier on the other end of the line explained that the only thing I needed to do was return my military equipment. "Great," I said. "I have a flight scheduled to leave this evening, so I'll get a cab back to post, and drop off my equipment." "Sorry," he replied. "The Central Issue Facility, where you should return your equipment, won't be open until next week. Don't worry about your flight, we'll get you home. We're pretty full out here, but there's an old barracks building on post where you can stay for a few days." He was referring to the run down barracks that had chased me away the night before.

I remembered the poor soldier I met in the chow hall at the CRC months earlier who was trying to get a flight back to Boston, and stuck in CRC purgatory. On a whim, I asked the solder on the other end of the phone, "If I can get someone else to turn in my gear, can I catch the flight tonight and bypass CRC?" "Sure ma'am. Some people do that. Pick someone you trust, because if it doesn't get turned in, you'll get a hefty bill." Then I asked, "Do you have the phone number for the JAG on call?" He did. I took the phone number down.

I didn't call right away, because I was uncomfortable asking anyone for such a favor. I left the hotel, and walked to a coffee shop where I read the paper for a while and tried to assess my options. The newsprint between my fingers felt like a long lost friend. I didn't want to impose, but I was so hungry for home. I wanted to drive my own car, sleep in my own bed, and unpack my bags. I wanted my own life back! I was dubious about staying in the abandoned

> **JAG Fact**
>
> *Every JAG office appoints a "JAG on Call." Generally, the duty rotates on a weekly basis from one JAG lawyer to another. The JAG officer on call carries a pager and cell phone and responds to any emergencies. There aren't a lot of legal "emergencies."*

barracks building, foregoing my scheduled flight, and waiting on the CRC to rebook it. With hundreds of soldiers processing through the CRC, it could be days, maybe even weeks, I feared.

Finally, I went back to the room and dialed the phone. The voice on the other end picked up. "Captain Matt Neiman, JAG on call," he said. I started with "This isn't an emergency. I'm a JAG officer, too, and I wouldn't make this call if I didn't need your help. I apologize in advance, and please feel free to decline, but here's my predicament...." I went on to explain my situation.

Before I could even finish my sentence, Matt interrupted and said, "Do you want me to come and pick up your equipment? I can turn it in next week. Really, it isn't any trouble." I exhaled in relief. I was so glad that I reached a friendly, fellow JAG, and that he understood. "I'll pick you up in a few hours." I hung up the phone. Then I did a little victory dance around the hotel room. "Whoopee, I'm going home today!"

Matt and his wife Amy met me at the hotel, took me to lunch, and then drove me to the airport. It was the final leg of my long journey. I felt instantly befriended, and was truly touched by their kindness. Soldiers help soldiers— this is especially true among JAG officers.

The next week Matt turned in my equipment. I had lost a laundry bag somewhere along the way and the army billed Matt $7.00. He notified me, and I put a check in the mail for the amount. I also included a Starbucks gift card, and again thanked him and Amy for their kindness.

My bill for the laundry bag was only $7.00. It seemed a little nit-picky, considering that I had voluntarily deployed, worked six to seven days a week in a dusty hut, and lived in cramped quarters. But I paid the bill.

The army's stingy billing practices eventually backfired. The army charged troops returning from Iraq for lost or damaged equipment, even when the reason was combat related. Military equipment is lost, stolen, or destroyed in the chaos and confusion of war. The army billed one soldier for a new uniform because his uniform was *stained with blood* from fighting in combat![1] Another soldier, who was billed hundreds of dollars for lost equipment said, "I'm so proud to be in the military ... at the same time I just could not believe that when I got back after sacrificing so much that I owed the Army money."[2] Another explained, "Maybe you were lying down with a coat behind your head and you come under fire. Your first reaction isn't to grab [your] coat, fold it neatly, and make sure it's properly stowed when you're being shot at."[3]

The military defended its billing practices by explaining that soldier can challenge the bill by completing a several page long "reasonable wear and tear form." It requires their Commander to approve the damage or loss. But, most soldiers don't want to bog their Commanders down with bureaucratic forms or wait for a signature. Often, they just pay the bill.[4]

The army charged one guardsman from Oregon $4,000.00 for gear that he lost in his one-year plus tour fighting in Iraq. According to the soldier, he turned over the equipment to the Army before he left Iraq. The army launched an investigation to find out what happened to the soldier's gear. But, not sur-

---

1. Jim Hoffer, *Vets Charged for Lost and Damaged Gear*, 7 ONLINE NEW YORK CITY NEWS, March 22, 2007. Story available online at http://abclocal.go.com/wabc/story?section=local&id=5074904.

2. *Id.*

3. *Id.*

4. *Id.*

prisingly, soldiers weren't reachable, or couldn't recall, what happened to another soldier's canteen or body armor.[5]

The Neimans can't possibly know how much their gesture meant to me. I was finally home. As my plane descended over the Washington, D.C. area, a John Denver tune played repeatedly in my mind, "Hey, it's good to be back home again. Sometimes this old farm feels like a long, lost friend. Yes, hey it's good to be back home again...."

---

5. Beth Slovic, *Friendly Fire*, WILLAMETTE WEEK ONLINE, December 4, 2007.

CHAPTER FOURTEEN

The Fallen and Wounded

After my deployment to Guantanamo Bay, I returned to Walter Reed to finish what remained of my active duty obligation to the army. (The army requires soldiers to serve a certain number of years on active duty, followed by a several year commitment in the reserves. JAG Officers are bound to serve on active duty for three years, and then in the reserves for an additional five years, for a total eight year military commitment).

A few weeks after I returned to duty at Walter Reed, the Hospital Commander, Major General Kevin Kiley, (who was later promoted to Lieutenant General and became the Surgeon General of the Army), appointed me as the deputy of a new facility at the Walter Reed Army Medical Center (WRAMC), called the Medical Family Assistance Center (M-FAC).[1] Military installations around the United States and abroad have "Family Assistance Centers" to help deploying soldiers and their families; but Major General Kiley was the first to establish such a center within a hospital to assist families and returning casualties from the war in Iraq. Generally, injured soldiers went from a field hospital to Landstuhl Medical Center in Germany, and then to Walter Reed in Washington, D.C. when they were stable enough to make the flight.

The prior U.S. conflict, the Gulf War, ended so quickly and there weren't many casualties. In fact, it had been over thirty years since the U.S. had a significant number of casualties. Frankly, the military was out of practice.

The army could easily account for the seriously wounded, because they were inpatients and the hospital automatically provided their meals and quarters. However, the process was more difficult with the less seriously injured—the outpatients. The military placed them in the hotel on post, called the Mologne House. They were temporary residents at WRAMC, and in somewhat of a TDY capacity—temporary duty. When soldiers travel to attend military training, or for a job related reason, the military issues them "Temporary Duty Orders" so they can receive reimbursement for meals, lodging, gas, and other

---

1. Information about Walter Reed's Medical Family Assistance Center is available online at http://www.wramc.amedd.army.mil/Soldiers/MedFac1/FAQs.cfm.

incidental expenses. Generally, when on Temporary Duty Status, the soldier pays all expenses up-front and then files a travel voucher to receive compensation for meals and lodging.

That system doesn't work with casualties. Soldiers arrived at Walter Reed with only the hospital gowns on their backs. Some didn't even have an ID, let alone clothes, credit cards, or cash. The army assigned these injured outpatient soldiers to a hotel on WRAMC grounds, which was a short walk from the hospital. But the system was seriously flawed. If the army failed to account for a soldier when he got off the bus and went to the Mologne House (the name of WRAMC's hotel), the soldier could remain at the Mologne House, sick and alone, for days without any follow-up or care—or even a way to pay for meals.

One afternoon a wandering outpatient knocked on my door and said softly in an embarrassed tone, "Excuse ma'am ... but I ... well, I need ... do you know where I can get some clean underwear? It's just that I've been here for a few days and...." "No problem," I said, and called the Red Cross representative, who came running like always. I felt sad for this wounded soldier. How could this happen in the U.S. Army, I wondered?

Major General Kiley created the M-FAC to "solve problems." Team members consisted of representatives from several departments, including nursing, finance, JAG, Chaplains, Red Cross, USO, Personnel, Psychiatry, Army Community Service, and a Housing representative from the Mologne House, among others. We went to work solving the problems, but learned that navigating through army bureaucracy can be difficult. When time was of the essence, and soldiers or their families suffered on account of bureaucratic hold-ups, volunteer organizations like the Red Cross and USO graciously stepped in every time. They accepted public donations of everything from mouthwash to socks to auto magazines, and yes, even underwear. It generously distributed them to injured troops.

When the army didn't pay soldiers on account of one bureaucratic error or another, Barbara Green of the American Red Cross was on hand with her checkbook to buy them a meal. Repeatedly, the Red Cross bailed out the Army while we tried to get "all systems go." The same is true of the chaplains office, which provided countless cafeteria meal vouchers for hungry soldiers who couldn't pay; the USO, which provided hotel-room vouchers for family members; and Army Community Service (ACS), which distributed $100.00 cash to every casualty to offset the cost of "hospital incidentals."

My job at the M-FAC was to identify and resolve legal issues, but in reality, my responsibilities were much greater. I scheduled soldiers to man the phones, worked with the casualty affairs office to find personal items that were lost somewhere between the battlefield in Iraq and Washington, D.C., visited injured soldiers, talked to distressed parents on the telephone who had just learned that their soldier was being medically evacuated to our hospital, and I even did menial tasks like selecting the carpeting for our new facility. In the army, we are *Soldiers First, Lawyers Always*.

Sometimes we took matters into our own hands. One soldier had stabilized, and his doctors had released him from the hospital. However, he was waiting on travel orders that never came (another example of "hurry up and wait"). For days, he waited. Finally, one Friday afternoon, he came to the M-FAC office, frustrated and looking for help. An Army nurse, Colonel Cauldwell, and I went to work making phone calls. We were both operating outside our normal areas of expertise. She offered to drive him to the airport herself. Eventually, we got him home. She said, "Captain, thanks so much for your help." I smiled, thinking of my own recent situation at Fort Benning, and replied, "I've been there."

In the army, when a general wants something done, soldiers usually "make it happen." When Major General Kiley decided to establish a Medical Family Assistance Center he hired contractors who worked overnight to transform a storage closet into an office space. For a few days, soldiers and contractors busily painted walls, purchased office furniture, set up phone and computer lines, and did everything necessary to get the office in shape for opening day. Word quickly spread around Washington, D.C. that Walter Reed was about to establish a combat wounded center, and the dog and pony show began. Congressional representatives and high-level officials from the Pentagon paraded through the center to get a glimpse of the center in the making.

But Major General Kiley's intentions were ahead of the army's capabilities. He ordered soldiers to make a beautifully printed sign clearly outlining all of the benefits that combat wounded troops would receive. The sign said that soldiers would receive monetary stipends, free uniforms, free hotels for their family members, taxi vouchers for transportation around D.C., meal vouchers, so on and so forth. But it was fiction. One senior officer who was aware of the problem said, "We will put the sign in the closet, and only bring it out when the dignitaries visit our center." That is exactly what happened.

Eventually, Walter Reed (actually, *volunteers* at Walter Reed) did many, but not all, of the things on that list. And the sign only saw the outside of its closet when a dignitary was at the hospital that Walter Reed wanted to impress. I, and other young soldiers working with me, were disheartened that the army took credit for things that volunteers did.

The problems that I observed at WRAMC, I later learned, were just the tip of the iceberg. Walter Reed didn't know how to account for wounded outpatients from the outset, and the problems only worsened with time. By 2006, the Washington Post broke a shocking news story about deplorable conditions at Walter Reed. The outpatient facility (the Mologne House) soon reached maximum capacity and the army needed a place to keep recovering wounded outpatients. It put them in Building 18, a rundown brick building across the street from the hospital. In Building 18, soldiers lived in squalor. Some units had only sporadic running water, toilets didn't flush, heating and air conditioning units were often on the fritz, and there were even holes in the floors and ceilings. One injured soldier remarked that he could stand in his shower, look up, and see into the bathroom above him.[2]

Hearing about the conditions at Walter Reed on the television reminded me of the rundown building I encountered at Fort Benning when I returned from Gitmo. The army just wasn't equipped to manage and accommodate so many troops.

To make matters worse, the army started requiring injured troops living in Building 18 to report to 7 a.m. morning formations. Every morning soldiers limped across a dangerously busy Washington Street (Georgia Avenue), and reported to a large gymnasium on the Walter Reed Complex, where they stood in formation so the army could count them.[3]

It was only a matter of time before the press learned about the outrageously deplorable conditions at Walter Reed. But instead of apologizing and promising to do better, at first the army *defended* the deplorable conditions at Building 18. The Surgeon General (Lieutenant General Kiley, who was the former Commander at Walter Reed) foolishly came to Walter Reed's defense.

In the end, the army relieved both Lieutenant General Kiley and the Commander of Walter Reed (Major General George Weightman) from duty for allowing soldiers to suffer on their watch and for failing to fix systemic problems at Walter Reed. No one person is solely responsible for what happened at Building 18. The problem harkened back to what I observed when the first injured troops arrived at Walter Reed. The army bureaucracy just could not manage numerous wounded troops.

Secretary of Defense Gates created a commission to study the problems at Walter Reed. According to that Commission, the problems at Walter Reed stemmed mostly from the inundation of wounded troops at a time when Walter Reed was least able to manage them. At the same time that hundreds of wounded troops arrived at Walter Reed, both the facilities and personnel were declining because, around that same time, the U.S. government had identi-

---

2. Dana Priest and Anne Hull, *Soldiers Face Neglect, Frustration at Army's Top Medical Facility*, THE WASHINGTON POST, February 18, 2007, A01.

3. Id.

fied Walter Reed for base closure in approximately 2011. Knowing that Walter Reed would eventually close, the Pentagon was directing money and resources *away* from Walter Reed, at a time when these resources should have been flowing *toward* Walter Reed. What resulted is, as former Secretary of the Army Jack O. Marsh called it, "the perfect storm."[4]

But the "perfect storm" theory does not explain the problems that I observed at Walter Reed in the spring of 2003—two years before the Base Realignment and Closure Commission recommended closing the Walter Reed Campus.

---

4. CRS Report for Congress, Walter Reed Army Medical Center (WRAMC) and Office of Management and Budget (OMB) Circular A-76: Implications for the Future, August 21, 2007.

CHAPTER FIFTEEN

Captain Marton and Private First Class Lynch

I met some remarkable soldiers while working at the M-FAC. One, Captain Andras Marton, was a JAG officer who was seriously injured while deployed to Kuwait when one of his fellow U.S. soldiers threw grenades into several tents. Although the attack came in the middle of the night, at approximately 1:30 a.m., Captain Marton was well trained and instinctively reached for his flak vest, which saved his life, but did not spare him injuries. The blast ripped through the tents, killing two officers, and wounding thirteen others. Eventually, a military court convicted the attacker, Asan Akbar, a U.S. Muslim soldier, and sentenced him to death for brutally attacking his fellow soldiers.

Akbar volunteered to join the army, but didn't support the U.S. mission in Iraq. Some soldiers recalled Akbar making statements like, "You guys are coming into our countries and you're going to rape our women and kill our children."[1] If he objected to liberating his fellow Muslims in Iraq, he could have sought reassignment to a noncombat job, or even a discharge from the army. Army regulation 600-43 establishes criteria for soldiers to claim conscientious objector status.[2] It takes the Army about 90 days to process each application and render a decision. Instead of following the regulation, he viciously attacked his fellow soldiers while they slept.

During the Vietnam War, soldiers occasionally turned on their commanders and killed them—an offense called "fragging" an officer. Troops "fragged" their commanders when they lost faith in their leadership. It is a horrific crime.

---

1. The Associated Press, *Motive a mystery in grenade attack, Army says he may have acted out of resentment*, CNN.com, March 24, 2003. Available at http://www.cnn.com/2003/LAW/03/24/101.attack.ap/.

2. Army Regulation 600-43, *Conscientious Objection*, Department of the Army, 21 August 2006. (The regulation existed before August, 2006. The Army made administrative changes in 2006, but the process was available to Akbar in an earlier regulation published on May 15, 1998).

We learn to trust and take care of each other—honor, duty, loyalty—the creed that sustains us.

Captain Marton suffered extensive injuries, and the army admitted him to Walter Reed for several operations and months of grueling rehabilitation. He had a strong spirit, and a positive attitude that was infectious to others around him. He came to my office because the army took his personal belongings when he was in a field hospital in Kuwait. It bagged them, put his name on them, and then promptly lost them. Among the misplaced items was a precious family heirloom—I believe it was a locket. Captain Marton was desperate to find the locket. I consulted the casualty affairs office, made a few phone calls, and tried unsuccessfully to run it down. Sadly, nobody knows what became of the locket. Captain Marton recovered, and went on to be an outstanding prosecutor—some say he is one of the best in the Army JAG Corps.

While working at the M-FAC, I also met a remarkable young soldier, Private First Class Jessica Lynch. Reality and humility grounded her, and she did not care about fame. The media occasionally characterized her and her family as simple, but they weren't. The Lynchs knew that Jessica faced a long road of recovery. They just wanted her to get well, and that was all that mattered.

One day I was in the M-FAC clinic when Private Lynch's father walked through the door. He was a slight man, with a quiet, friendly demeanor. He was there to pick up Jessica's mail, which came by the sack-full, several times a day. Her mail was on a big table toward the back of the room, and it overflowed on to the floor. Crowning the table, in the very center, was an enormous bouquet of flowers. It was as large as a casket spray. "Who's that from?" he asked, pointing to the garden display. "Not sure," I said. He looked inside the attached card, to find flowery words of praise and encouragement for America's new hero. It was from a well-known journalist—a household name who was obviously vying for an interview. "Huh," he said, in a disinterested tone and put the card back.

He turned his attention to a large photo album, sitting among the cards and letters. He opened the cover, and inside were photos and signatures from Jessica's friends back home in small town Palestine, West Virginia. Mr. Lynch smiled, and his eyes lit up as he pointed to a few pictures, and told me about the girls in each one. "Jessica went to high school with this girl … this little girl lived down the street from us, they played together." He continued looking through the album, silently, running his fingers over pictures that took him to an earlier, much happier time.

"How is she doing?" I asked. "Well," he said after a pause, "not that good. She's sad. She's been through a lot, and she just lost her best friend. They went to boot camp together, and they were battle buddies." He was referring to Sergeant Piestwa, Private Lynch's closest friend, who drove the Humvee that

Jessica was riding in when the convoy wandered into enemy territory and shots erupted. Sergeant Piestwa expertly maneuvered the heavy humvee, until it careened out of control and crashed, killing her and several others. Jessica Lynch said later that Sergeant Piestwa was the true hero. (Incidentally, Piestwa was the first Native American killed in combat during the Iraq war).

"Well, we're glad she's home," he said, carrying an armload of flowers, stuffed animals, and the picture book, as he walked out the door and back to Jessica's room.

Private Lynch's family practically moved in to the Walter Reed hospital. I saw them at all times of day around the hospital, in the morning and late at night. They were constantly with Jessica. One afternoon I ran into them in the elevator. Jessica's mom had long cascading blond hair. She was an older version of Jessica. She seemed frustrated and asked why Jessica couldn't determine her own visitors. Apparently, Private Lynch wanted to see a West Virginia Senator, before seeing a higher-level official at the Pentagon, which broke with protocol. "Some official" at Walter Reed decided whom Jessica would see, and when she would see them. Everyone in Washington wanted a glimpse at America's new hero, and her family was getting frustrated with all of the army protocol. I understood and sympathized with their frustrations. Jessica was a soldier, but she was also their little girl. I was surprised at comments by a fellow officer who coldly stated, "This is a military hospital and Private Lynch is a soldier. We're not even required to let her family in here. We're being kind, but we still call the shots."

One may wonder why a recovering Private Jessica Lynch, or any returning POW, would need an attorney. Ordinarily she wouldn't, but for a gracious American public who literally flooded her room with flowers and extravagant gifts. There are ethics rules about soldiers accepting gifts, if offered by a company that does business with the military or offered solely because one is a soldier. If an offer is extended to all service members (such as Veteran's Day specials at local restaurants, or military discounts), then there is not an ethics violation. If, however, the vendor extends the offer to just one soldier, because they are a soldier, then accepting the gift may violate the army's ethics rules.

In the Iraq War, gifts even found their way to the battlefield. One morning I logged on to my computer, and received a message sent the previous night from somewhere in Iraq. It included an image of a life size Winnie the Pooh bear with a patriotic ribbon tied around its giant neck. It was a garish sight.

The Pooh bear was a gift intended for General Tommy Franks from a patriotic American, and (for an unknown reason) somebody asked our JAG office at Walter Reed for a legal opinion about whether General Franks could accept the giant Pooh bear. (Perhaps the Iraq office referred this case to our office because it was concerned with greater matters).

The sender claimed it was a birthday gift for Franks' grand-daughter (whom the sender did not know and had never met), but the regulations take care of that rather obvious loophole. Under the regulations, gifts given to family members are imputed to the soldier. We "researched" the sender and the cost of the giant bear, and determined that General Franks could not accept the teddy bear, which had a very hefty, several hundred dollar, price tag. This is just one example of the military's gift rules in action. It is also an example of the lighter, less interesting, side of life in the JAG Corps.

As with most rules, there are exceptions. One exception allows soldiers to keep perishable gifts like flowers or candy, so long as they share with others. This happened a lot on Jessica's wing. She shared everything. She knew that others were suffering too, and gladly shared her gifts. Eventually, Private Lynch asked America to please just send cards.

Government ethics provisions don't apply to those who have left the military. That is, the ethics regulations bind Private Lynch but they do not bind private citizen Lynch. If the donor agrees to wait, soldiers can accept gifts once they've left the army that they can't accept as soldiers, so long as there is no negotiated quid-pro-quo. One of my jobs was to advise Jessica Lynch (and other troops) about these rules.

I remember sitting in Private Lynch's hospital room along with her parents and Major With. Major With explained to Jessica that the government ethics rules limited what gifts she could accept. Jessica innocently looked up at Major With from her hospital bed with curious blue eyes and said, "But I don't understand. If somebody wants to give me a present, why can't they?"

This young private seemed to have more common sense than is reflected in the Government's ethics rules. It makes sense that a military officer who awards contracts to government contractors should be free from bribery and influence. But what influence does a private in the army have? Enlisted soldiers, and most officers, have no ability to award private contractors, or influence business decisions that would benefit contractors. The rule was overly broad and didn't make sense. When Illinois Congressman Kirk heard about the prohibition on wounded soldiers accepting gifts, he said, "Gifts to wounded soldiers should not be limited to folded flags."[3] Congressman Kirk and other legislators urged Secretary Rumsfeld to lift the "senseless restriction."[4]

---

3. Cheryl Reed, *Repeal of GI gift caps going to Congress*, CHICAGO SUN TIMES, Nov. 4, 2005.

4. Russel Lissau, Lawmakers aiming to ease limits on gifts to soldiers, DAILY HERALD, Nov. 5, 2005.

Eventually, Congress amended the Federal Law, so that the Secretary of Defense can accept gifts on behalf of service members who "incur a wound, injury or illness while in the line of duty."[5] The Department of Defense also amended its rules. The provision, called the Gifts to Wounded Soldiers Exception, allows wounded soldiers to accept gifts valued at up to $1,000.00.[6] Service members (and their families) can even accept gifts that exceed the $1,000.00 value so long as a Government Ethics Official approves the gift. This is to ensure that the do-gooder is really a do-gooder and not seeking something in exchange from the soldier or the military. This provision is retroactive to September 11, 2001, and it is a welcome change.

Overall, the tremendous outpouring of support to casualties at Walter Reed was nothing short of amazing. Veterans organizations came in droves, carrying bags of games, books, and magazines. Even celebrities came. Sheryl Crow's room-to-room performance of her chart-topper "All I Wanna Do is Have Some Fun" had soldiers talking for weeks. Jennifer Love Hewitt came too. It was rumored that one of the soldiers caught her eye—and she gave him her private (no doubt unlisted) phone number. Nobody knew for sure, but that is what people said.

A Vietnam veteran with a scruffy beard and red-suspenders came to Walter Reed a lot that spring. He said, "Just call me Big John." He talked about how America turned its back on Vietnam veterans when they came home from the war. "I don't want that to happen to these guys," he insisted. When he visited the troops, he brought them McDonald's milkshakes.

Even the Easter Egg Roll (an annual Easter egg hunt on the White-House grounds) paid a special tribute to Walter Reed's casualties, who received personal invitations and a ride to the White House gate. Many soldiers were too sick to go, but a few family members went. I remember one adorable toddler who wore a colorful spring dress and swung her Easter basket at her side, with her curls bouncing in unison as she walked through the main lobby of Walter Reed, bound for the Easter Egg Roll.

> **JAG Fact**
>
> *Each soldier has a "battle buddy" in training. Buddies are responsible for each other. This helps the army know when the enemy has captured a soldier. It also ensures that another soldier always "has your back." Sometimes it pairs a stronger soldier with a weaker one.*

America was in love with her heroes, and every soldier returning from combat was a hero. My JAG colleague, Major With, looked sincerely at Private Lynch and said simply, "Private, you are my hero." Heroism transcends rank.

---

5. 10 U.S.C §2601 (2006).

6. DoD 5500.7-R, §3-400 (March 23, 2006).

Jessica insisted that she was no hero. Later, she revealed that her weapon jammed, and that she was scared. She didn't fire a single shot. Instead, she hit her knees and prayed. She insisted that her best friend Lori Piestwa was a hero. The army did not require Sergeant Piestwa to deploy. She chose to deploy along with her friend and battle buddy, Private Lynch. At her homecoming ceremony in Elizabeth, West Virginia, Jessica said, "Most of all I miss Lori Piestwa. She was my best friend, she fought beside me, and it was an honor to have served with her. Lori will always be in my heart."[7]

What does it really mean to be a hero? Does one have to be heroic on the battlefield? Is bravery under fire a prerequisite? What we've learned from previous wars is that soldiers typically fight or flee. We can't predict what we will do in battle. Some soldiers have "fought" in battle only to later discover that they didn't fire a single shot. Some freeze. Others flee. And, some exhibit incredible acts of heroism that they later deny, or don't even remember. It doesn't matter to me, or most Americans, what happens on the battlefield. Jessica Lynch, and every other soldier who serves in this—or any—war is a hero. They are all heroes.

The media requested to interview a wounded soldier, and Walter Reed agreed. In the interview, the wounded soldier, accompanied by his young wife, recounted his experiences as a combat wounded soldier. The soldier said something like, "We are especially grateful for the kind support from Taco Bell. Thank you, Taco Bell for all the free tacos! They're great, and we love 'em!" (This was before the military amended its gift rules. Under the rules in effect at the time, it was only legal for the soldier to accept up to $20.00 worth of tacos from Taco Bell).

It was an important time for Americans, and everyone wanted to ease the burden of soldiers and their families. America just couldn't do enough for her fallen troops.

---

7. Linda D. Kozaryn, *Army Pfc. Jessica Lynch: Home to the Mountains*, Armed Forces Press Service, July 22, 2003.

Here I am pictured with former Senator Robert Dole, who was interested in one of my client's physical evaluation board hearings. This photo was taken at the U.S. Army Physical Disability Agency located at the Walter Reed Army Medical Center.

CHAPTER SIXTEEN

Casualty Affairs Office
Drops the Ball

One morning while searching for an exception to the rigid gift rules that would allow an injured soldier to accept a computer from a grateful American, my phone rang. "Captain Miller," I said picking up the receiver. The voice on the other end sounded profoundly distressed. I knew this was an important call.

In a barely audible tone, the voice on the other end said, "Yes, captain. I'm calling because my son has been injured and is coming to Walter Reed." Her son, a soldier, had been injured in a grenade blast. His condition was so critical that the military could not transport him to a field hospital. Instead, the army transported him to a naval ship at sea, close to where he was injured.

The physicians on board saved his life, but for days he remained unconscious and teetering on the brink of death. Apparently, the medical officer aboard the ship had contacted the soldier's mother over e-mail. For days, she had waited with bloodshot eyes in front of her computer, hanging on for e-mail updates. She said through tears, "I'm just so glad that he's alive." The latest communication from that doctor was that the army would fly her son to Walter Reed and admit him. She packed her bags and went to the airport. Later I learned that the military expected her son to arrive on a flight that very afternoon. The physician awaiting him at Walter Reed requested to see the family before providing their son's room number, so that he could prepare them.

The family arrived at Walter Reed and remained for several days while the soldier underwent countless procedures and fought for his life. Since their son was critically injured, his immediate family members are entitled to reimbursement from the government to travel to his side and stay for a few days. The army summons family members entitled to this benefit by using what it calls "invitational travel orders." The Army's Casualty Affairs Office issues them. In this case, although the soldier was critically ill and clinging to his life, there was some administrative problem with the orders.

For days, the family met with Casualty Affairs Officers, submitted additional paperwork, and made every effort to sort through the problem. The Casualty Affairs Office denied their request. Officers above my rank became involved as we tried to settle the discrepancy. Nonetheless, the bureaucratic objections to reimbursement persisted. At one point his mother, understandably distressed from it all, said something like, "My son may be dying, and I just can't be concerned with these problems. The army should help pay our expenses, but I can't control that, and I won't worry about this any longer." Feeling overwhelmed, she left the family assistance office. I immediately contacted a representative at the American Red Cross, who went after the family with a checkbook in hand to help offset their expenses. The Red Cross was on the ball; the military was not. I think, eventually, the problem was resolved when Lieutenant General Kiley became involved, and the government reimbursed the family for their expenses.

This story underscores a few important points. The military has a Casualty Affairs Office to help soldiers and their family members when soldiers are critically ill or have died. Generally the process works. However, when the army wrote the rules, it controlled information about critically injured soldiers, and the Casualty Affairs Office was the first to know.

The Global War on Terrorism marks a time where technology allows soldiers to be in touch with their families, literally, from the battlefield. Soldiers often call their family members on satellite or cell phones or, as in this case, using the Internet on ships at sea. Soldiers are able to say things like "Mom, we're under attack," or even "My God, I've been hit!"

Families, understandably, make travel plans. This interferes with the casualty affairs regulations that require the family to be *invited* by the physician before they initiate travel, and require the *Casualty Affairs Office* to arrange that travel. Previously, the Casualty Affairs Office controlled all information to the family, so the family couldn't learn about a soldier's condition before the Casualty Affairs Office did. The military had to revise the rules and procedures to accommodate this new eventuality in the Global War on Terror. This family, unfortunately, was caught in the transition from old to new.

I enjoyed working with soldiers at the M-FAC, and I extended my military commitment a few times so that I could stay longer. It became clear that this war in Iraq would not end in a quick victory, like Desert Storm. I finally decided that I couldn't wait-out the war. I wanted to be closer to my family. I was dubious about another round of negotiations with the army Assignments Officer and I was quickly losing faith in the army's senseless bureaucracy. After much thought and deliberation, I left the army and returned home to Wyoming to take a position with the governor's office.

CHAPTER SEVENTEEN

Home, Home on the Range

I walked into the governor's office, smoothing my skirt and fixing my hair. I had just rolled into town the night before, and the governor didn't expect me to start work for another week. I didn't even have a place to live yet. That morning I received a call from the governor's chief of staff who said that the governor wanted me there for a meeting in a few hours. So, I pulled a suit out of a packed cardboard box, and went back to work. After wearing a uniform every day for the past several years, having a choice of dress was strangely liberating, but also a nuisance.

I walked through a door marked "Gov Dave" and started the next chapter of my life. In my position, I led a staff of bright, young policy analysts, as we explored ways to make Wyoming better. I was the only military veteran on the governor's staff, so I handled military-related issues. It was a budget year, and I worked closely with Wyoming's adjutant general to propose and support legislation benefiting service members. That year, nearly every military-related bill became law—thanks mainly to the adjutant general. We also hosted a Veteran's Conference, where all of the veteran's service organizations came together to discuss the needs of Wyoming's young veterans and establish clear goals.

Airmen and soldiers in Wyoming were hard-hit by the war in Iraq. The Army National Guard and Air National Guard deployed several groups of soldiers and airmen. Wyoming's Air and Army National Guard units invited Governor Freudenthal, their commander in chief, to attend all deployment ceremonies. Generally, these farewell events occurred in the early morning hours, around 3:00 a.m. Sometimes only one, or a few, service members were deploying. "It's the least I can do—they're going to war," the governor would say. I attended the deployment ceremonies with him. Countless mornings we rode in the darkness together, making small talk, and easing through intersections with flashing red lights. The car would warm up about the time we arrived at the air base. Governor Freudenthal's remarks were always appropriate—different each time—and sincere.

The governor had a clever sense of humor, and soldiers appreciated his rugged, down to earth honesty. One deployment ceremony occurred at the height of budgetary struggles between the Governor and members of the legislature. During the ceremony, Governor Freudenthal went to the front of the military formation and said something like, "You all look pretty rough and tough this morning. Could I talk you into coming back to the Capitol with me to kick the shit out of the legislature before you go to Iraq?" The room erupted in laughter.

We met some inspiring young men and women at those deployment ceremonies. One couple, J.D. and Kelly Parker, exemplified sacrifices that soldiers make. They were both soldiers in the Army National Guard. At one ceremony, J.D. (the husband) boarded the bus for his deployment, and his wife, Kelly, stood in uniform and saluted as he drove away. Her pregnant tummy bulged under her uniform. She was eight months pregnant with twins. She was positive and strong. She said, "I'm not the first one this has happened to, and I'm not the last.... It's my responsibility. It's time for me to earn my paycheck."[1]

Once I traveled with the Governor on a Black Hawk helicopter to Fort Carson, Colorado. Some of Wyoming's troops were training at Fort Carson, and about to deploy. Their training was similar to the type I underwent at Fort Benning, Georgia, before I deployed to Guantanamo Bay. I informed the governor about the crowded conditions at Fort Benning, and how there weren't enough beds for everyone deploying from there. The governor then pressed those briefing us about pre-deployment exercises, to make sure that the accommodations were sufficient. They assured the governor that Wyoming's troops were in good hands at Fort Carson.

I enjoyed working for the governor and supporting his rigorous agenda to help Wyoming's soldiers and veterans. However, I couldn't help but feel sidelined while much younger soldiers sacrificed and went to war. I wondered if it was wrong to leave the Army during a time of war. I wondered if I had made the right decision.

Early one morning when I was brushing my teeth over the sink, and listening to the news on the TV, I heard something about detainee abuse and Guantanamo Bay. With my toothbrush still in my mouth, I ran to the TV and watched the news coverage.

The news reported alleged abuse of detainees at Abu Ghraib, and reported "Major General Miller went to Abu Ghraib to Gitmoize the mission." Later that day I received a phone call from a good friend of mine, who had served with me in Guantanamo Bay. "Kyndra," she said, "did you hear that Major General Miller is going to Iraq to straighten out the mess over there?" She be-

---

1. Cara Eastwood, *Goodbye again: husband sent to Middle East shortly before twins are due.* CHEYENNE TRIBUNE EAGLE, February 22, 2004.

lieved as I did, that the term "Gitmoize" was a favorable term. But it wasn't. The media was quick to pin blame for Abu Ghraib on General Miller, arguing that harsh interrogation tactics migrated from Guantanamo Bay to Abu Ghraib—without evidence to support that claim.

Another morning, around that same time, I sat in my office sipping coffee and going through my e-mail when the phone rang and the voice at the other end said, "Good Morning Ma'am, I'm calling for Captain Miller." A chill went up my spine. I knew it was the army calling, because nobody had addressed me as "Ma'am" or "Captain Miller" for over a year, since I left the army and traveled west. Time stopped and I could literally feel my life turning in a new direction.

I cleared my throat, "Yes, this is Captain Miller." The caller was an army sergeant, who explained that he was calling from a U.S. Army Reserve unit in the state of Utah. "Ma'am" he said, "This is a courtesy call letting you know that you can expect to receive orders in the next week to ten days returning you to active duty to support a Utah reserve unit." There was a short pause before he continued, "Ma'am, well … we're deploying to Iraq."

I had been off active duty for less than one year, and apparently was on the short-list to be reactivated. "But, I live in Wyoming … why are you calling from Utah?" The Sergeant explained that my "home of record" was still Evanston, Wyoming, the small Wyoming town bordering Utah where I grew up and graduated from high school. "Evanston is within the same reserve region as Utah, that's how you came up on our list," he explained.

I couldn't believe it. The army was calling JAG Officers—lawyers—to active duty! I knew it could happen, I just didn't *think* it would. "So sergeant," I interrupted him, "This is for sure? I'll definitely receive orders in the next week or so?" He hesitated. "Well, I'm pretty sure."

I ended the call and started making calls of my own. I called every JAG office I knew to discern whether the army was really activating JAGs. Finally, I reached a knowledgeable lieutenant colonel in Washington, D.C., with the Judge Advocate General's Reserve Office. "What's your name again, captain?" he asked, "and your social security number?" I gave him the information and could hear him clicking away on the computer keys. "Oh yes. I understand now," he said, reading from the screen, "you have a top secret security clearance, is that right?" "Yes, sir. It was required for my assignment in Guantanamo Bay," I said. "And, what about operational law experience, have you been deployed before?" he asked. "Well, Guantanamo Bay was considered a deployment, and my position title was Operational Lawyer. So, yeah, I guess so." "Well, the army is looking for JAG officers with top-secret security clearances. Utah is probably being square with you. There is a good chance that you'll, indeed, get those orders." I was speechless.

It costs approximately $15,000.00 for the army to process a Top Secret (TS) Security Clearance because it requires extensive background checks and voluminous paperwork. Processing top-secret clearances also take time—it can take a year or more for the army to investigate and grant a TS clearance. In my case, it even sent investigators to the neighborhood where I grew up to talk to neighbors, and it chatted with old boyfriends from years earlier. Once granted, a security clearance is valid for ten years. I was on the army's "short list" for reactivation due to my clearance. However, it afforded me a few options. I could wait for military orders activating me for eighteen to twenty-four months; or I could volunteer and get a choice of assignments and a shorter tour.

There wasn't much of an option, really. I "volunteered." The governor broke the news of my reactivation to his cabinet during a meeting at the governor's residence. He said, "I knew I shouldn't have hired a darned woman. They always want time off to get married, have babies, *fight our wars.*" The room erupted in laughter.

Within a few weeks (after again waiting on protracted orders) I traded my cowboy boots for combat boots and drove back across the United States toward Washington, D.C., to serve a tour on the Criminal Investigation Task Force (CITF), where agents call themselves "terrorist hunters." In my rearview mirror, I watched the small Wyoming town fade into nothingness. I was on a new course.

This is a photograph of Wyoming's Governor, Dave Freudenthal (second from right) meeting with members of the Wyoming Guard. Second from the left is Wyoming's adjutant general, Major General Edwin Wright.

CHAPTER EIGHTEEN

Twisted Logic, Terrorism 101[1]

"Thank you," I said to the man behind the counter at the convenience store, as I took the road map and my receipt. How did I get so off track? I wondered. Somewhere I had missed a turn, and realized my error when I passed a huge road sign welcoming travelers to the Poconos. "The Poconos!" I exclaimed — "isn't that in New York?"

My mistake was irritating. I had been on the interstate for the better part of four days and had managed to stay on course, until now. I flung open the map, spread it across the steering wheel, and tried to figure out where I was and where I needed to go. It was Friday afternoon, before the 4th of July weekend. RV caravans bounced along the narrow mountain roads, mocking me as they headed for the Poconos.

My cell phone rang, and I pushed aside a crumpled McDonald's bag and a few CD cases to find it lying in the passenger's seat. "Hello," I said. It was my dad, calling to check in on me. He called just to make sure I was all right, and to keep company. "Well, dad," I said, "the Poconos are lovely this time of year!" He laughed, "Oh no, how did ya do that?" I blamed it on the riveting conclusion of *The Da Vinci Code* book on CD that had captured my attention for the last several hundred miles.

I finally got back on track, and continued toward Washington, D.C. My carefully laid plans to round the D.C. beltway before holiday rush hour traffic were in vain. The wrong turn not only required significant backtracking, but also it landed me in the middle of a monumental D.C. traffic jam, where I inched along for hours.

Long after my anticipated arrival time, I pulled up to the hotel in Springfield, Virginia, where the Army told me to go. It looked modest but had a decent outdoor pool. I went to the front desk and gave my name to the receptionist. She was a beautiful young woman and wore a traditional Mus-

---

1. More information about the Criminal Investigation Task Force is available on the CITF "General Information Fact Sheet" which is released to the public. They have a full-time public affairs office assigned to answer questions, and respond to the media.

lim head covering, long sleeves, and long pants. When she couldn't locate my reservation in the computer, she called to someone in the back, her brother, who approached with a faxed letter, said with an accent, "It is right here. Captain Miller will be with us for many months. She is assigned to the Criminal Investigation Task Force." Then he asked for a copy of my orders. He sat the faxed document on the counter, and I glanced over at it. It was a letter, on letterhead, with a logo, from the Criminal Investigation Task Force (CITF), where I would be working.

I was surprised that the task force revealed so much information, and even had its own logo. Anyone could discern who I was, where I worked, and generally, what we did. It was also very inconsistent, because a few weeks earlier I received a call from a very clandestine CITF attorney, who explained that I would be working at an "undisclosed location" with "deep undercover agents" who investigate worldwide leads regarding terrorists. He provided a broad overview of the mission, but omitted even minor details because we were on an "unsecured phone line." He even provided me a cover story to tell security guards if they asked where I was going. This was to avoid revealing the location of CITF, or that I worked there. All of that seemed very odd, since right before me, sitting on the hotel countertop, was letterhead from our organization clearly revealing what he told me to conceal.

On Monday morning, I wore my uniform for the first time in over a year, and saluted someone in the parking lot. "That's odd," I thought. "There are a lot of soldiers at this hotel." We each got in our vehicles, and all started driving in the same direction. At first, I thought it was a coincidence, and expected drivers to turn off eventually. But my suspicions were true. Many in this caravan were assigned to CITF, and that's where we were all going. I could not believe that an organization claiming to be so secretive would keep all of its "undercover" personnel at one hotel (in a predominately Muslim community), and then have them report to work at the same time of day, all wearing uniforms. What the CITF letterhead did not reveal, one could easily learn through a little reconnaissance. Anyone looking for the hive would simply follow its bees. For this reason, eventually, CITF began using more than one hotel. Apparently, the problem originated because CITF hired a supply and logistics person to make our hotel arrangements. He simply accepted the housing contract from the lowest bidder. He didn't have a TS Security Clearance and didn't fully understand the need for secrecy.

The CITF building itself was unmarked, difficult to find, and extremely secure. One thing is for sure, any reconnaissance efforts would definitely stop at the gates of this facility. Nobody without the proper clearance could conceivable pass through its gates and doors.

Once inside, I noticed that most personnel were wearing civilian clothes. But some, including all of the attorneys and the enlisted soldiers, were in uniform. Someone explained that only the agents are under-cover. Everyone else wore uniforms. That seemed odd. Wouldn't the uniforms blow the cover? Aren't they at risk to be targeted? For this reason, some soldiers who were required to wear uniforms kept them in the building, and commuted in civilian clothes. (Incidentally, marines do this as a matter of practice. They only wear their uniforms at work.)

For several days, I attended CITF training to learn about the organization. The Secretary of Defense created it on February 1, 2002. Its purpose was to investigate detainees held in Guantanamo Bay and to follow investigatory leads around the globe.

CITF has four regional offices: Washington, D.C., Guantanamo Bay, Iraq, and Afghanistan. Agents have worldwide jurisdiction and are hand-selected from each branch of service. Army, navy, and air force investigators work together.

Everyone assigned to the CITF has security clearances that allow them to view highly classified documents. Agents typically investigate six to eight cases at any given time, and have active leads pending in several countries around the world. Each case has thousands of documents, interview notes, and cryptic evidence. Much of it requires translation and subject-matter expert analysis. Skilled intelligence analysts work with every investigator to decipher information and help guide the investigations.

I also learned about our enemies: their motivations, their cover stories, their operations, their recruitment efforts. I was impressed how much the U.S. knew about the inner-workings of terrorist organizations like Al Qaeda, and how long Al Qaeda had been conspiring to bring the United States to its knees.

Because the length of military tours at CITF varies, and because the military assigns personnel to CITF for as little as four months, CITF has the arduous task of training agents about the complexities of Radical Islam, including their methods of operation, not to mention the cultural aspects of the Muslim religion. CITF offers a robust week of training for all personnel assigned there, which it created out of whole cloth. The training program is thorough and impressive. Its training course has caught the attention of the U.S. Army Intelligence Center at Fort Huachuca Arizona, the Defense Academy for Credibility Assessment, the Joint counterintelligence Training Center, the Federal Law Enforcement Training Academy, the U.S. Army Medical Command, and others, where it has offered tailored courses.[2]

---

2. The person primarily responsible for launching, and managing, this successful training program is Chief Warrant Officer 4 L.J. "Jim" Powlen. More information is available at Chief Warrant Officer 4 L.J. "Jim" Powlen, *Criminal Investigation Task Force*, MILITARY PO-

Part of the training includes a two-day workshop about radical Islamism. The trainers are world renown, and train CIA agents about the ins and outs of terrorist organizations. One of them opined that Iran remains the most significant long-term threat against the United States, and predicted that eventually U.S. attention would turn there. He explained that our enemy is not terrorist organizations, but instead an ideology that binds those organizations—Radical Islamism.

He turned the lights down, illuminated a large projection screen, and warned us about the graphic footage we were about to see. He invited anyone to leave that wanted to. A few, but not many, went to the back of the auditorium. I decided to stay.

He then showed the brutal beheading footage of Daniel Pearl. Pearl's captors violently shoved him to the ground and held him down. Another grabbed a handful of his hair, and began relentlessly sawing at the side of his neck. I turned away for a moment, thinking it would be over soon. But it wasn't.

The beheading was brutal, and slow. It was nothing like the guillotines of Revolutionary France. Daniel Pearl was very much aware of what was happening, and he was clearly terrified. He struggled, and eventually the life left his eyes. Terrorists with no regard for human life slaughtered Daniel Pearl like an animal. They slaughtered him for being an American, and they slaughtered him for being Jewish. To these terrorists, he was a worthless infidel who deserved to die. They were possessed with fiery hate.

Later, U.S. forces captured Khalid Sheikh Muhammad (KSM), who beheaded Daniel Pearl. In court, KSM said, "I decapitated with my blessed right hand the head of the American Jew, Daniel Pearl, in the city of Karachi, Pakistan. For those who would like to confirm, there are pictures of me on the internet holding his head."[3]

After watching the horrific beheading footage of Daniel Pearl, the room was notably silent. The instructor then said in a somber tone, "The next video you are about to see is a woman being stoned in Iran. Women are typically stoned for two offenses. Either she had an affair, or she rejected Islam."

The trainer then narrated the brutal video footage. Several men wrapped her body from head to toe in a white shroud, with her arms wrapped inside against her body. She looked like a mummy. The shroud completely covered her eyes

---

LICE PB 19-7-01, also available online at http://www.wood.army.mil/mpbulletin/pdfs/ Spring%2007%20pdfs/Powlen.pdf.

3. Verbatim Transcript of the Combatant Status Review Tribunal Hearing for ISN 10024, Khalid Sheikh Muhammad, March 10, 2007, U.S. Naval Base, Guantanamo Bay at p. 18. Also available at http://www.defenselink.mil/news/transcript_ISN10024.pdf.

and face. Then several men carried her to a deep hole in the ground. They placed her inside the hole, feet first, up to her mid-thigh. "Note how they pat the dirt gingerly around her legs. Several of the men caressed her, and talked to her as they were putting her in the hole," the instructor said. Then the men stepped away. It was ironic that raw brutality could follow this delicate handling ritual.

A crowd of men encircled her, and began screaming and yelling. They chanted, punched the air, and became more and more enraged. The anger of one seemed to fuel the others. Finally, they picked up sharp jagged rocks from a pile and threw them forcefully toward her body. Like wild animals, they yelled, and threw rocks, and yelled some more. The footage transported me back in time, to a much earlier, more primitive era. But, it wasn't an earlier time. This incivility happens all over the Muslim world today. They call it a "ritual stoning." It is allowed (indeed required in some instances) by Sharia (Islam) Law.

> **JAG Fact**
>
> *Some detainees held in Gitmo have admitted to participating in such stonings. One 33-year-old Afghan "admitted that he had supervised a ritual stoning to death of three people charged with adultery but said he had not chosen the people or the penalty."*
> —Guantanamo Bay Getting their Day, but Hardly in Court, N.Y. TIMES, Sept. 11, 2004

Eventually her shroud turned pink with blood, and then red. The delicate gauze began to fall away from her body. Her arms were eventually free and she screamed and tried to cover her face. Her hands were bloody. She bent forward, put her forehead to the ground and wailed. The stoning continued. The instructor interrupted, "This goes on for a long time. It usually takes about a half an hour for someone to die from stoning." Then, he turned it off, and we took a break. The image of this brutal attack and her extreme suffering still haunts me.

The footage sickened me. I had never seen anything nearly as vicious or brutal. The most shocking aspect is that this and similar atrocities are committed in the name of religion—Radical Islamism. Our enemy is powerful and formidable. It shows no mercy, and it governs through fear, oppression, and hate. The U.S. government does not air footage of our darkest enemies in the midst of their most brutal atrocities—like that inflicted on innocent Daniel Pearl and the woman stoned in Iran. Perhaps the American public deserves to know these things.

Perhaps the U.S. lulls its citizens into sleepy, ignorant deference. Don't Americans have a right to know and understand the hate that drives our enemies? Nearly six years after the World Trade Towers tumbled to the ground in a mass of billowing smoke and twisted steel, the U.S. government still does not speak the name of our enemies. Instead, it calls them "insurgents" and "rebels," which adds legitimacy and civility to a group that is neither of those things.

Those in Iraq and Afghanistan who target innocent civilians and don't wear uniforms are *terrorists*. Having lost in popular elections, they attempt to regain control of their country by killing innocent civilians and employing indiscriminate bombs in shopping markets and eateries. There is nothing legitimate about their actions. They are not *insurgents*. An *insurgent* is one who rises up against the government which offers no democratic outlet, such as a rebel or a revolutionary, and is synonymous with the term freedom fighters. Our early ancestors, such as George Washington and Thomas Jefferson, would probably fall into this category. Importantly, they rose up against a legitimate *government*, and did not clandestinely *murder civilians* as those in Iraq and Afghanistan do. Calling them insurgents, or freedom fighters, misstates their conduct and legitimizes their actions. Instead, they are fanatics who draw inspiration from innocent human suffering and legitimize their brutality through the twisted logic of Radical Islamism.

We claim to be in a *Global War on Terrorism*, and to that end we should call those who murder civilians what they are—Radical Islamist terrorists.

CHAPTER NINETEEN

Leads Turn Cold While Agents Turn Over

It was a rainy, autumn morning, perfect weather for hot coffee and donuts. I went to Dunkin' Donuts and picked up an assorted dozen for my team and a steaming hot latte for me. Nothing pleases investigators more than an assorted dozen donuts. Investigators I supported would brief me this morning about some important leads, and I didn't want to show up empty handed.

"Donuts," I called as I walked in the door of CITF, balancing the giant box in one hand, while hot latte dripped down the side of my cup in the other hand. To my chagrin, there was a box already on the counter, and another at the round table where our meeting would be. Several analysts were already in front of their computer screens, employing their impressive analytical skills to chart movements and associations of terrorists they were researching.

"Morning, Sam," I called to one of the analysis whose desk was on the other side of mine. "Hi," she said, and then called me over to look at something interesting she had discovered.

Sam had long, straight, brown hair and a pretty, freckled face. She dressed comfortably, but always looked nice. Sam never deviated from her work. In fact, she rarely left her cubicle, which she had transformed into a darkened cove. She had made a dark covering that she put over her cubicle. She strung it with white holiday lights and plastic chili peppers. It was strange, but allowed her to get "in her zone." Her workstation was unique, with all sorts of odd little relics that provided insight to her complexity.

"What's the cucumber for?" I asked as I approached from behind and saw it lying on her desk. "Oh, that's my lunch." One of the investigators near us laughed, and explained that Sam often brought a single vegetable for lunch — "Yesterday she had a green pepper," he exclaimed. "Yeah, yeah," she commented dryly, dismissing our banter and returning our attention to her find.

She had discovered another alias that one of the detainees used. Detainees commonly have six, eight, or more *kunyas*, or aliases, with several spellings for each. It helps them operate covertly. Often, fellow operatives don't know the identity of their cohorts. Reinventing oneself is easy in countries that don't maintain official documents. Many of the countries where detainees come from don't have birth certificates, photo IDs, social security numbers, finger print databases, DNA testing, or other legal instruments evidencing that Muhammad is, indeed, Muhammad.

Sam always found interesting things, but occasionally hid her light under a basket (or in this case, her private darkened cove). She didn't usually interject herself in outside conversations, but always seemed to have the answer within arm's reach, when asked. I learned to use this phrase, "What do you know about that, Sam?"

I wasn't surprised to learn that Sam discovered a new *kunya*. "Good job," I said, "Bring it to the meeting." "OK," she grumbled. Sam didn't like meetings. They interfered with her delicate hunting.

We spent the rest of the morning pouring through files, charts, records, statements, pictures, and other types of evidence. The lead investigator described a recent interview, and analysts provided intelligence to help shape the investigation from this point forward. I was there to answer legal questions. The case was incredibly complex, with eyewitnesses that couldn't be located, and evidence that Special Forces seized (and photographed) but lost track of somewhere along the way.

Just then, a scruffy haired agent came around the corner wearing a polo shirt and cargo pants. "Hey ma'am," he said, "just got back from Iraq—what a trip!" He was a seasoned CITF investigator who had been with the task force for several years. He was the kind of agent who despises "desk work," and excelled "in the field." He had just spent six months investigating leads from CITF's Iraq location. "I didn't join the army to sit at a desk," he explained. His bags were still packed, and he was already looking for another opportunity to deploy. One of the other agents said, "Have a seat, we're talking about Muhammad." "Naw, man," he said, "I can't sit still for that. No offense," he said to one investigator, "but I've been there, done that with the agent before you." Then he walked away.

At first, I found his demeanor a bit cavalier, even dismissive. But later I discovered that Davis operated from a point of experience and understanding. CITF is a task force and only designed to exist temporarily, until the War on Terror ends. The military deploys investigators to CITF for an average of six months at a time, and then they leave. Often this is barely enough time for an agent to become familiar with the facts of their case. Before they have time to follow any leads, it is time for them to go. Their replacements then go through the same process, and six months later, they leave too. Consequently, the cases evolve at a glacial pace. Too much turnover severely affects CITF's overall success and interferes with bringing the cases to prosecution. While the CITF train-ing is exemplary, there is no substitute for experience and time on the job.

Some agents have opted to extend their tours with CITF and stay longer, and a few, like Davis, have managed to receive quasi-permanent assignment to CITF, which guarantees that their position at CITF for two to three years. These agents are exponentially more productive than the others. They know their cases well, and they have learned to work around U.S. bureaucracy to obtain valuable evidence.

Successful agents take time to establish rapport with the detainees they're in-vestigating. I knew one CITF agent and one FBI agent who were Muslims, and both knew how to coax the truth from detainees' lips. One word captures their effective, secret ingredient to successful interrogations—patience. They each spent hours visiting with the detainee, sharing tea, bringing gifts of dried fruits, and talking endlessly about family, Allah, and the Quran.

In a thick accent, the FBI agent explained to me how he laid with the de-tainee on the ground, side-by-side with their hands clasped behind their heads, together looking up at a starry sky and talking about the greater things in life. He offered the detainee Muslim companionship, trusted brotherhood, and endless hours of conversation. Eventually, the detainee comfortably lying on his back, effortlessly, freely, voluntarily, admitted terrorist crimes to his trusted new friend—the FBI.

The CITF Muslim, Agent M., also spent countless hours visiting with the detainee he was investigating. He made long trips to Guantanamo Bay, just to "check on" his detainee, and "build rapport." Some other agents were skepti-cal of this slow as molasses method, and wondered when he would get to the point. "When are you going to make that guy talk?" some would say. "He'll talk," Agent M. would respond with unwavering confidence.

Agent M. established rapport through compassion and fellowship. The de-tainee asked Agent M. if he could move to a different cell, and Agent M. had him moved. Then the detainee explained that he wanted to take classes, and Agent M. arranged for the detainee to learn English and take other classes in his native language. After that, the detainee cooperated.

Agents don't need to be Muslim to establish rapport with their detainees; they just need to understand their subjects, learn a new culture, and remain ever pa-tient and calm. This rapport saves U.S. lives. In one case, the detainee told his investigator about a terrorist training camp, even identified the precise loca-tion on a map, and provided hand-written diagrams of the area. Days before the investigator would travel to the terrorist training camp to take pictures and gather evidence, the detainee insisted to talk to him. He warned the agent that the training camp was "bugged" with land mines and told the investigator precisely where terrorists buried bombs, and how to avoid the deadly explosions. Ironically, the information that protected the Agent also inculpated the detainee.

Many cultural mores govern terrorist investigations. Agents must be patient, and establish trust with the detainee. The CITF Commander, Colonel Britt Mallow, once said, "Interviews and interrogations are not about making someone talk. They are about making them *want* to."[1]

But, establishing rapport takes time. The CITF revolving door method is wholly ineffective, and doesn't allow agents sufficient time to make any significant headway on their cases. Those agents who commit to longer tours have time to establish rapport, and get good information. Those assigned to CITF for only a few months generally come up to speed on their cases about the time their tour ends.

CITF should be a permanent duty assignment, and the military should assign investigators there for at least three years. It should assign each investigator only a few cases, and investigators should work their cases consistently every day to exhaust every lead. Turnover is expensive, inefficient, and completely incompatible with investigating these extremely complex cases. Otherwise, leads turn cold while agents turn over.

---

1. Bill Dedman, *Gitmo Interrogations spark battle over tactics: The inside story of criminal investigators who tried to stop abuse,* MSNBC.com, Oct. 23, 2006.

CHAPTER TWENTY

Bureaucratic Bog Down

The agent sitting at the desk next to mine slammed down his phone and ex-claimed, "I hate the freakin' FBI!" He'd been trying to get information from the FBI for weeks without success. Originally, CITF and FBI agents worked cooper-atively. However, as time went on the relationship became less cordial. In 2004, CITF and the FBI signed a "Memorandum of Understanding" to govern their re-lationship and even hired a "liaison" to improve coordination between the two or-ganizations. Despite these efforts, most agents report that conflicts persisted, and information sharing between the two organizations was far from ideal.

One may wonder why CITF agents, who investigate detainees in Guantanamo Bay, would need assistance from the FBI, which ordinarily investigates domestic terrorism. The reason is a simple one: many of the cases have leads in the United States. In fact, several detainees have traveled, at one time or another, to the United States, where they have gone to school on student visas. Ten percent of them were educated in western universities, including Texas A&M, the University of Texas, and Arizona schools. Many have lived in the United States temporarily and worked or have family members still living in the United States, some within miles of CITF. In these instances, the FBI often runs parallel investigations. When the FBI refuses to cooperate and share information from these investigations with CITF agents, the trail gets cold at our own doorstep.

Accessing information from intelligence agencies, such as the CIA, was also very difficult. After negotiating for years, it finally acknowledged a "checkered past" and agreed to work with military prosecutors. However, it specified that military prosecutors could not share information with their CITF investiga-tors. This unnecessary caveat drove a wedge between prosecutors and CITF agents, who should have freely shared information.

CIA officials claim that they're just not equipped to accommodate scores of investigators within their facility. One CIA official explained that other CIA functions would "grind to a halt" if they honored every law enforcement request for information. But these weren't run of the mill law enforcement requests. These were investigatory requests related to terrorists held in Guantanamo Bay during a war on terror.

Even accessing information in the custody of government facilities was problematic. For almost two years, while I worked with CITF, agent access to detainee health records was a point of contention. Some believed that detainees had privacy rights that prohibited the U.S. government from examining the detainee's medical records created and maintained by the U.S. military at the U.S. detention camp.

Officials at Guantanamo Bay were increasingly reluctant to provide detainee medical records to CITF agents, for fear that interrogators would exploit phobias or detainees' medical conditions during interrogations in order to get information.

However, this fear was unsupported by fact. After an extensive investigation, *The Church Report* "found no instances where detainee medical information had been inappropriately used during interrogations, and in most situations interrogators had little interest in detainee medical information even when they had unfettered access to it."[1] A separate investigation, directed by the Surgeon General of the Army, Lieutenant General Kiley, similarly concluded that "In general, the medical records for detainees were managed the same as records for the AC (active component)."[2] This means that the military handles detainee medical records the same way it handles soldiers' medical records.

In 2005, both *The Church Report* and the Surgeon General's Investigation concluded that the Department of Defense should decide who has access to detainee's medical records, and under what circumstances. Although both studies independently concluded that DoD should answer these important questions, DoD failed to act.

By January 2006, CITF officials and Guantanamo Bay officials still could not agree whether CITF agents investigating detainees in Gitmo could review their medical records. Consequently, detainees enjoyed a greater privacy right in their medical records than U.S. soldiers did.

Even when the government allows its investigators access to certain evidence, military rules governing classification often limit the way that investigators can use that evidence. A document's security classification (such as Confidential, Secret, or Top Secret) limits who has access to the document. For instance, only persons with a Top Secret Clearance may see documents marked (or "classified") as Top Secret. Almost anyone in the military can see

---

1. *The Church Report*, Unclassified Executive Summary, at 20.

2. The investigation is approximately 250 pages, and the findings were approved by the Surgeon General, Lieutenant General Kevin Kiley in a Memorandum for Record on May 24, 2005. The entire investigation, and approving memorandum is released at www.armymedicine.army.mil/news/detmedsopsrpt.pdf.

Confidential documents, fewer are eligible to see Secret documents, and still fewer have access to Top Secret documents. The military adopts numerous transportation and storage rules to ensure that only people with the appropriate clearance have access to certain documents.

When the War on Terror began, soldiers who discovered evidence in Afghanistan and Iraq often erred on the side of caution by marking everything as Secret or even Top Secret.

Consider the following hypothetical. An Army Special Forces team searching for Osama Bin Laden in the mountains of Afghanistan comes across a terrorist safe house. In the house, they discover books and videos about Islamic Jihad, bomb making materials, chemical weapons manuals, an assortment of foreign passports, cell phones, a ceramic pot full of U.S. dollars, and notebooks including names and addresses. Which items should be classified Secret or Top Secret? All of the items, especially when taken together, could reveal useful information about our terrorist enemies and could lead to other suspects. In an effort to protect the evidence and national security, the team marks everything as Top Secret and transports it to a secured evidence room. Classifying this evidence makes sense.

But, the problem arises two years later when investigators capture Muhammad, a known terrorist, in Iraq and transport him to Gitmo. During his interrogation, Muhammad admits to being the emir (leader) of a terrorist training camp. He claims to have trained dozens of radical Islamic terrorists in a safe house. The analyst and interrogator suspect that Muhammad worked at the very safe house that Special Forces exploited earlier. He is being cooperative, and the interrogator wants to ask Muhammad to review and identify the passports. But, the passports are classified Top Secret. Muhammad, a detainee, does not have a clearance, so showing Muhammad the passports and classified information would violate federal law.

Classification rules impair investigations because the U.S. government prohibits agents from sharing classified documents with detainees. For instance, some detainees have drawn diagrams and maps during interrogations that range from terrorist training camps to suicide vests to bomb-making diagrams. The army originally classified those documents as Top Secret. Therefore, agents cannot later share those drawings with the detainee who drew them in the first place. Only a bureaucratic mind could comprehend why we could not show a detainee a drawing that he made a few days earlier. Only a bureaucratic mind can comprehend why we could not show Muhammad evidence gathered in the safe house where he worked.

The same is true of other evidence, including video tapes where detainees or other terrorists filmed themselves planning and carrying out terrorist attacks. Agents cannot show the "classified" tapes to detainees who appear in the footage. CITF and other agencies have begun to address the problem of over-classification, but convincing an agency to declassify items originally classified by another can be tedious. The agency wishing to declassify information must contact the first agency that originally classified each item with a compelling justification for declassification. Often these requests disappear into a bureaucratic black hole, and ultimately officials are reluctant to sign their names on the dotted line and authorize declassification. They figure that it is better to overclassify evidence than exercise judgment and risk making a mistake. For them, it is safer to be risk adverse.

Presumably, our involvement in an active war creates a disposition against declassifying documents. The stakes are extremely high, because intelligence sources and U.S. soldiers are still in-theatre and in harm's way every day. Still, common sense should dictate.

The Department of Defense created CITF and designated it to take the lead in investigating cases in the global war on terrorism, but intense friction exists between agencies. CITF agents often don't have access to information, or the information is classified and they're unable to use it during interrogations. Despite the fact that the 9-11 Commission identified problems of agency data sharing and cooperation as a contributing factor to the attacks on September 11th, poor coordination and bureaucratic bog down nonetheless continue to impede investigations.

As the lead investigatory team in the War on Terror, CITF should have access to *any and all* information collected by *any* government agency that relates to investigating detainees held in Gitmo. Further, the government should adopt procedures allowing CITF to quickly declassify certain evidence for use in interrogations or at trial.

CHAPTER TWENTY-ONE

Due Process for Detainees

I spent most of that summer, 2004, in a cramped and busy office in the heart of CITF's facility, hidden and protected from the rest of the world. The sun rose and set, and rain came and went, without our acknowledgment as we worked. Our building was a concrete cave, surrounded by a wire wall. Behind our curtains, instead of windows, were giant charts outlining the connections between terrorists' organizations and detailing events that turned Muslim boys into hardened, trained terrorists.

"Any takers for a smoke break?" one of the analysts called as she closed a four inch file marked Secret. "I'm in," one of the agents said. "Yep, me too," said another. We took breaks every few hours, to cut the monotony and see the outside world. I went along, just for the break. I don't smoke, but I had a fistful of M&Ms from the M&M dispenser on our team leader's desk.

We did not discuss cases outside of the building. You never know who might be listening. But we often discussed the law, which, of course, is not classified. I may have answered more legal questions during smoke breaks, drives in the car, and over Chinese buffet lunches, than I did sitting at my desk.

"Why can't we just prosecute the guy for war crimes?" one CITF agent asked. We all knew which detainee he was talking about. This detainee admitted to multiple terrorist acts and identified countless other terrorists in his supposed network. While his claims were credible and consistent, CITF agents and analysts could not corroborate them. I explained, "Under the law, we need more than just a confession. True, his testimony is evidence, but how compelling would it be without any evidence to back up the confession?"

The United States does not prosecute defendants who admit to crimes without sufficient evidence that the defendant in fact committed that crime. That is what we had here—admissions without any evidence. "The chief prosecutor has been very clear. He doesn't want to waste time trying to prosecute cases without any corroboration. We can only try cases that are corroborated," I explained. Requiring corroboration is a fair standard. Although it is extremely difficult to gather evidence in the midst of a battle, the U.S. has decided that maintaining the rule of law is more important than obtaining convictions.

Even though it is expensive, and often even impossible, to corroborate a detainee's criminal acts, the U.S. applies that standard nonetheless.

One quick-witted analyst said flatly, tapping ashes from her cigarette, "You assume there will be trials. These detainees will never see a courtroom." Another added, "Especially if we keep releasing them."

They were referring to the military's over-reaction to a recent Supreme Court case, *Hamdi v. Rumsfield*.[1] The case was simple and narrow, and only applied to U.S. citizens captured in the War on Terror. However, the U.S. military applied it broadly, and put in motion a damaging chain of events that compromised national security, interfered with ongoing investigations, returned suspected terrorists to the battlefield, and far exceeded requirements in the Geneva Conventions or those articulated by the U.S. Supreme Court. It all began with the story of Mr. Hamdi, an American who sided with terrorists and faced off against U.S. troops in the hills of Afghanistan.

Who Is Mr. Hamdi and How Did He Get to the U.S. Supreme Court?[2]

> **JAG Fact**
>
> *The Supreme Court operates under a majority rule. There are nine justices. If five of them agree, that is the law and we call it a "majority decision." If they can't agree, the opinion with the most justices is called a "plurality."*

Several months before September 11, 2001, Mr. Hamdi, an American citizen, traveled to Afghanistan. We don't know why he went to Afghanistan in the first place. His father alleged that it was to perform "relief work," but Hamdi never made that claim. He said that he wanted to get military training so he could to go Israel and kill Israelis. He wanted to join the Saudi Army, which rejected him, so he went to Afghanistan.[3]

Sometime after the United States invaded Afghanistan, U.S. forces captured Mr. Hamdi fighting alongside a Taliban unit. He was armed with an assault rifle.[4] Like many detainees captured in battle, the U.S. military eventually transferred Mr. Hamdi to Guantanamo Bay, Cuba. When U.S. officials discovered that he was an American citizen, they transferred him to a Naval Brig in Norfolk, Virginia. The U.S. treated him as an American citizen be-

---

1. *Hamdi v. Rumsfeld*, 124 S. Ct. 2633 (2004).

2. *Hamdi v. Rumsfeld*, 124 S. Ct. 2633 (2004).

3. Ronald Rotunda, *The Detainee Cases of 2004 and 2006 and Their Aftermath*, 57 Syracuse L. Rev. 1, at fn. 86, 2006).

4. *Hamdi v. Rumsfeld*, 124 S. Ct. at 2635–36. (2004).

cause he was born in the United States. Neither of his parents were Americans, but the Fourteenth Amendment states that "all persons born or naturalized in the U.S, and subject to jurisdiction thereof, are citizens of the United States and of the State wherein they reside." The court has interpreted the language to make all persons born in the United States U.S. citizens (except those born of foreign embassy personnel who are not subject to U.S. jurisdiction).

What to do with this American Al Qaeda caused a series of court cases that eventually reached the United States Supreme Court. The nine Supreme Court Justices could not reach a majority decision concerning Hamdi's status. However, Justice Sandra Day O'Connor wrote a plurality opinion that was joined by three other justices (Chief Justice Rehnquist, Justices Kennedy and Breyer). O'Connor's opinion first discussed the definition of "enemy combatant" and defined the term as one who the government alleges was "part of or supporting forces hostile to the United States or coalition partners" in Afghanistan and who "engaged in an armed conflict against the United States" there.[5] Justice Thomas would defer to the military for all battlefield captures.

Having settled on a workable definition of "enemy combatant," the court then, confirming its earlier decision in the WWII cases, concluded that the United States may detain enemy combatants during wartime without charging them with any crime.[6]

However, regarding U.S. citizens like Hamdi, the court required the military to adopt some procedures that ensure the detainee is an enemy combatant.[7] The procedures could be basic, and the government can assume that the detainee is an enemy combatant. That is, unless the *detainee* presents compelling evidence *otherwise*, the U.S. can hold him, so long as it affords the detainee a fair opportunity to present his view of things. The plurality specifies that the purpose for such a hearing is to protect the "errant tourist, embedded journalist, or local aid worker"[8] by giving detainees a fair opportunity to be heard and it allowed the government to leave the burden of proof on the detainee.

---

5. *Hamdi v. Rumsfeld*, 124 S. Ct. at 2645, quoting brief for respondents at 3 (O'Connor adopted the Government's suggested definition).

6. *Hamdi v. Rumsfeld*, 124 S. Ct. at 2645.

7. The plurality opinion stated "We hold that although Congress authorized the detention of combatants in the narrow circumstances alleged here, due process demands that a citizen held in the United States as an enemy combatant be given a meaningful opportunity to contest the factual basis for that detention before a neutral decision maker." *Hamdi v. Rumsfeld*, 124 S. Ct. at 2635.

8. *Hamdi v. Rumsfeld*, 124 S. Ct. at 2649.

The court did not say that detainees were entitled to lawyers. This is not surprising. After all, when a grand jury decides whether probable cause exists to indict a person, the grand jury can question that person but no lawyer will be present. If that person has a lawyer, the lawyer can sit in the next room and wait. This probable cause hearing does not allow any lawyer to be present.

The Supreme Court plurality opinion emphasized that the procedures could be simple and should not interfere with an ongoing war. Along these lines, the hearing could occur some time after capture; and it could consider documents drawn up by soldiers who captured the detainee on the battlefield. The court suggested that proceedings in an existing Army Regulation 190-8, section 1-6 would satisfy the minimal process due.[9] Therefore, the U.S. can hold a U.S. citizen captured on the battlefield so long as the U.S. government affords him an opportunity to rebut the government's presumption that he is an enemy combatant.[10]

The plurality didn't reach a conclusion about what procedures the government should afford detainees held in Guantanamo Bay—non-U.S. citizen enemy combatants. That is, are the Taliban members that fought alongside Hamdi entitled to similar hearings? Perhaps not. If the Supreme Court intended the approximate 600 detainees to receive a Hamdi-like hearing, presumably they would have said so. Additionally, the plurality wouldn't have cautioned that its holding was narrow.

Although *Hamdi* did not require status hearings for non-U.S. citizens, the Department of Defense nonetheless decided to grant such hearings to *all detainees* held in Guantanamo Bay. Within one week after the Supreme Court issued its opinion in *Hamdi*, Paul Wolfowitz, Deputy Secretary of Defense, created the Office of Administrative Review for Detained Enemy Combatants (OARDEC), under the Navy Secretary Gordon England.[11]

---

9. The *Hamdi* plurality states, "There remains the possibility that the standards we have articulated could be met by an appropriately authorized and properly constituted military tribunal. Indeed, it is notable that the military regulations already provide for such process in related instances, dictating that tribunals be made available to determine the status of enemy detainees who assert prisoner-of-war status under the Geneva Convention. See Enemy Prisoners of War, Retained Personnel, Civilian internees and other Detainees, Army Regulation 190-8, 1–6 (1997)."

10. For additional discussion of *Hamdi's* limited applicability to U.S. citizens picked-up on the battlefield see, Ruth Wedgewood, *The Supreme Court and the Guantanamo Controversy*, Terrorism, the Laws of War and the Constitution, 159–183, edited by Peter Berkowitz (Hoover Institution Press) (2005).

11. Memorandum for the Secretary of the Navy, from Paul Wolfowitz, Deputy Secretary of Defense, Establishing Combatant Status Review Tribunal, 7 July 2004.

OARDEC held hearings for every detainee, called Combatant Status Review Tribunals (CSRTs) based on O'Connor's plurality opinion, Geneva Convention Article 5 procedures, and Army Regulation 190-8 as a guide. However, the CSRT proceedings went further than the Supreme Court required in *Hamdi*, by appointing each detainee a personal representative to assist with the hearing.[12] This is unprecedented and not required by any law.

From July until October of 2003, the U.S. military held CSRT hearings for all of the approximately 600 detainees held in Guantanamo Bay. However, unilaterally adopting an untested process came with risks and wrinkles and, ironically, resulted in greater procedural protections for *non-citizen* detainees than the Supreme Court required for *citizen* detainees like Hamdi.

CSRT Hearings: Letting Detainees
in on the Case against Them

For Guantanamo Bay detainees, a cooperative interview could result in small but coveted privileges—the most favored was a Big Mac meal from the McDonald's at Guantanamo Bay. During that era, detainees were cooperative and kept teams of interrogators and interpreters busy for hours—often around the clock. Detainee files grew thicker with every interview and some interrogators and analysts struggled to keep up.

Eventually the detainees stopped talking. Perhaps they ran out of things to say. However, investigators have reported that cooperation waned when the government brought detainees before CSRT boards and showed them all the evidence against them. Several investigators reported frustration that their detainee clammed-up after the CSRT and asked me, their lawyer, why we gave them CSRT hearings and revealed all of the reasons we were holding them. I remember one conversation where the investigator asked, fairly, "Aren't we interfering with our own investigation? After all—we don't give a synopsis of statements to U.S. soldiers accused of crimes on military bases. Aren't we showing our cards?"

As a CITF attorney, I reviewed several CSRT documents that the government planned to share with detainees in upcoming hearings. The documents were very inclusive, and some agents and attorneys opined that only the minimum

---

12. Memorandum for Secretary of the Navy, from Deputy Secretary of Defense, Paul Wolfowitz, Order Establishing Combatant Status Review Tribunal, 7 July 2004. See paragraph "(c) Personal Representative. Each detainee shall be assigned a military officer, with the appropriate security clearance, as a personal representative for the purpose of assisting the detainee in connection with the review process described herein."

amount of information should be included. Under *Hamdi* the U.S. had no obligation to hold hearings for non-U.S citizen detainees *at all.*

Furthermore, even under *Hamdi* the U.S. is only obligated to explain why the detainee was being held, and allow the detainee to rebut that presumption. Instead, in lengthy documents the U.S. outlined nearly all evidence against the detainee. For example, the CSRT summaries could merely state, "You are being held because you were captured fighting U.S. forces with an AK 47 in the Tora Bora region after the Taliban fell." Instead, the documents outlined *all* information about the detainee discovered through interrogation and investigation. For instance, "You provided security for Osama Bin Laden; you've drawn pictures of bombs and suicide vests for interrogators; you've been identified by other detainees learning to throw grenades at known terrorist training camps; you admitted to smuggling weapons and money from Al Qaeda to Taliban forces."[13] Not only did the CSRT hearings grant a higher standard of due process for non-citizen detainees than U.S. citizen detainees are due under *Hamdi*, they compromised interrogations by letting detainees in on the case against them.

Despite objection from some JAG attorneys the CSRT process was on an abbreviated time-line, and there was little interest in scaling it back. Therefore, over the course of a few damaging months, the U.S. government gave every detainee a CSRT—and let him in on the case against him. Big Mac meals lost their effectiveness as detainees' view of the larger picture came into focus.

Furthermore, misapplication of the *Hamdi* decision and AR 190-8 led the public to conclude, erroneously, that the U.S. held detainees based on their admissions made *after* capture. That was not the case. The U.S. held detainees as enemy combatants, and information learned after the fact went either toward capturing other terrorists, or toward building a criminal case against the detainee. When the military compiled evidence against the detainee, and presented it before a CSRT, it only frustrated both purposes.

To prove that it was fair, the United States opened CSRT hearings to the media, and naively expected them to understand that CSRTs are much different from criminal trials, or Military Commissions. That is, CSRTs require very little procedure because they only permit the U.S. military to hold enemy combatants until the end of hostilities. The military holds combatants in every war. It holds them without charge because, as Supreme Court Justice Black once said, "it is no crime to be a soldier."[14] Military Commissions, on the other hand, are wartime trials that afford defendants multiple protections because the result can

---

13. These examples are hypothetical and not drawn from any specific case.
14. *Johnson v. Eisentrager*, 330 U.S. 763, 793 (1950).

lead to punishment. The government will not try all enemy combatants for war crimes. In fact, it only expects to bring 50 to 60 detainees to trial for war crimes.

And so, without adequately educating the American public, the United States opened the gates of Guantanamo Bay, brought detainees before CSRT boards with the media looking on, and held CSRT hearings. Not surprisingly, the media complained that detainees did not have lawyers; that they appeared in prison uniforms, which suggested guilt; and that the U.S. held detainees without sufficient evidence to bring them to criminal trial. They were correct on the facts, but misled on the law. These CSRT hearings were administrative hearings that the U.S. Supreme Court requires for U.S. citizens. The Court did not say what was required for all non-citizen detainees, but one would think that non-citizens would receive no greater rights. The flood of negative press blackened the eye of Uncle Sam and compromised security by opening Guantanamo Bay, which in its earliest days the military closed to virtually *all* non-military personnel.

In some instances, during their CSRT hearings detainees admitted to war crimes that they had previously denied. CITF agents sought access to CSRT records and transcripts to determine what information detainees had revealed to CSRT boards that might shed light on criminal investigations. However, for over three years the administrative board handling CSRT cases denied these requests. During the first CSRT hearings on August 29, 2004, one official repeatedly stressed, "Interrogators and intelligence personnel have no access to information obtained in the process, and the guards don't enter the room."[15] However, no law, including International law, the Geneva Conventions, any Supreme Court ruling, or the Military Order governing CSRT hearings, requires the government to keep information about detainees from investigators. No law requires, or allows, the government to keep detainees' secrets. The origin of this policy is unclear. One wonders why the government chooses to fight a war with one arm tied behind its back. The government was giving more information to the detainees than it was giving to its own investigators.

Late in 2005, officials again insisted that military prosecutors and investigators could not access CSRT records. The stated reason for this rule was to "draw a line" between administrative and criminal proceedings—again without any specific authority. U.S. law does not require such line drawing between criminal and administrative proceedings. For instance, if a U.S. person appears before a worker's compensation board and provides testimony con-

---

15. Kathleen T. Rhem, *Reporters Offered Look Inside Combatant Status Review Tribunals*, AMERICAN FORCES PRESS SERVICES, August 29, 2004.

cerning his alleged work-related injury that later becomes the subject of a criminal fraud investigation, the investigators are not barred from reviewing testimony from the worker's compensation hearing. In fact, refusing access would only provide criminal immunity for statements made in administrative hearings. Despite this reality, officials refused CITF access to these documents, and impeded investigations.

Finally, in 2006, after the United States finished CSRT hearings for all detainees then held at Gitmo, and several years after investigators first attempted to obtain CSRT transcripts, the policy changed. From that point forward, the government would permit CITF to review all documents and transcripts related to CSRT determinations. The policy change came, again, without explanation. However, a senior official at CITF welcomed the policy change and advised his subordinates against "looking a gift horse in the mouth." He then advised them to prioritize their requests for documents and submit them right away, before "they change their minds."

One hearing room where detainees had their Combatant Status Review Tribunals in Guantanamo Bay. Photo located at www.defenselink.mil.

Hearing room where detainees had Combatant Status Review Tribunals in Guantanamo Bay. Photo located at www.defenselink.mil.

CHAPTER TWENTY-TWO

Paroling Terrorists
Back to the Battlefield

"We don't want to be the world's jailers."[1]

Fallout from initiating CSRT boards had catastrophic results. The U.S. let detainees in on the case against them, and detainees began recanting every admission they had previously made. Other detainees, who had good rapport with their interrogator and were on the cusp of admissions, closed up as tight as clams and completely refused to cooperate. Not only did the CSRT hearings interfere with developing cases, they generated harsh criticism by the media, and public support for holding detainees in Gitmo waned.

> **JAG Fact**
>
> *The law does not require the U.S. to have elaborate hearings before holding detainees in Gitmo. But, the military gives each detainee a Combatant Status Review Tribunal (CSRT) and an Annual Review Board (ARB) hearing. Without any legal authority requiring it, the military paroles detainees back to the battlefield—to fight against U.S. forces!*

Oddly, despite this fallout, the U.S. didn't acknowledge, or perhaps didn't realize, that initiating CSRTS for all of the detainees was a mistake. Instead, it went one step further and created yet another layer of review, a super-CSRT for all detainees, which it called Annual Review Boards, or ARBs, also under the direction of the Office of Administrative Review for Detained Enemy Combatants (OARDEC).[2] Essentially, ARBs are annual parole board hearings for every detainee. If the board decides a detainee "no longer poses a threat," it can release

---

1. Answer from Rear Admiral McGarrah (orally and on power-point slides), head of OARDEC, when asked why DoD adopted ARBs, which have no basis in international or U.S. law. Public Forum, George Mason University Law School, February 16, 2006.

2. Memorandum from Gordon England, Department of Defense Designated Civilian Official, dated September 14, 2004. Subject: Implementation of Administrative Review Procedures for Enemy Combatants Detained at U.S. Naval Base in Guantanamo Bay, Cuba.

him. Ironically, the procedures governing the ARB are significantly more complicated than CSRT procedures.

The U.S. government spent over 15 million dollars the first year to hold ARBs for every detainee, and reviewed over 300,000 documents during these hearings.[3] Despite the effort and cost of ARBs, there is no legal authority or requirement for them. The leader of OARDEC acknowledges this fact, calling ARBs "unprecedented, historic, and discretionary."[4]

International law, including the Geneva Conventions governing treatment of POWs, does not require these blanket parole board hearings. Indeed, the original Geneva Conventions of 1929 did not provide for parole in any instance. In the 1949 revisions to the Conventions, the option of granting parole at the discretion of the detaining power was included, "particularly in cases where this may contribute to the improvement of their state of health." Those who are paroled are "bound on their personal honor scrupulously to fulfill ... the engagements of their paroles or promises."[5] *On their personal honor?* It's hard to imagine how that term could be applied to anyone who has been captured fighting with the Taliban or Al Qaeda, or any other organization that routinely massacres civilians.

Parole opportunities under the Geneva Conventions are limited and "no longer posing a threat" is not a justification for release. Similarly, the army regulation governing detained personnel allows repatriation, but only of the sick and wounded and only in limited circumstances. Under that regulation, only those suffering from "disabilities as a result of injury" equivalent to losing a limb or those with chronic conditions, and a prognosis that precludes recovery within a year, are eligible for direct repatriation.[6] The ARB process that paroles our enemies back to the battlefield is not grounded in international law, the Geneva Conventions, Army Regulations governing retained personnel, or even good old-fashioned common sense.

Not only is the ARB a voluntary and unprecedented creation of DoD, the decision to return an enemy combatant to the battlefield endangers U.S. soldiers. Several detainees released under the ARB process have rejoined the battle against U.S. and coalition forces. The Military has recaptured some detainees

3. Comment by Rear Admiral McGarrah, Commander of OARDEC, public forum, George Mason University, February 16, 2006.

4. *Id.*

5. Third Geneva Convention, Relative to the Treatment of Prisoners of War, 12 August 1949, article 21.

6. Army Regulation 190-8, *Enemy Prisoners of War, Retained Personnel, Civilian Internees and Other Detainees*, 1 October 1997, paragraph 3-12(l). The regulation goes on to state "Prisoners who are not sick or wounded will be repatriated or released at the cessation of hostilities as directed by OSD." Paragraph 3-13.

and killed others on the battlefield. Some remain at large. The numbers are not precise, because until soldiers either capture or kill a paroled detainee it is impossible to discern whether they've taken up arms against the United States. Additionally, there is no way to determine if, or how many, U.S. soldiers were injured or killed at his hands before being killed or recaptured. However, we know that approximately 5–10% of detainees released in the ARB process have rejoined the battle—a fact acknowledged by the Department of Defense. In fact, the Deputy Secretary of Defense, Detainee Affairs Division stated in a public briefing, "some of those released to date have already returned to the fight."[7]

I've heard people say that the detainees are harmless, and if they join Al Qaeda after the U.S. releases them, it is only because their experience in Guantanamo Bay made them want to join Al Qaeda. The facts do not support this assumption. Detainees whom the U.S. releases claim they have always been committed members of Al Qaeda and brag about this to reporters.

One released detainee killed a judge leaving a mosque in Afghanistan,[8] and another assumed leadership of an Al Qaeda-aligned militant faction in Pakistan, bragging to reporters that he "tricked his U.S. interrogators into believing he was someone else."[9] Another Pakistani, Muhammad Mahsood, threatened violence against U.S. forces only days after it released him. He said, "We would fight America and its allies, until the very end!"[10] Mahsood backs his claim with action, claiming responsibility for kidnapping of two innocent Chinese engineers. He eventually freed one and killed the other. Considering that two known Pakistanis have reentered the battle, it is curious that the Department of Defense characterizes detainee releases to Pakistan as "successful," insisting that coordination with local villagers ensures that detainees will not return to the battlefield.[11]

The military has released even high-level members of Al Qaeda. Early in 2006, the U.S. released a known Al Qaeda loyalist known as "Tabarak" from Guantanamo Bay to Moroccan custody, where he was set free four months later. Tabarak was a chief aid to Osama Bin Laden and helped plan and execute Bin

---

7. Deputy Secretary of Defense Detainee Affairs Policy Division slides presented in public forum, George Mason University Law School, February 16, 2006.

8. THE WASHINGTON POST, November 11, 2005.

9. John Mintz, *Released Detainees Rejoining the Fight*, WASHINGTON POST, October 22, 2004, Page A01.

10. *Released Detainees Rejoining the Fight*, by John Mintz, Washington Post Staff Writer, October 22, 2004, A01.

11. Deputy Secretary of Defense, Detainee Affairs Policy Division, public forum, George Mason University Law School, February 16, 2006.

Laden's escape from Tora Bora during December 2001.[12] During the escape, he made phone calls from Bin Laden's satellite telephone. Neither U.S. nor Moroccan authorities will comment about the specifics of Tabarak's release. Therefore, we cannot verify whether the ARB played a role in Tabarak's release. However, in either case, the U.S. released a dangerous Al Qaeda operative from its custody without any explanation.

It makes sense that released detainees would reenter the fight, and scholarly research supports their propensity to do just that. Canadian authorities have extensively documented recidivism of radical Muslims. In January 2006, a senior Middle East Analyst for the Canadian Security Intelligence Service (CSIS), identified only as "P.G." testified in an open court hearing about his agency's belief that members of Al Qaeda or other related militant Islamic groups "maintain their ties and their relationships to those networks, for very long periods of time. These ties are forged in environments where relationships mean a great deal, and it is our belief that the dedication to the ideology, if you will, is very strong, and is virtually impossible to break."[13] He further opined that militants who have attended terrorist training camps or opted for radical Islam must be "considered threats to Canadian public safety for the indefinite future."[14]

P.G. also opined that incarceration tends to harden, not soften, their radical Islamic beliefs. He cited to several examples where radical Islamists emerged from prison more dangerous and committed to principles of radical Islam than they were going in. For instance, Ayman al-Zawahiri, served a prison term in Egypt for his role in the assassination of Anwar Sadat, and after Egypt released him, Al Qaeda elevated al-Zawahiri to become Osama bin Laden's principal deputy. Mussab al-Zarqawi, leader of Al Qaeda's affiliate in Iraq, previously spent seven years in a Jordanian prison for extremist activities.[15] Essentially, P.G. concludes that it is categorically "unsafe to ever release a jihadi militant."[16] Some U.S. officials share this position. A former special assistant for detainee policy stated, "You can't trust them when they say they're not terrorists."[17]

Despite the lack of legal authority or historical precedent for releasing able-bodied enemy combatants during wartime, and their proven propensity for

---

12. *Al Qaeda Detainee's Mysterious Release*, WASHINGTON POST, January 30, 2006, at A1.

13. Mark Hosenball, *Once a Terrorist, Always a Terrorist*, NEWSWEEK WEB EXCLUSIVE January 18, 2006.

14. *Id.*

15. *Id.*

16. *Id.*

17. John Mintz, *Released Detainees Rejoining the Fight*, WASHINGTON POST, October 22, 2004, A01.

recidivism, Admiral McGarrah nonetheless supports the ARB parole process because "We have no desire to be the world's jailer."[18] By February 2006, the U.S. government had released 270 detainees from Guantanamo Bay.[19] By March 2007, the total number of detainees released or transferred from Guantanamo Bay had climbed to 390.[20]

Therefore, the story of one captured American Al Qaeda was the first gossamer strand of what became a colossal bureaucratic web. The U.S. government reacted to the Supreme Court's narrow holding in *Hamdi* by adopting layer upon confusing layer of procedures that the court did not contemplate, and the Geneva Conventions don't require.

A Word about Uighurs

Most detainees that the CSRT board deems "no longer a threat" to the U.S. are transferred, or released to their home countries. However, the U.S. will not release detainees to countries that are likely to torture the detainee. Several detainees held in Guantanamo Bay are Chinese Uighurs. They commit terrorist acts primarily directed at the Chinese government. However, although they agitate against an oppressive government, they are violent terrorists, who accept funds from known terrorist groups, including Al Qaeda. They have also conducted training in known Afghani terrorist training camps.

The U.S. government has determined that they are "no longer a threat" in ARB hearings, but the U.S. could not find a country to take them. The United States Government asked over twenty-eight countries to take the Uighurs, but they refused due to the Uighurs' violence and terrorist ties.

Eventually, during the summer of 2006, Albania announced it would accept the Uighurs. Before that, no other country including Saudi Arabia wanted to take these fellow Muslims into their home country. There are people who actually argued that the U.S. should give them asylum. If we took these people into our country, we could expect them to blow up the Chinese Embassy or kill Chinese in this country. There are various ways to receive U.S. citizenship; being a terrorist that no other country would take should not be one of them.

---

18. Statement of Admiral McGarrah, Commander of OARDEC, public forum, George Mason University, February 16, 2006.

19. Data provided by the Department of Defense, Deputy Secretary of Defense Office, Detainee Affairs Policy, public forum, George Mason University, February 16, 2006.

20. U.S. Department of Defense News Release, No. 253-07, March 6, 2007. Available at http://www.defenselink.mil/releases/release.aspx?released=10582.

Some have criticized the U.S. government for capturing Uighurs to begin with. However, like other detainees, soldiers captured them during active hostilities in terrorist training camps. Under the Geneva Conventions, they are enemy combatants and engaged in hostilities against the United States. The fact that they are dangerous is confirmed by the fact that no other countries will accept them. Critics that characterize the Uighurs as innocent misrepresent the facts.

CHAPTER TWENTY-THREE

Iraqi Justice

While the U.S. wove its bureaucratic web and slowed down CITF led investigations, Iraq made huge strides forward in bringing terrorists to justice. Iraq created the Central Criminal Court of Iraq (CCCI) to try "insurgents" for criminal acts against Iraqi and coalition forces. The procedures differ from those in U.S. courts, but protect fundamental rights, such as the right to an attorney, the right to remain silent, and the right to appeal a guilty verdict. Defendants can even request a new trial if new evidence that tends to prove their innocence arises after their convictions.

Select CITF agents work closely with the Central Criminal Court of Iraq (CCCI) trying terrorists for violent crimes, including bombings and grenade attacks against coalition forces and Iraqis. CITF agents investigate and help build cases going before the new CCCI.

By August 2006, with CITF assistance, the Iraqi court held 1,340 trials of insurgents, which resulted in 1,144 convictions with sentences including three ranging up to death.[1] Many are convicted of "unsettling the stability and security of Iraq." Others are convicted on illegal weapons charges, and still others of "illegal border crossing" in violation of Iraq's passport laws.

Aside from helping the CCCI investigate and convict terrorists, CITF agents stationed in Iraq help find kidnapped hostages. One agent reports that they "drop everything" and support an exhaustive around-the-clock effort to locate and rescue victims.

With U.S. assistance, an unstable Iraq is more successful at investigating and trying terrorists still in Iraq than the U.S. is at bringing detainees held in Guantanamo Bay to justice. Some CITF agents gave up on CITF in the U.S. and requested deployments to Iraq, where they could "actually do something."

---

1. *The Iraq Central Criminal Court Convicts 16*, MULTI-NATIONAL FORCE-IRAQ, August 7, 2006, Rls. A060807a, available at http://www.mnf-iraq.com/index.php?option=com_content&task=view&id=1826&Itemid=21.

CHAPTER TWENTY-FOUR

Helping Prosecutors

It was late October 2004, and crisp fall weather settled over Washington, D.C. Leaves turned magnificent colors, and then fell to the ground where soldiers' boots carried them into the CITF building. Leaves scattered at the entranceway reminded us of the world outside our concrete walls.

The cool autumn wind usually keeps me inside. But not this year. The Army's Physical Fitness Test (called a PT test) was only a few weeks away. So every day after work, I laced up my running shoes, covered my ears with a knitted earband, and hit the running trail. The army requires all soldiers to take and pass a PT test every six months. Failing the test can keep a soldier from promotion to a higher rank. The army even has a process to discharge some soldiers who don't pass the test. Physical fitness is an important component of military life.

I dreaded the first whip of wind, but soon felt energetic and invigorated. That season I trained on long, winding, gravel running trails that curved through the trees with steep hills and long dips. The cool air nettled my lungs, but the fall aroma always smelled so good that it was worth the sting.

I had a lot on my mind, and running along the winding, wooded trail put things in perspective. For this reason, the times when I am most fit coincide with the times when I have the most on my mind. I literally ran through my first year of law school, and was a spindly 100 pounds by Thanksgiving break.

On this day my thoughts mainly turned to work. A few weeks earlier, I had received a call from a military prosecutor working at the Office of Military Commissions (OMC). The DoD created this prosecution office soon after it began holding detainees in Guantanamo Bay. Their job was to prepare cases and try detainees for war crimes violations. Once CITF has finished investigating its cases, OMC was supposed to bring them to trial. However, the trial process had a very, very slow start. For months on end obsessive officials at the Department of Defense wrung their hands and grappled with the rules that would govern these historic trials. It struggled to see what it could not, and to diagnose problems that didn't yet exist.

The voice at the other end was friendly and upbeat. I gathered that he was young, probably about my age. The chief prosecutor assigned him to review a case that my team was investigating, and he asked if I could help prepare it for trial. I agreed, and we began working closely together.

My supervisor at CITF supported the idea, and allowed me to work several days a week at the Office of Military Commissions (OMC), and the remaining days at CITF. Usually, hybrid work arrangements are difficult to manage in the army, but the supervising attorneys in each office were cordial and agreed that it made sense to share attorneys on the eve of military commission prosecutions. So I wore two hats, and became even more absorbed in detainee-related legal issues.

At the same time that we prepared our case for trial, two others were well underway. David Hicks, an Australian, and Salim Hamdan, a Yemini, two detainees at Guantanamo Bay, were nearing the eve of their trials. They would be the first detainees tried before a military commission since the trials following World War II. OMC prosecutors worked long, hard hours drafting trial motions. We expected these trials to be modern day Nuremberg trials. We were anxious to make history and bring terrorists to justice.

I listened to the regular tempo of my feet on the trail, like a musician's metronome. I was going to interview a witness tomorrow—someone who interrogated the detainee during a Special Forces raid in Afghanistan. Although this witness wasn't working for the military anymore, and a few years had passed, the CITF agent managed to track her down. She was reluctant at first, but finally agreed to meet with us. Interviewing a real person—taking the case from paper files to preparing witnesses to testify—made it all seem real and worthwhile. In my mind, I went through a list of questions to ask.

Thump, thump, thump. I was one hill from the finish line. With only thirty seconds remaining, I picked up the pace, and crossed the muddy finish line with only a few seconds to spare. I heaved like a panting mountain cat, trying to catch my breath. I ran the practice trail within the required time limit, but barely. There's no reason I couldn't do it on the day of the PT test.

CHAPTER TWENTY-FIVE

Military Commission History and Rules

Working with the prosecution team was the natural next step in my career progression. At Guantanamo Bay, I learned about detaining and interrogating enemy combatants. Then, working alongside CITF agents, I learned how the U.S. investigates terrorist leads that originate in Guantanamo Bay. Now, working with prosecutors, I would help to try detainees before War Crimes Tribunals.

> **JAG Fact**
>
> *JAGs have been involved in every major conflict since the Revolutionary War. They prosecuted President Lincoln's assassins after the Civil War, and helped organize international war crimes tribunals in both Japan and Germany after World War II.*

In the Global War on Terror, some suggest that war crimes trials (or what the military calls military commissions) are novel, untested, and offend fundamental principles of due process. But these claims aren't true. Countries around the world have used war crimes trials to try war criminals for centuries, and the U.S. Supreme Court has approved them.

The Archduke of Austria held the first war crimes trials in 1474. A tribunal of twenty-eight judges tried and convicted Peter von Habenbach, whom Austria had appointed to restore order, but who did so by terrorizing the people. The war crimes tribunal tried, convicted, and ordered Habenbach beheaded for violating the "laws of God and man." Habenbach alleged that he was simply following orders but the tribunal rejected his defense.[1]

The United States and other nations have repeatedly used international tribunals in lieu of civilian courts.[2] The most notable use of war crimes tribunals was by the victorious allied nations, who tried hundreds of Nazi and Japanese war criminals around the world after WWII.[3]

---

1. Linda Grant, *Gallery Exhibit highlights the first international war crimes tribunal*, HARVARD LAW BULLETIN, p. 72, Spring 2006.

2. GREGORY E. MAGGS, TERRORISM AND THE LAW, CASES AND MATERIALS, 383 (Thompson West Publishing) (2004).

3. *Id.* at 383, *citing* the International Military Tribunal, Nuremberg; The Dachau Trials; the International Military Tribunal for the Far East; and other Military Tribunals of Japanese and German defendants.

Aside from participating at Nuremberg and other international tribunals, the United States independently held military commissions and tried war criminals. Two cases were elevated to the United States Supreme Court, *Ex parte Quirin* and *Application of Yamashita*.[4]

Understanding the *Quirin* Case

The year was 1942, and the United States was at war with the German Reich. After receiving specialized training, eight German saboteurs boarded two submarines in French ports, and began their trip to the United States. Hidden under miles of dark water, they made the journey across the Atlantic ocean undetected. At least one of them was a U.S. citizen.

Their submarines came ashore in the middle of the night, under the cover of darkness. One landed in New York, the other in Florida. Each four-man team off-loaded explosives, fuses, and timing devices. Some were wearing German uniforms. They buried their uniforms in the sand, and dressed as civilians in order to blend-in and escape detection. At this point, they became spies, unprivileged combatants under the laws of war. Roving among unsuspecting civilians, they began surveying buildings. Their plan was to attack the United States, from within its own borders.

Within days of coming ashore, they contacted two Americans. They met for drinks and discussion with one of them, Anthony Cramer. However, even years later it remains unclear whether Cramer knew of their plan or whether he helped them carry it out.

On the verge of their planned attacks, one of the saboteurs lost his nerve and decided to abandon the plan. He took a train to Washington, D.C., intending to confess. After a long wait, he met with officials at the FBI and informed them of the plan.[5] However, when FBI Director J. Edgar Hoover announced their capture, he left out the untidy fact that the FBI only knew about the plan because of the voluntary admission of one of the participants. Instead, Hoover credited the FBI's investigatory powers for discovering the

---

4. *Ex parte Quirin*, 317 U.S. 1 (1942); *Application of Yamashita*, 327 U.S. 1 (1946).

5. Charles Lane, *Liberty and the Pursuit of Terrorists*, THE WASHINGTON POST, November 25, 2001, *stating*, "The trial was held in secret not only to protect legitimate intelligence sources and methods, but also to conceal the embarrassing fact that J. Edgar Hoover's FBI had failed to uncover the plot until one of the Germans came to Washington and offered a detailed confession."

saboteurs.[6] The trials were secret. If they had been public, the entire nation would know that the U.S. caught the saboteurs by accident. The Nazis would have known that this plan failed by happenstance, and they would have been more likely to try to infiltrate saboteurs again.

The U.S. convicted Cramer of treason, but the Supreme Court later reversed that conviction.[7] The other American was Hans Haupt, whose son was one of the saboteurs. He provided shelter and a car for his saboteur son and, unlike Cramer, definitely knew about the plan. The U.S. convicted him for providing shelter, sustenance and supplies, and the Supreme Court upheld his conviction.[8] The government tried Cramer and Hans Haupt in Civilian Article III Courts (the type that hears cases of U.S. citizens). It tried the saboteurs in military courts.

A war crime tribunal convicted the saboteurs of the following crimes:

1) Violating the laws of war;
2) Relieving or attempting to relieve, or corresponding with or giving intelligence to, the enemy;
3) Spying; and
4) Conspiracy to commit the former three crimes.

On an expedited schedule, the Supreme Court decided to hear the saboteurs' appeals. The main question was whether prosecutors could try the saboteurs by military commissions or whether they were entitled to trial by civil courts with all the rights afforded to U.S. citizens. The Court first issued a short opinion rejecting the claims of Quirin and the others. The Court said it would write a full opinion in the fall, after returning from vacation. A few days after the Court issued this initial opinion, the Government executed the German saboteurs, long before the Supreme Court issued its lengthier opinion.

The Supreme Court held that "the detention and trial of [the saboteurs]—ordered by the President in the declared exercise of his powers as Commander in Chief of the Army in a time of war and of grave public danger—are not to be set aside by the courts without the clear conviction that they are in conflict with the Constitution or laws of Congress constitutionally enacted."[9] In a unanimous opinion, it found no such conflict. The court determined that the president's constitutional power to wage war necessarily included the power to hold

---

6. Tony Mauro, *A Mixed Precedent for Military Tribunals 1942 case of Nazis on U.S. soil gives administration the authority for terrorist trials, but leaves room for doubt*, LEGAL TIMES, November 19, 2001.

7. *Cramer v. United States*, 325 U.S. 1 (1945).

8. *Haupt v. United States*, 330 U.S. 631 (1947).

9. *Ex parte Quirin*, 317 U.S. 1, 9 (1942).

war crimes trials, and punish war criminals. Further, Congress had explicitly sanctioned military commissions in its articles of war.

Aside from deciding that the president could initiate military commissions, the Supreme Court also discussed the specific charges brought against the saboteurs. Looking to military history, it found that wearing a uniform was central to lawfully waging war, and that historically spies lurking around behind enemy lines were put to death. The Court did not define the outside jurisdictional boundaries of military commissions, but found that clandestinely entering the United States to wage war, without wearing a uniform, most certainly violated the laws of war.[10] The Supreme Court upheld the convictions in a full opinion that it issued the next fall.

In the current war on terror, President Bush's order creating the military commissions copies the order that President Roosevelt had issued over fifty years earlier to try the Nazi saboteurs, an order that was unanimously upheld by the Supreme Court.

Understanding the *Yamashita* Case[11]

In 1946, four years after military commissions convicted and executed the Nazi saboteurs, another military commission case made its way to the Supreme Court. General Yamashita was a commanding general of the Imperial Japanese Army in the Philippines during WWII, who eventually surrendered to the United States and became a prisoner of war (POW). A military commission tried, convicted, and sentenced him to death by hanging for allowing his soldiers to commit brutal atrocities against people of the U.S. and its allies. On over one hundred occasions, his soldiers attacked unarmed civilians and POWs, and destroyed public, private, and religious property.

Yamashita's defense at trial, and on appeal, was that he couldn't be held responsible for crimes committed by his soldiers. The Supreme Court disagreed, and determined that international law permits holding commanders responsible for "permitting their soldiers to commit" extensive and widespread atrocities. Justices Murphy and Rutledge authored strongly worded dissents, criticizing the Court for permitting "revenge and retribution, masked in formal legal procedures for purposes of dealing with a fallen enemy commander...." They argued that General Yamashita could not be held responsible for acts without proving he specifically committed, ordered, or condoned, the atrocities.

---

10. *Ex parte Quirin*, 317 U.S. 1, 16 (1942).
11. *Application of Yamashita*, 327 U.S. 1, 66 S. Ct 320, 90 L. Ed. 499 (1946).

Despite the spirited disagreement about whether General Yamashita formed the requisite criminal intent to be held liable, the Court reaffirmed *Quirin* and made clear that trial by military commission was permissible. It concluded that the articles of war, authorized by Congress, allowed military commissions. The court called military commissions "an appropriate tribunal for the trial and punishment of offenses against the law of war." It acknowledged significant judicial deference to military commissions, stating, "If the military tribunals have lawful authority to hear, decide and condemn, their action is not subject to judicial review merely because they have made a wrong decision on disputed facts. Correction of their errors of decision is not for the courts but for the military authorities which are alone authorized to review their decisions."[12]

Inside Nuremberg

The most famous WWII military tribunals occurred in Nuremberg, Germany. At the close of World War II, the allied powers met numerous times to determine how to redress the Nazi atrocities. The British, French, and Soviets thought the offenders should be quickly executed, and in 1944 Winston Churchill said that offenders should be "hunted down and shot."[13] Alternatively, the Americans pushed for justice through a court of law. Eventually, the others came around to America's way of thinking and decided to bring Nazi defendants before war crimes trials.

In August of 1945, the four powers (Britain, France, America, and the Soviet Union) set out to write rules to govern the trials. They wrote and signed what would become the governing document for the Nuremberg trials, the "London Charter of the International Military Tribunal."

The document's purpose is set forth in Article I "for the just and prompt trial and punishment of the major war criminals of the European Axis."[14] The tribunal's "constitution" sets forth 30 succinct articles governing the overall tribunal process, and 11 simple rules drafted by the Tribunal itself to put meat on its bones.

Generally, each tribunal consisted of four judges with four alternates appointed by each participating country (U.S., France, Britain, and Russia).[15]

---

12. *Ex parte Quirin* at 8.

13. See information at www.courttv.com/archive/casefiles/nuremberg/law.html.

14. Nuremberg Trial Proceedings, Charter of the International Military Tribunal, August 1945, article 1, appearing at www.yale.edu/lawweb/avalon/imt/proc/imtcost.htm.

15. Charter for the International Military Tribunal, August 1945, article 2.

Neither the prosecution nor defense could challenge members of the tribunal. It was not like a regular criminal court where each side can challenge and remove some jurors on grounds that they cannot be fair. The members agreed among themselves on a president.[16]

Judges made all decisions, including whether to convict the defendant, by a majority vote. In the event of a tie vote, the president's vote carried the issue. The tribunal had jurisdiction over any defendant alleged to have committed, or conspired to commit, crimes against the peace, war crimes, or crimes against humanity.[17] Defendants were entitled to appointed attorneys, or they could represent themselves and cross-examine any prosecution witnesses.[18] The tribunal allowed any evidence, so long as it was "probative,"[19] which means evidence that would help members decide an issue relevant to the case. The tribunal decided whether a defendant was guilty or innocent, and if guilty, issued a just punishment.[20] No higher court reviewed the sentences (there was no appeal) and the court carried out the punishment expeditiously.

The Nuremberg rules were succinct and straightforward and only included eleven rules in all.[21] In fact, the rules themselves specifically exclude the "technical" rules of evidence, instead directing the tribunal to "adopt and apply to the greatest possible extent expeditious and non-technical procedure, and ... admit any evidence which it deems to be of probative value."[22]

Article 16 is entitled "Fair Trial for Defendants." It provides for only the very basic rights, including defendant's right to a copy of the charges in his own language, the right to provide an explanation relevant to the charges, the right to conduct his own defense or have assistance of counsel, and the right to present evidence and cross-examine witnesses called by the prosecution. The tribunal could exclude defendants and/or their attorney from proceedings for being disruptive or demonstrating willful contempt of the court.[23] The rules

---

16. Charter for the International Military Tribunal, August 1945, article 4(b).

17. Charter for the International Military Tribunal, August 1945, article 6.

18. Charter for the International Military Tribunal, August 1945, article 4.

19. Charter for the International Military Tribunal, August 1945, article 19.

20. Charter for the International Military Tribunal, August 1945, articles 26–27.

21. Richard May and Marieke Weirda, *Trends in International Criminal Evidence: Nuremberg, Tokyo, the Hague and Arusha*, 37 COLUM. J. TRANSNAT'L L. 725, 729 (1999).

22. Charter of the International Military Tribunal, August 1945, §4, article 19.

23. Charter of the International Military Tribunal, August 1945, §5, article 18(c), indicating the Tribunal shall "deal summarily with any contumacy, imposing appropriate punishment, including exclusion of any Defendant or his Counsel from some or all further proceedings, but without prejudice to the determination of the charges." See also Nuremberg Trial Proceedings, Rule of Procedure, Rule 5, stating "... The Tribunal, acting through

even allowed prosecutors to try defendants in absentia.[24] Prosecutors used that provision to convict a defendant it presumed was already dead.

One controversial rule at Nuremberg specifically precluded defendants from raising certain defenses. Defendants could not argue that they were just following orders, and they could not justify their atrocities by showing that other countries committed similar offenses.

Under these rules, prosecutors tried twenty-four leading Nazi figures in the first trial, which was widely publicized.[25] The world watched as prosecutors aired dramatic video footage of the death camps that revealed Nazi atrocities, and displayed shrunken human heads that Nazis used as paperweights—yes paperweights. The trial revealed to the world Hitler's "final solution"—annihilating the Jews. After the first trial, the U.S. also tried another 182 defendants in 12 separate cases in Nuremberg, but the press lost interest and these trials didn't receive much media coverage.

Some praise the international military tribunal at Nuremberg for its simplicity, while others criticize it. Nuremberg prosecutors expeditiously brought egregious war criminals to justice for their heinous crimes against humanity. On the other hand, some criticize the Nuremberg procedures for lacking jurisdiction and imposing ex post facto laws, laws written after the crime is committed. A law must exist before it can be broken. Otherwise, the state can arrest and punish an individual for an act that is not a crime today but will be tomorrow.

On the ex post facto issue, Nuremberg prosecutors adeptly pointed out that the first person tried for murder could have claimed that the charge was ex post facto. There is a first time for everything. In addition, commentators acknowledge "customary international law," which makes certain acts crimes, without specifically requiring that they be codified.

Despite mixed reviews of Nuremberg's legal machinery, it established international precedent. One month after the executions, the UN General Assembly passed Resolution 95(I), adopting "the principles of International Law recognized by the Charter of the Nuremberg Tribunal and the judgment of the Tri-

---

its President, shall provide for the maintenance of order at the trial. Any defendant or any other person may be excluded from open sessions of the Tribunal for failure to observe and respect the directives and dignity of the Tribunal."

24. Charter of the International Military Tribunal, August 1945, article 12, "The Tribunal shall have the right to take proceedings against a person charged with crimes set out in Article 6 of this Charter in his absence, if he has not been found or if the Tribunal, for any reason, finds it necessary, in the interest of justice, to conduct the hearing in his absence."

25. Professor Gregory E. Maggs, Terrorism and the Law, 383 (Thompson/West Publishing) (2005).

bunal." The resolution lay dormant until in 1993 the UN Security Council created the war crimes tribunal to prosecute atrocities in Yugoslavia.[26]

The rules and procedures for war crimes tribunals are more relaxed than the rules applicable to civilian courts, due to wartime realities. Gathering evidence during a time of war is extremely difficult. Witnesses die or scatter, documents are destroyed, and evidence may change hands many times over before it is cataloged. Put simply—the notion of "securing the crime scene" is unrealistic in the midst of battle.

However, relaxed rules do not mean the process is unfair. The door swings both ways. Rules that allow prosecutors to admit anything deemed "relevant" are reciprocal. The defense can do the same thing. Maybe the relaxed rules benefit defendants, as much as or more than they benefit the prosecutors. For instance, at Nuremberg, defendant Hermann Goering frustrated prosecutors by lengthy, wandering responses on cross-examination. The judges permitted so much latitude that the chief prosecutor, Supreme Court Justice Jackson, became frustrated and was unable to cross-examine Goering effectively.

Uncharacteristic of Justice Jackson, his composure crumbled when he protested, "I respectfully submit to the tribunal that this witness is not being responsive to his examination! ... It is perfectly futile to spend our time if we cannot have responsive answers to our questions.... This witness, it seems to me, is adopting, in the witness box, and in the dock, an arrogant and contemptuous attitude toward the tribunal which is giving him the trial which he never gave a living soul, nor dead one either."[27] Nonetheless, the Court upheld Goering's right to have his say—though it violated cross-examination custom.[28]

Considering *Quirin*, *Yamashita*, and the Nuremberg trials, the United States entered the Global War on Terrorism backed by significant legal precedent to hold military commissions. They are a well-established means of bringing war criminals to justice, and affording defendants fair trials while accommodating battlefield realities.

Robust Procedures for Present-Day War Crimes Trials

In the war on terror, some criticize the Department of Defense for initiating "kangaroo courts" with an uneven playing field. Nevertheless, the mil-

---

26. Joseph E. Persico, Nuremberg, Infamy on Trial, 443 (Penguin Books) (1994).
27. *Id.* at 278.
28. *Id.* at 276.

itary commissions' procedures to try detainees, just like the administrative ones to hold them, are significantly more robust than ever before. The rights that the U.S. government grants the detainees are far greater than the rights of the defendants in *Quirin* (the Nazi saboteur case), which the Supreme Court upheld.

The president's November 13, 2001 order laid the groundwork for military commissions, and in Section 4 instructed the secretary of defense to draft rules governing the commissions. At a minimum, the president directed full and fair trials with a commission that decides both fact and law, admission of any evidence having probative value to a reasonable person, protection of classified information, conviction and sentence by a two-thirds majority; and review of the trial record by either the secretary of defense or the president himself.[29]

Responding to the president, the secretary of defense then drafted military commission order number one, which succinctly sets forth military commission procedures. Section five, entitled *Procedures Accorded the Accused*, guarantees the accused several rights that include:

- A copy of charges in defendant's language
- The presumption of innocence until proven guilty beyond a reasonable doubt
- Detailed defense counsel
- Access to information the prosecution intends to use at trial and any evidence tending to exculpate the defendant
- Guarantees that the defendant is not required to testify against himself, but may testify on his own behalf (the right to remain silent)
- The defendant's right to be present except when it violates laws governing classified information or when the defendant is disruptive
- Access to information used in sentencing
- The right to present evidence and make a statement at a sentencing hearing
- Open public trials
- Prosecutors cannot charge defendants twice for the same crime (double jeopardy).[30]

We learned from Nuremberg and other international criminal tribunals that procedures don't need to be elaborate to be fair. The general rules set forth in

---

29. President's Military Order (November 13, 2001), available at http://whitehouse.gov/news/releases/2001/11/20011113-27.html.

30. Military Commission Order No. 1 (revised version), August 31, 2005, available at www.defenselink.mil/news.

Military Commission Order Number One protect fundamental rights, and lay the groundwork for fair but efficient trials that take into account battlefield realities. In fact, these rules grant defendants more rights than criminal defendants receive in many European countries, which routinely accept hearsay and don't require proof beyond a reasonable doubt in order to convict.

In 2006 Congress passed the Military Commissions Act,[31] and the Department of Defense then drafted new rules to govern military commissions. The new rules are called the Manual for Military Commissions, and these rules incorporate procedures originally set forth in Military Commission Order Number One, and additional procedural protections adopted by Congress.[32]

---

31. 10 USC 948a.

32. *See* DoD Press Briefing on New Military Commissions Rules, January 18, 2007, available at http://www.defenselink.mil/Transcripts/Transcript.aspx?TranscriptID=3868.

CHAPTER TWENTY-SIX

Back to Guantanamo Bay— Not a Modern Day Nuremberg

For November, it was a warm afternoon in Washington, D.C. I decided not to take my coat— I wouldn't need it where I was going. I reached for a few last-minute items and wheeled my bag into the hallway. I pressed the elevator button and glanced at my watch. There was plenty of time before my flight.

I was on my way, once again, to Guantanamo Bay, Cuba. As I stood alone in the elevator, I couldn't help but reflect on my seven-month tour in Guantanamo and was grateful that this one was a much shorter trip, only a few weeks. While I was actually assigned to CITF, I had worked closely with the prosecution team preparing motions for the *Hicks* and *Hamdan* trials. At the last minute, the prosecution office asked me to join them in Guantanamo Bay for hearings on the trial motions, though I was not technically part of the prosecution team. I would finish my tour with CITF in a few short months and hoped to earn a spot as a prosecutor on Military Commissions prosecution team. This was a significant first step toward that goal.

When the military created the Office of Military Commissions (OMC) in 2003, it hand-selected prosecutors from each branch of the services—they were the best. Chief Prosecutor Colonel Robert Swann, who had a solid reputation in the Army JAG Corps, both as a litigator and an army judge, led the team. Throughout his career, Colonel Swann served in many difficult missions abroad, including a tour in Korea far apart from his wife and three children. In fact, when he assumed the chief prosecutor role, he moved alone to Washington, D.C., leaving his family hundreds of miles away. He lived in a modest apartment, slept on an air mattress, ate take-out, and made the 13-hour drive home to see his family when he could.

He was talented in other ways, too. As a child, Colonel Swann captivated audiences as the adorable, fair-headed, freckled-face child star of a Walt Disney movie called "Emil and the Detectives."[1] The OMC analysts—able to find any-

---

1. James Gunter, *SS Berlin Bureau, Roles in Disney Movie Go to Six American Children in Germany*, THE STARS AND STRIPES, Sept. 6, 1963.

thing—located a color photograph of Colonel Swann as a boy on the movie set, and tacked it to the bulletin board. People who passed by would look at it and say, "Isn't that the Colonel … well, I'll be darned."

Also at the helm was Deputy Chief Prosecutor, Carol Joyce, a career Marine Corps Officer. She was small in stature, but had a gigantic presence. From one end of the office to the other, you could hear her holler for the Gunney Sergeant from her desk when something went awry … *Gunney!* She was direct, confident, and seemed to know exactly what she was doing. Colonel Joyce is the kind of officer we all aspire to be.

Colonels Swann and Joyce led a team of hard-working prosecutors and support staff from all branches of service. (Like Gitmo, it was a joint mission, with all services represented.) All were assuming the monumental responsibility for holding the first military commissions since World War II. There are countless stories I could tell about these prosecutors, their families, and what brought them to the Office of Military Commissions. However, early on, the prosecution office received credible threats from known terrorist groups. Since that time, the Department of Defense has carefully guarded the identity of all prosecutors but for the office leaders. Some even adopted cover stories, and in a few instances kept even their family members in the dark about their jobs. Some terrorist web sites have said that these military prosecutors and their families are legitimate targets.

After a plane ride to Florida, another to Guantanamo Bay, and a misty boat ride across the bay with some FBI agents, I finally reached my destination—the Gitmo courtroom. It was in the very building where I had worked two years earlier, only with a significant face-lift. Offices that were once small and dingy had been combined and transformed into a beautiful courtroom with wooden railing, counsel tables, and a distinguished elevated platform for panel-members.

Some key prosecutors had arrived several days earlier, and motions hearings were already well underway. I looked around in the back of the courtroom for an empty seat and a familiar face. Among the sea of reporters was a man in a bright bow tie who immediately caught my eye. I assumed he was a reporter, or perhaps a consultant for the defense team. He was notably distinguished, with an academic flair about him. While intrigued, I avoided the empty seat next to him, just in case he was a reporter looking for the inside scoop. (I later learned that this fascinating person was a Constitutional law expert, and author of numerous law school books, Professor Ronald Rotunda. He was not with the prosecutors, the defense team, or the Appointing Authority. Instead, he was on leave from the George Mason Law School as a consultant to the Department of Defense (DoD). He was here on its behalf to observe the trials).

The president of the tribunal, Colonel Peter Brownback, banged his gavel and called the court to order so that arguments could resume. The defendant, David Hicks, was clean-shaven, and looked professional in his suit and tie. I later learned that he wore an $800.00 *Brooks*

> **JAG Fact**
>
> *The U.S. purchased an $800.00, hand tailored, Brooks Brother's brand suit for Australian detainee David Hicks.*

Brothers suit, compliments of the U.S. government. This was in sharp contrast to defendants at Nuremberg, who wore U.S Army issued black fatigues, class X, which indicated "unfit for further use."[2] Hicks didn't look at all like pictures I'd seen in the media. He was fit, healthy, and muscular. I later overheard an enlisted soldier remark in the hallway, "He's been working out."

Like most war crimes courts, there wasn't one judge but instead a panel of three members, with equal voting power. The only lawyer among them was Colonel Brownback, who was the president of the panel. Beforehand, I wondered if the issues would be too complex for non-lawyers. Would they be able to grasp complicated legal concepts, and would they pose relevant and probing questions?

I observed right away that all panel members were quite competent. They were fully engaged in the debate and posed fine questions. They probed issues like whether international law recognized the crime of conspiracy; whether "terrorism" was a crime; whether the panel could call legal experts as witnesses to educate the panel about international law; and whether detainee-defendants have the same Constitutional rights as U.S. citizens. Lawyers for both sides discussed and argued these, and other, questions before the tribunal.

I was a bit surprised that the only lawyer on the panel, Colonel Brownback, seemed less judicious than the other two. He interrupted the lawyers to pompously interject that he was a combat veteran, and point at the ribbons on his uniform. He even called Defense Counsel Major Mori of the U.S. Marine Corps, "Sunshine." At other times, he was demeaning towards prosecutors, too. He was an equal opportunity disparager. I noticed some reporters making notes, and realized that Colonel Brownback's comments potentially had worldwide reach, and could fuel critics who looked for things to criticize.

At Nuremberg, the panel members (all judges from different countries) displayed exceptionally judicious temperaments. The most courteous among them was Judge Lawrence, himself a medal-winner. He had won the Distinguished Service Order as a gunner during WWI. His impartiality and "attachment to fair play" was so prominent that it confused the defendants. One account re-

---

2. JOSEPH E. PERSICO, NUREMBERG, INFAMY ON TRIAL, 56 (Penguin Books) (1995).

calls, "Clad in a black robe and striped pants, he would bow first to the prosecution and then to the defense before taking his seat. By now, the attitude toward him of the defendants and their lawyers approached worship." Participants and defendants respected "the man's gift of maintaining total authority without ever raising his voice."[3]

A Blow from Washington, D.C.

> **JAG Fact**
>
> *Habeas corpus is a legal term that means, "show me the body." Lawyers file "habeas corpus" petitions when they believe the government has violated the law by detaining their client. These petitions require a judge to decide whether the government has violated the law.*

After panel members entertained all motions in the Hicks case, a bailiff brought Mr. Hamdan into the courtroom and his motion hearings got underway. However, they did not get far. Across the ocean, in Washington, D.C., Judge Robertson, on the Federal District Court, was releasing his opinion in Hamdan's habeas corpus case. In a far-reaching opinion, he alleged that President Bush lacked authority to create military commissions, that Hamdan had rights under the Geneva Conventions, and that the military commissions procedures violated Hamdan's due process since they permitted closed hearings to protect classified information. Judge Robertson enjoined (stopped) the proceedings. When word reached the courtroom in Guantanamo Bay, the court promptly recessed.

Legal assistants scurried around distributing copies of this opinion to all of the attorneys as we filed out of the courtroom. Prosecutors crowded into a small office without enough chairs, and stood reading the opinion. Some of the lawyers vociferously questioned Judge Robertson's ability to stop a military proceeding. Could a federal judge interfere with an ongoing war? we wondered. Does this open the door for judges to make operational decisions in the theatre of war? Is a military court obligated to adhere to rulings by a federal district judge that affects court proceedings not before the civilian judge? All of these, and other questions, swirled around the room, as we discussed potential next steps. Some of the lawyers suggested that the trial should proceed until directed otherwise by the *military* chain of command.

Colonel Umberg, a JAG Reservist from California (who was elected to the California Legislature while he was deployed, due to the campaign efforts of his spouse), disagreed with this assertion. He thought that it would be akin to

---

3. Joseph E. Persico, Nuremberg, Infamy on Trial, 211–212 (Penguin Books) (1995).

asking the Supreme Court to overrule *Marbury v. Madison* (the historic Supreme Court case that allows higher courts to review the decisions of lower courts, what we lawyers call "judicial review").

Moments later, Colonel Brownback called both parties back into the courtroom. Then without giving either side an opportunity to respond or brief the potential effect of Judge Robertson's ruling, abruptly adjourned the proceedings without comment. Whirling from the strange turn of events, attorneys and paralegals began packing our evidence for the trip back to Washington, and legal support staff hurriedly dialed telephones, hoping to reserve seats on the next flight off the island. At the hour when attorneys fully expected to argue their motions, they were packing their bags and going home.

There were not enough flights off the island, so we went home in several different groups dispersed over several days. The last thing I wanted was an extended stay in Guantanamo Bay. However, it was much more comfortable this time around than before. The housing quarters were much nicer, and even furnished, and we had enough cars so nobody had to walk or wait for a ride. Those left behind ate and drank well that week, and we commiserated about Judge Robertson's bold opinion that brought these procedures to a screeching halt.

After packing our materials in giant, black plastic boxes and locking safes, it was finally time for the last group to return home. Strapped in the noisy belly of a C-130 military plane for the flight out of Cuba, I couldn't help but revisit Colonel Brownback's "*Sunshine*" comment. While I sat there, thinking about how Colonel Brownback's comment demeaned the proceedings, others were writing and "blogging" about his comment. USA TODAY reported that Brownback's comment "drew criticism." An instructor at West Point didn't hold back in his assessment of Brownback's comment. He said the comment, "demonstrates his [Brownback's] lack of judgment, judicial demeanor, and unsuitability for this post."[4]

I also thought about Colonel Brownback's abrupt decision to recess the proceedings, without hearing from either side. Procedurally, it was very odd. The case filed before Judge Robertson was a habeas proceeding. For normal U.S. citizens the federal court would not hear a habeas case from a state court until after the criminal defendant was tried and convicted and exhausted his appeals. Military trials are the same way. The federal court will not hear a habeas motion until a lower court tries and convicts the soldier, and the soldier exhausts all appeals. However, those whom the government prosecutes for war crimes apparently have more rights.

---

4. Tony Locy, *Guantanamo Proceedings Full of Challenges*, USA TODAY, Nov. 8, 2004, *quoting* Gary Solis, a retired Marine lieutenant colonel who teaches at the U.S. Military Academy at West Point.

Shouldn't he have heard arguments from both sides about whether a ruling from a D.C. District Court can stop a military proceeding? The mere fact that Judge Robertson declared a halt to Military Commissions didn't mean he had the authority to do it. I thought to myself, "An appellate court will have to sort all this out" as I tried to unwind from a week of anticipating hearings that never happened.

Judge Robertson's opinion enjoined (stopped) Hamdan's case. However, within days the Department of Defense decided to stop *all other* pending proceedings. It was not obligated to stop them, and doing so only artificially inflated the importance of Judge Robertson's lone opinion. What goes unreported is that another D.C. District Court judge (Judge Leon) issued a ruling opposite from Robertson's opinion (*Khalid v. Bush*),[5] in favor of the government. In that case, Judge Leon said that Congress authorized the president to capture and detain enemy combatants, that non-resident aliens captured and detained outside the U.S. had no constitutional rights, and that capturing and detaining enemy combatants did not violate any statute or treaty.[6] It is unclear why the DoD decided to apply the lone negative opinion to all of its cases, even when no court order required that, and apply that ruling even to the case it won before Judge Leon.

Morale Plummets and
CITF Agents Get a Pep Talk

There was significant fallout from DoD's decision to halt all detainee proceedings. Morale at both CITF and OMC plummeted, and soldiers began to doubt the mission and likelihood of ever bringing the cases to trial. The Public Affairs Office inundated CITF employees with countless media clips, taken from published newspapers around the world, on a daily basis. They were all negative. One agent stopped reading all news stories, explaining, "They've got it all wrong, and it is depressing." But the prosecution office and officials responsible for organizing military tribunals never answered the critics. Instead, they just complained to each other.

The negativity was palpable. The CITF commander, Colonel Mallow, knew that he had to turn around the morale. One morning, he called a meeting with

---

5. *Khalid v. Bush*, 355 F. Supp.2d 311 (D.D.C. 2005).

6. Subsequent litigation has overtaken this case and the Supreme Court will decide these issues sometime in 2008.

all CITF personnel, who crowded into the same auditorium where months earlier we had seen the gruesome video footage of Daniel Pearl's beheading.

From the front of the room, Colonel Mallow addressed his troops with seasoned eloquence, reminding us about the events of September 11th and the worldwide terrorism threat. He reminded investigators that their job is just to discover the truth. Whether or not the cases ever come to trial doesn't interfere with that mission. He urged them to drive ahead, and not allow negative media reports and trial interruptions to discourage investigations. Colonel Mallow then read from a book that recounted stories of September 11th victims. "You're doing it for them," he said. Colonel Mallow's words didn't change things right away, but slowly over the course of a few weeks, CITF re-energized and continued working.

It was not surprising that Colonel Mallow knew what his troops needed. He was a good leader who always demonstrated sound judgment. From the beginning, Colonel Mallow opposed aggressive interrogations tactics. In late 2002, when the military considered incorporating aggressive interrogation techniques, Colonel Mallow made clear that he, and those under his command, would not employ such techniques. He released a policy that directed, "All deployed CITF personnel are instructed to disengage, stand clear, and report any questionable interrogation techniques.... CITF maintains that its personnel will not utilize non-law enforcement techniques to participate, support, advise, or observe aggressive interrogation techniques or strategies."[7]

---

7. Josh White, *Tough Interrogation Tactics Were Opposed Pentagon Task Force Was Told Not to Use Techniques Approved in 2002, Records Show*, THE WASHINGTON POST January 13, 2006.

Building in Guantanamo Bay where Military Commissions were held. DoD photo by Chief Petty Officer Dave Fliesen.

The Military Commissions Court Room in Guantanamo Bay. Bench where panel members sat. DoD photo by Chief Petty Officer Dave Fliesen, U.S. Navy.

Military Commissions Courtroom, Guantanamo Bay, DoD photo by Chief Petty Officer Dave Fliesen.

Closed-circuit television system tested during rehearsal for Military Commissions in Guantanamo Bay. During commissions, live video feed is sent to an auditorium for news media to observe. DoD photo by Chief Petty Officer Dave Fliesen.

CHAPTER TWENTY-SEVEN

Inside Military Commissions

After a time of dating Professor Ronald Rotunda, the man I had recently met at the Guantanamo Bay hearings, he and I married on June 18, 2005. I then finished my tour at CITF and Colonel Swann, the Chief Prosecutor, offered me a position on the prosecution team at the Office of Military Commissions (OMC). I changed the name on my uniform from "Captain Miller" to "Captain Rotunda" and began another tour.

Soon after I started working at OMC, the D.C. Circuit Court heard the *Hamdan* case on appeal and reversed Judge Robertson. (This was the habeas corpus case that led the U.S. government to stop trials in Gitmo.) It ruled in favor of the government and found that military commissions could proceed. I assumed the cases would resume quickly, and we would be back in Guantanamo Bay within weeks. That did not happen. Instead, the Department of Defense hardly said anything about winning the case on appeal, and it continued at a tentative, glacial pace. It drew little attention to the opinion and acted if we had lost the case. For example, after the Circuit Court approved the rules governing Military Commissions, the U.S. government changed them.

Unfair to Change the Rules in the Middle of the Game

I sat between two other prosecutors in a cramped office, made smaller by the stacks of books and binders along every wall. One prosecutor, a naval officer with an infectious laugh and a hilarious sense of humor, adopted a more serious demeanor than usual and made his point. "The rules we have just don't work. We need one judge who understands the law and can make decisions. Having three panel members, when only one of them is a lawyer, is awkward. The government should appoint Colonel Brownback (the lone lawyer on the panel) as the judge. Otherwise, these trials will be extremely slow because even the simplest decisions will require all three to deliberate."

I disagreed, "War crimes tribunals historically appoint panel members to make decisions, not one judge. Nuremberg is a fine example of that. Specially trained judges are only necessary when complicated rules of evidence apply. The rules governing military commissions are simple and straightforward. They allow either side to use whatever evidence it wants to use, so long as it is relevant. We just don't need a lone judge. The panel members are doing a fine job. The procedure we are using is similar to what we used during WWII, and the U.S. Supreme Court approved that in the *Ex parte Quirin* case. Later, Justice O'Connor in *Hamdi*, said that *Ex parte Quirin* is the law today."[1]

I made my final argument, "Besides, that ship has sailed. It is just too late. These trials have started, and the U.S. has brought the defendant before these panel members and charged him with war crimes. It has told the defendant— and the world—that these trials will be one way. Now you think they should be another? Do you really think it is appropriate to call a time-out and have everyone switch places? U.S. critics allege that these trials are 'kangaroo courts,' and changing the rules in the middle of the game only bolsters that argument."

Just then, Colonel Swann, the chief prosecutor, who enjoyed a good debate, approached our office and stood in the doorway. He listened attentively and then said something like, "Defense counsel probably won't criticize the Government if it changes the procedural rules in their favor. After all, they requested a judge/jury system." He was correct about the facts. Defense committed a whole motion[2] and parts of another,[3] to arguing that a panel system (as opposed to a judge/jury system) was "fundamentally flawed" and archaic. Additionally, defense challenged Colonel Brownback's impartiality during jury selection,[4] arguing that only a military judge, with authority to instruct on the law, could ensure an unbiased panel.[5] Each time defense criticized the panel system, it applauded the judge/jury system, commenting, "The presence of highly qualified military judges at courts-martial ensures that trials are conducted fairly and in accordance with the law, and the rights of the accused protected."[6]

I responded, "Then the panel should simply grant defense's motions. The U.S. government should not intervene and change the rules on its own. Defense

---

1. *Hamdi v. Rumsfeld*, 542 U.S. at 518, 124 S.Ct. at 2640.

2. Defense Objection to the Structure and Composition of the Commission, September 9, 2004.

3. Defense Motion to Dismiss for Lack of Jurisdiction: Commission System Will Not Afford a Full and Fair Trial, October 4, 2004.

4. Unofficial Transcript of Voir-Dire, *Hicks*, at 13, August 24, 2004 *see also* Unofficial Transcript of Voir-Dire in *Hamdan* case, (pages un-numbered) August 24, 2004.

5. Defense Memorandum of Law in Supporting its Challenges for "Good Cause" For the Removal of Members of the Military Commission, September 7, 2004.

6. Defense Motion to Dismiss for Lack of Jurisdiction: Commission System Will Not Afford a Full and Fair Trial, p. 5 (October 4, 2004).

counsel will not thank the U.S. government. It will criticize the government for having a process that allows it to change all the rules in the midst of trial."

I believed then, as I do now, that reinventing the rules in the middle of a trial was wrong in principle, and not strategically perceptive. The U.S. government opted for a hacksaw approach, when it could have simply granted defense counsel's motions, with the delicacy of a surgeon's scalpel.

Just then, a seasoned former Marine Corps JAG in a crisp shirt and red tie emerged from his office next door to add, "The government needs to just get out of the way and quit intervening. It just won the Hamdan case on appeal. The Circuit Court decided that the existing rules are fine. We need to drive on, with the rules as they are, and get these trials done. Changing the rules will just create another issue for defense to appeal."

We continued in this fashion. Two attorneys argued for changing the rules, and two argued for staying the course. It was a clear draw. Finally, Colonel Swann ended the debate and said, "Look, we don't know what will happen. The government hasn't said it will change the rules. This is speculation, and out of out of our hands. We should just wait to see what the Department of Defense decides to do with it." He was right. Nothing was official, but rumors were circulating around the prosecution office that the government was about to announce changes to the rules.

After we finished the debate, I went to lunch with the marine who had emerged from next door to take my side in the debate. As we walked to the sandwich line, we continued our discussion. I said, "If the government decides to appoint a judge, it shouldn't appoint Judge Brownback. He wasn't very judicious at the hearing in Guantanamo Bay. The way he tapped his chest, and referred to defense counsel as "Sunshine" was embarrassing to the U.S. It can do better than that."

The marine then said, "You know he has a reputation, don't you?" He went on to explain that Judge Brownback has a reputation for bravado in the courtroom, and liked the "hands on" approach. Without going into detail, he explained that a Military Appeals Court had once reversed Colonel Brownback in a high-stakes death penalty case. Colonel Brownback made significant judicial errors that resulted in an injustice.[7] I thought that was very interesting.

> **JAG Fact**
>
> *The rank of general is the highest achievable rank in the army. There are four levels of General. One star is a "brigadier general." The next highest levels are major general, Lieutenant general and then general. The saying "Be My Little General" helps troops remember the order.*

7. See *U.S. v. Kreutzer*, 59 M.J. 773 (Army Ct. Crim. Appl, 2004), *aff'd*, 61 M.J. 293 (Armed Forces, Aug. 16, 2005). Also discussed in Chapter 29.

A day later, despite misgivings about changing procedural rules in the midst of trial, the hammer fell. On August 31, 2005, Brigadier General Hemingway, the legal advisor for the Appointing Authority, abruptly announced new changes to Military Commission Order No. 1. He called the changes "smoother and more efficient" and said they guarantee "a more efficient and orderly process" and acknowledged that the government had been working for some time to "produce a better and more efficient system."[8]

The most significant change to the rules was the provision elevating the presiding officer from panel member to "judge"[9] with the lone ability to rule on questions of law, just like judges in civilian courts. To the surprise of prosecutors who supported this change, defense counsel criticized the change within hours of the announcement. Major Mori and Mr. Dreitel, attorneys for defendant David Hicks, said, "The most recent manipulations of the military commission procedures represent a desperate attempt to salvage the failed commission process and [are] a confirmation that Mr. Hicks will not receive a fair trial."[10]

On the same day as Brigadier General Hemingway's announcement, a news report observed, "The Pentagon announcement amounted to changing the rules in the middle of the game. You can't have any kind of fair system of justice that can change at any moment...."[11] I wondered, how can the government fail to see what is immediately obvious to others?

True, the military commission rules allowed the Secretary of Defense to "amend this Order from time to time,"[12] but allowing jurors today to become judges tomorrow just didn't seem fair. How can defendants get a "full and fair" trial when the proceedings, and even the judge and jury, change from day to day? It turned the trial into a game of duck-duck-goose.

Ultimately, U.S. Supreme Court concluded that it was patently unfair for the Department of Defense to change the rules after the trial began. Specifically, it stated, "Further evidence of this tribunal's irregular constitution is the fact that its rules and procedures are subject to change midtrial, at the whim of the

---

8. Brigadier General Hemingway, Special Defense Department Briefing on Military Commissions, August 31, 2005, referring to changes as "better ... more efficient ... and smoother."

9. Brigadier General Hemingway, Special Defense Department Briefing on Military Commissions, August 31, 2005, describing the process as "more aligned with the judge/jury model."

10. *US Makes Changes to Guantanamo Terrorism Trials* (Reuters), August 31, 2005. (Hard copy on file with the author).

11. *Id.*

12. Military Commission Order No. 1, § 11.

Executive. See Commission Order No. 1, §11 (providing that the Secretary of Defense may change the governing rules "from time to time")."[13]

The government, by changing the rules on its own, instead of granting the defendant's motion, created a crucial error that led to the Supreme Court reversing the victory that the military had won in the D.C. Circuit.

Other Panel Members—Benched?

Ironically the new rules were not more "efficient," as General Hemingway claimed they would be. Instead, they raised unanswered questions that created endless confusion. What would happen with those trials already underway? Would they start over? What about the existing panel members? Would they just scoot over, so others could join them? Could the military reasonably pick up the trials where it left off? Was it creating yet another error for defense to appeal?

These questions, and others, puzzled everyone. One reporter asked Brigadier General Hemingway, "Are you going to start—the trials that have already begun, are you going to start over with those? Are those going to proceed?" Another then asked whether those trials underway would "begin again from scratch." General Hemingway responded, "Well, it depends on what you mean by 'scratch.' If the appointing authority appoints additional members as in at least one of the cases counsel have asked for, then you would have additional voir dire examinations. If you consider that to be, beginning from scratch, to that extent, there would be a beginning. But we're not going back, new charges and starting all over again, which is what I would think would be a complete new beginning." Even General Hemingway, the government's messenger, seemed confused.

In a trailing question, another reporter asked when the trials would "resume or begin, however you want to"—and the General responded, saying, "That's the "$64,000 question."

Adding new panel members seemed unfair, but Military Commission Rules allowed it. Specifically, Military Commission Order Number 1 (both the original and revised versions) permitted the Appointing Authority to fill vacancies *after* the trial has begun, so long as the new member familiarizes him/herself with prior proceedings and evidence.[14]

---

13. *Hamdan v. Rumsfeld*, 126 S.Ct. 2749, 165 L.Ed.2d 723, fn. 65.

14. The language reads in relevant part "… Any vacancy among the members or alternate members occurring after a trial has begun may, but need not, be filled by the Appointing Authority, but the substance of all prior proceedings and evidence taken in that case shall be made known to that new member or alternate member before the trial proceeds."

Adding members may seem unfair, but the Military Manual for Courts Martial (MMCM) that governs soldiers' trials has similar provisions. Under those rules, the military can add new panel members in a few limited instances, to maintain a quorum.[15] The rules allow one member to be substituted by another, even after a court martial is assembled, primarily for military exigency.[16]

However, what was going on in the case of the military commissions was different. The government's motivation here was not to "maintain a quorum" or respond to "military exigency." Instead, supposed efficiency is what motivated the government. It wanted to adopt rules that are more efficient in the middle of a trial. There was no military exigency—even according to the Government. When a reporter asked if the changes amounted to "minor tinkering" General Hemingway said, "Well, I will leave it to members of the media to characterize this as a major change or a minor tinkering...." If the changes were essential, or driven by "military exigency," the government could have said that. But it didn't.

---

15. Rules for Courts Martial, §505(2)(B).
16. Uniform Code of Military Justice, art. 29.

Photograph of Brigadier General Thomas Hemingway updating reporters about changes to the Military Commissions rules at the Pentagon, August 2004. DoD photo by Helene C. Stikkel.

CHAPTER TWENTY-EIGHT

The Taliban:
A License to Kill

Soon after September 11th, 2001, President Bush declared to the world that the United States would not distinguish between terrorists and those who harbor them. Instead, it would treat them alike. Two months later, he issued a presidential order saying essentially the same thing. It established three categories of persons who the military could try before a military tribunal. The three categories were: 1) members of Al Qaeda, 2) persons who engaged in, aided or abetted, or conspired to commit acts of international terrorism and 3) a person who knowingly harbors anyone in category one or two.[1]

However, despite this clear guidance, prosecutors disagreed about whether the U.S. government could charge members of the Taliban with war crimes and bring them to justice before war crimes tribunals. Prosecutors used phrases like "merely Taliban" and "pure Taliban" to define a category of detainees that it believed were untouchable. Despite three distinct categories set forth by the president, these prosecutors believed that the government could only try before war crimes tribunals members of Al Qaeda, or those who aided, abetted, or conspired with them, even though the Taliban had aided, harbored and supported Bin Laden and Al Qaeda. Following this guidance, investigators and analysts spent countless hours searching for the smallest detail that would link

---

1. The term "individual subject to this order" shall mean any individual who is not a United States citizen with respect to whom I determine from time to time in writing that:
    1) there is reason to believe that such individual, at the relevant times,
        i) is or was a member of the organization known as Al Qaida;
        ii) has engaged in, aided or abetted, or conspired to commit acts of international terrorism, or acts in preparation therefore, that have caused, threaten to cause, or have as their aim to cause, injury to or adverse effects on the United States, its citizens, national security, foreign policy, or economy; or
        iii) has knowingly harbored one or more individuals described in subparagraphs (i) or (ii) of subjection 2(a)(1) of this order; and
    2) it is in the interest of the United States that such individual be subject to this order.

the Taliban detainee to Al Qaeda. When they couldn't establish such a link, otherwise solid cases remained indefinitely on the back burner.[2]

One prosecutor hesitated to charge a detainee, suspected of kidnapping and murdering an aid worker in Afghanistan, until he learned that the detainee was not a member of the Taliban, but Al Qaeda instead. The prosecutor commented, with relief, that he could "slide under the jurisdiction bar" in the president's military order.[3] That seemed odd, because the president's order clearly said that all terrorists, including but not limited to members of Al Qaeda, and those who aid, abet, or harbor them, could be tried before military commissions. There was no "jurisdiction bar" other than a self-imposed one.

Presumably, if the president intended to limit jurisdiction to just members of Al Qaeda, he would have replaced the phrase "acts of international terrorism" with "members of Al Qaeda." It is significant that the language permits jurisdiction over "terrorists" in prong two, without specifying members of Al Qaeda. This is particularly true since there are many terrorist organizations, independent of Al Qaeda. The state department list of "terrorist" groups continues to grow and includes Hezbollah, Hamas, and others posing a significant risk the United States. Many of them have traveled to Iraq and Afghanistan to attack Americans and Coalition Forces.

Known terrorist groups should not escape accountability for their war crimes simply because they call themselves "Taliban" instead of "Al Qaeda." Limiting jurisdiction to only members of Al Qaeda invites other terrorist organizations to violate the laws of war, knowing they will escape accountability. The president's order would allow Al Qaeda or those associated with Al Qaeda to face trial by military commission, but the prosecutors applied such a rigid definition to the phrase "or associated with Al Qaeda" that nobody would qualify. It created a loophole for members of the Taliban.

The broadest, and most ignored jurisdictional prong is the last one, which allows the U.S. to hold and try anyone who "knowingly harbors" either of the first two (members of Al Qaeda or those who aid, abet, or conspire to commit acts of international terrorism). In the days after September 11th, Presi-

---

2. Prosecutors at the Office of Military Commissions expressed this view. Cases presenting compelling facts, but without a strong Al Qaeda link received low priority level. Most attorneys opined that these cases could never proceed to military commissions due to lack of jurisdiction. Brigadier General Hemingway, the Legal Advisor to the Appointing Authority, in a public forum held at George Mason University Law School on February 16, 2006, confirmed the DoD position that the order is "narrow" and that "only members of al Qaeda or those directly aiding, abetting, or conspiring with al Qaeda are eligible for trial by military commission."

3. Discussion, Office of Military Commissions, Jan. 2006.

dent Bush repeatedly characterized the Taliban regime as "harborers" and warned that failing to turnover Bin Laden would lead to treating Bin Laden and the Taliban as one in the same. On September 20, 2001, President Bush addressed the nation, stating, "The leadership of Al Qaeda has great influence in Afghanistan and supports the Taliban regime in controlling most of that country." He condemned the Taliban for "sponsoring, sheltering and supplying terrorists" and made clear that they should turn over members of Al Qaeda or "share in their fate."[4] Thousands headed his warning and fled Afghanistan in the days after the president's address. Five years later, on the anniversary of September 11th, the president again made clear that terrorists and those who harbor terrorists would suffer the same fate. Nevertheless, his subordinates never carried out this directive, and prosecutors ignored the broadest jurisdictional prong that gave them license to try Taliban detainees before military commissions.

Importantly, both Congress and the U.S. Supreme Court acknowledge jurisdiction over members of the Taliban. The Authorization for the Use of Military Force (AUMF)[5] authorized the president to exercise necessary and appropriate force "against those nations, organizations, or persons he determines planned, authorized, committed or aided," in the September 11th attacks, "or harbored such organizations or persons in order to prevent any future acts of international terrorism." Both Justice Stephens in the *Rasul*[6] case and Justice O'Connor in the *Hamdi*[7] case interpreted the AUMF to include Al Qaeda and the Taliban regime. Justice Stephens states, "Acting pursuant to that authorization [Congressional AUMF], the President sent U.S. Armed Forces into Afghanistan to wage a military campaign against al Qaida and the Taliban regime that had supported it." Similarly, O'Connor in the Hamdi plurality states, "There can be no doubt that individuals who fought against the United States in Afghanistan as part of the Taliban, an organization known to have supported the al Qaeda terrorist network responsible for those attacks, are individuals Congress sought to target in passing the AUMF."

---

4. President Bush, Congressional Address, September 20, 2001. Available at ERLINK"https://www.archives.cnn.com/2001/us/09/2001gen.bush.transcript/"https://www.archives.cnn.com/2001/us/09/2001gen.bush.transcript/.

5. Authority for the use of Military Force, Pub. L. No. 107-40 §1-2; 115 Stat. 224; 50 USCA § 1541 (2001).

6. *Rasul v. Bush*, 542 U.S. 466, 479, 124 S.Ct 2686, 2690 (2004) stating "Acting pursuant to that authorization, the President sent U.S. Armed Forces into Afghanistan to wage a military campaign against al Qaeda and the Taliban regime that had supported it."

7. *Hamdi v. Rumsfeld*, 542 U.S. 507, 526, 124 S. Ct. 2633 (2004).

Therefore, based on the plain language of the president's military order, the language in the AUMF, and the Supreme Court's interpretation of the AUMF, members of the Taliban are triable before Military Commission. Simply put— they should not automatically escape jurisdiction. Otherwise, they have a license to kill.

Nonetheless, and despite the wealth of authority allowing prosecutors to try members of the Taliban, contention in the prosecution office persisted, as some prosecutors insisted that the president only intended to try members of Al Qaeda. When faced with clear language contradicting this view, one prosecutor justified his argument by explaining that the president's lawyers drafted that order—not the president *himself.* Essentially, lower ranking officers and government employees ignored the president's clear directive and created artificial jurisdictional filters.

A Judge and His POM, POMs

The government ignored clear presidential orders, and instead went to work creating new, local rules. Once Colonel Brownback became the judge, he appointed an assistant, retired Army Judge Colonel Keith Hodges. Together, they wrote more rules. They intended to add meat to the bare bones of the president's military order through local rules. These new rules they called Presiding Officer Memorandums, or "POMs." But the rules went too far. In some instances, they granted more rights than necessary, and in others, they departed from normal legal practice and standards for no particular reason.

For example, POM 11 issued on September 7, 2005, attempts to cure earlier problems with translators. Due to Arabic linguist shortages within the DoD, it relied on government-contracted translators. The government used native linguists to ensure solid language skills in the detainee's first language. Competent translators must have proficient skills in the detainee's language, but must also have outstanding English language skills to ensure accuracy. Getting qualified translators has been difficult for DoD.

POM 11 purports to provide "qualifications" for translators, but falls short of doing that. Under this POM, the government selects translators based on their resumes. However, the POM is silent on what a criterion renders a translator "qualified." Further, the process to verify a questionable translation is arbitrary. When one side objects to the initial translation, a second equally qualified translator reviews the translation and the second interpretation trumps the first.

It makes no sense that the government will automatically accept the second version as "the correct translation" for no reasons other than the second interpreter came later. Not only is the process ineffective and arbitrary, it is burdensome and invites interruptions and mini-trials about translator competence.

DoD shouldn't reinvent the wheel. Federal courts use translators all the time without such arbitrary and inefficient rules. Federal Rule of Criminal Procedure 28 allows the judge to exercise discretion in selecting interpreters. Absent abuse of discretion, a judge's selection of a specific interpreter is not reviewable.[8] Instead of creating a rule out of whole cloth, it makes logical sense that the POM should simply adopt the Federal Rule and allow the judge to exercise his discretion and pick a translator. It should also rely on objective criteria, such as a specific, current score on a standard language exam to determine whether a translator is qualified.

The Nuremberg Trials after World War II, which successfully prosecuted Nazis for war crimes, adopted simple, objective criteria for selecting translators. An assistant at Nuremberg developed a practical test to select interpreters. He asked each of them to name, in two languages, ten trees, ten birds, ten medical terms and ten automobile parts.[9] Those able to do this demonstrated knowledge of the language, and on-the-spot translation abilities. They were rare. Only about five percent of the prospects were able to listen and translate simultaneously.

> **JAG Fact**
>
> *War is complex, and lawyers are necessary to interpret various treaties and Law of War provisions. But the U.S. government over-lawyered the War on Terror with revolving-door rules, self-imposed jurisdictional bars, and procedural rules made up out of whole cloth called Presiding Officer Memorandums (POMs). Even prosecutors couldn't keep track of the ever changing rules!*

POM 14-1, issued on September 8, 2005, establishes a Commissions Library, which is an electronic database of information that counsel, the presiding officer, and appellate review panels could access. "Anything useful as a reference" that the clerk "deems appropriate" is the criteria for admission to the library. Capturing information on the Internet that is here today, gone tomorrow is one justification for the library. Another is that it "alleviates" the need for counsel to include attachments with filings. This POM is problematic, because it discourages creation of a complete trial record.

All U.S. courts require each party to submit their documents during the trial to create an official record. Simply "citing" to the document contained in the library is insufficient, and breaks with judicial norms. Prosecutors at Nurem-

---

8. *See Pietrzak v. U.S.*, 188 F2d, 418, cert. den. (1951).

9. Joseph E. Persico, Nuremberg, Infamy on Trial, 221 (Penguin Books) (1995).

berg understood the importance of a complete record and read every document into the record before they sought to admit it into evidence—a practice
that some criticized for slowing down the proceedings.

Under this POM review, panel members will have access to information never
offered or even presented at trial. Every appellate body in the U.S. court system is
limited to reviewing only information on the record—if it works for the Supreme
Court, it should work for Military Commissions. Furthermore, the library POM
is inconsistent with both MCO No. 1 and MCO No. 9, which indicates that appellate reviewers will examine the *record at trial* and evidence submitted at trial.

Perhaps the most problematic POM of the bunch is POM 1-1, issued on August 12, 2004, and rescinded over a year later on September 15, 2005. The original POM said that lawyers should raise objections to each POM within seven
days after Colonel Brownback issued it. This departs from judicial norms. Lawyers
do not raise hypothetical objections to laws immediately after Congress drafts
them. Instead, they object when problems arise in the context of a case. Many
defects may not be obvious from the outset. In addition, the government may
not appoint defense lawyers to represent particular defendants until months
after the judge creates a new POM. Do they waive a right to object?

This POM also invited ex-parte communications with the judge. Ex parte
communications occur when one party talks privately with the presiding judge
about the case. Under U.S. law, both sides (the prosecutor and the defense
lawyer) must be there.

POM 1-1 stated, "If counsel objects to a procedure established in any POMs,
such objections should be made within 7 calendar days directly to the presiding Officer (with a CC to Mr. Hodges)." Communications between one party
and a judge clearly run afoul of rules prohibiting ex-parte communications.
U.S. courts prohibit judges from communicating with attorneys for one side
of the case, unless the other side is present. This POM, which was in place for
over one year, not only invited ex-parte violations, it directed them. The prosecutors, for reasons unknown, never objected to this.

Although it is unclear why the government rescinded POM 1-1 in September 2005, a new provision replaced it that did not include the troubling seven-
day window to raise objections or the ex parte provision. However, it is curious
that such a provision remained part of the governing rules for over one year.

Discovery at Trial

TV shows often depict one side of a case admitting surprise evidence in the
middle of a trial. Surprise witnesses take the stand and their testimony leads

the judge to bang his gavel and declare, "Trial dismissed." It makes for exciting movies, but trials don't work that way.

Ordinarily a process called "discovery" occurs long before trials. "Discovery" is a legal term referring to the requirement of each opposing side to share basic information with the other side—so each can "discover" the evidence in the case.

In criminal cases, prosecutors review statements and evidence gathered by criminal investigators to decide if there is sufficient evidence of a chargeable crime. If so, the prosecutor either indicts the defendant in a federal court, or files charges in the local jurisdiction. Under Federal Criminal Procedural Rule 16(a)(1)(E), defendant's are entitled to "discover" evidence that meets the following criteria:

> **JAG Fact**
>
> *At Nuremberg, prosecutors kept all documents filed in a document room. Defense had full access to the information. Each evening during the trial, the prosecutor would post a list of documents that he planned to introduce the next day at trial on the door. Nuremberg preceded the Brady case, so prosecutors weren't required to release exculpatory information to the defense lawyers before trial. Present day military commission rules follow Brady.*

1) Is within the government's possession, custody or control **AND**

2) Is material to preparing the defense **OR**

3) Is evidence the government intends to use in its case in chief at trial **OR**

4) Is obtained from or belongs to the defendant

The Supreme Court, in a famous case entitled *Brady v. United States*,[10] held that, if requested by the defendant, the prosecution is required to disclose evidence favorable to the accused that is material to the guilt or punishment of the accused. Lawyers refer to this information as "Brady Material."

In criminal cases, defendants are not required to turn over any information to the prosecution. Prosecutors bear the burden of proof beyond a reasonable doubt, and, under the law, defendants are innocent until proven guilty. Defendants have no obligation or burden whatsoever. They don't have to discuss their case with prosecutors—or even admit any evidence at trial. Under the 5th Amendment to the U.S. Constitution, defendants have the right to remain silent, cannot be made to testify against their own interests, and guilt cannot be inferred by silence. Military Commission rules guarantee these rights as well.

The Military Commission rule that governs discovery mirrors the federal rule, and states, "The Prosecution shall provide the Defense with access to ev-

---

10. *Brady v. U.S.*, 373 U.S. 83, 87 (1963).

idence the Prosecution intends to introduce at trial and with access to evidence known to the Prosecution that tends to exculpate the Accused...."[11]

During fall 2005, in preparation for resuming the Hicks case, Presiding Officer Peter Brownback, through his assistant Mr. Keith Hodges, issued a detailed discovery order.[12] It required *greater* discovery than U.S. or the Military Commission rules required. The first sentence reads, "The Presiding Officer is aware that the discovery process—though perhaps not by that name—has been ongoing since at least 2004; in other words, parties have been sharing matters that *might* be used to prepare for trial or at trial." (Emphasis added). The very first sentence of this order suggests discovery requirement far beyond what any U.S. criminal court would require—evidence that *might* be used, as opposed to evidence that *will* be used in the prosecution's case in chief.

The order goes on and explicitly requires the prosecution to provide *copies* of evidence, as opposed to *mere access*. This is an important distinction because the evidence in these cases can be voluminous. In a U.S. criminal court, the burden to examine and make copies is generally on the defense and their support staff—*not* on prosecution.

Additionally, the order also requires the prosecution to provide names, contact information, and the subject matter that witnesses will address within fourteen calendar days of the order issuing. This is substantially different from the rules governing soldiers at courts martial, which only require attorneys to reveal the names and address of witnesses before the beginning of trial. In most courts, the defendant can then interview the witnesses to determine the subject matter of their testimony. (Although in criminal cases witnesses are not required to cooperate with defense counsel.) Under this discovery order, the prosecution generously provides that information.

Discovery is usually limited to information in the possession, custody, or control of the government, or opposing party. The Commission's discovery order requires prosecution to release statements not in the possession or custody of the government, but *known by* the prosecutors to exist. This provision applies to some statements, whether or not attorneys plan to use those statements during the trial, and even when the statements are not exculpatory. This requirement is onerous because the prosecutors are required to produce thousands and thousands of documents.

Perhaps the greatest departure from accepted legal procedures is the order's reciprocity requirement. Paragraph 15, remarkably, requires the *defendant* to

---

11. Department of Defense, Military Commission Order No. 1, ¶ E.
12. September 21, 2005.

provide information to the *prosecution*. This is curious, since ordinarily defendants are considered innocent until proven guilty and are not obligated to present any evidence at trial. The discovery order requires defense to provide evidence and copies of all information it intends to offer at trial, along with a list of witnesses and the subject matter of their testimony. Furthermore, the defense is required to present its information only seven days after receiving discovery materials by the prosecution. This requirement is one that doesn't exist under U.S. law, and the time frame is unreasonable. That is, defense counsel will have one week to assess the prosecution's case in chief and provide a defense. This requirement eviscerates the defendant's right of innocence until proven guilty, and his right to remain silent.

We should not be surprised if the defense will accept the broader discovery required of the prosecution, but will not ultimately reciprocate because it has no legal obligation to do so. Furthermore, the orders and instruction governing military commissions *do not* require defense to show its hand before trial. It is unlikely that this presiding officer's discovery order would stand up if challenged by defense counsel, because it conflicts with commission rules, and U.S. law. Nobody objected to the discovery order.

Definition of Conspiracy Departs from U.S. Law[13]

Under U.S. law, it is illegal for two or more people to plan a crime, even if they are ultimately unsuccessful in carrying out the crime. For instance, when at least two people plan to break into a home, and take some steps to accomplish the break-in, they have illegally conspired. They can still be held liable if they fail to break-in, or are caught before they carry out the crime. This is because U.S. law makes the *agreement itself* a crime. The agreement is the essence of the crime.

These "steps" toward committing the crime are called "overt acts" under U.S. law. When parties have agreed to commit a crime, even the simplest acts meet the "overt act" requirement. For instance, making a phone call, picking a lock, or even attending a meeting, can each be considered an "overt act."[14] In the above hypothetical, purchasing dark clothing to commit the break-in undetected, or driving through the neighborhood to "case" the home, could both be considered overt acts.

---

13. For a thorough discussion of conspiracy, see WAYNE R. LAFAVE, SUBSTANTIVE CRIMINAL LAW §12.2 (Thompson West Publishing) (2005).

14. *Id.* at §12.2(b).

Under U.S. law, any overt act committed by any one of the conspirators gives rise to the crime of conspiracy, and all in the group can be held responsible. In the above hypothetical, if one conspirator commits an overt act (i.e., purchasing dark clothing) the other conspirator can be held independently liable, even if he didn't himself commit an overt act. Only one conspirator needs to commit an overt for all conspirators to be liable for conspiracy.

But the law that applies to detainees in Guantanamo Bay is different and more stringent than conspiracy laws that apply to U.S. citizens. Prosecutors at the Office of Military Commissions applied their own definition of conspiracy by requiring that the particular detainee *himself* commit the overt act. Under this strange definition, a detainee could conspire to commit another 9-11 with members of Al Qaeda, and not be held liable for his role in the conspiracy unless prosecutors prove that that detainee *himself* took specific steps toward carrying out the attack. Therefore, rules that apply to U.S. civilians that commit conspiracy crimes are more likely to result in criminal convictions than those applied to alleged terrorists held in Guantanamo Bay.

While there was some disagreement among prosecutors about whether Military Commissions should adopt conspiracy rules that departed from U.S. law, the U.S. Congress passed the Military Commissions Act of 2006, and agreed with prosecutors. Under the new law, the crime of conspiracy is defined as "Any person subject to this chapter who conspires to commit one or more substantive offenses triable by military commissions under this chapter, and who knowingly does any overt act to effect the object of that conspiracy, shall be punished...."[15] Therefore, the U.S. has made clear that alleged terrorists in Guantanamo Bay are much harder to convict on conspiracy charges than U.S. citizens. To hold them liable for conspiracy, prosecutors must prove that that particular detainee himself "knowingly" committed an overt act. It is ironic that U.S. soldier Lynndie England was convicted under a traditional definition of conspiracy, but detainees held in Guantanamo get a special definition of conspiracy, making it harder—and even impossible—for the government to convict them.

Instead of simply trying cases under simpler rules, as we did at Nuremberg, the U.S. government went to work drafting onerous rules that were inconsistent with U.S. law, and creating new rules out of whole cloth. The combination of rules, orders, and something Mr. Hodges referred to broadly as "commission law," was confusing and time consuming.

The Supreme Court later, in *Hamdan v. Rumsfeld*, invalidated military commissions and opined that the U.S. government had not demonstrated that mil-

---

15. 10 USC § 950v (28).

itary necessity required expeditious hearings. It invited Congress to review, propose, and ultimately approve whatever procedures would govern military commissions.

It was inconsistent for the government to allege on one hand that military necessity required a presidentially authorized forum to expeditiously try suspected war criminals, while on the other hand delaying trials to write and rewrite the rules. The Supreme Court noted, "Any urgent need for imposition or execution of judgment is utterly belied by the record; Hamdan was arrested in November 2001 and he was not charged until mid-2004. These simply are not the circumstances in which, by any stretch of the historical evidence or this court's precedents, a military commission established by Executive Order under the authority of Article 21 of the UCMJ may lawfully try a person and subject him to punishment."[16]

---

16. *Hamdan v. Rumsfeld*, 125 S. Ct. 2749, 2785–2786 (2006).

CHAPTER TWENTY-NINE

Orchestrating Trials:
Colonels Brownback and Hodges

I took off my beret and put it in my handbag as I stepped into the elevator, and pressed the button for the floor where my office was located. "Good morning" a familiar voice said. I turned around to see Cheri, an analyst that worked at OMC. She was tall and slender, with long blond hair and impeccable fashion sense.

Cheri was also very smart and she worked hard. I realized her attributes early in my assignment with the prosecution team and recruited her to help with my cases. From the very beginning we worked well together.

"I've got that information you asked about," she said. She referred to some news reports I was seeking to corroborate an important aspect of my case. "That was quick; I'll stop by your desk."

I greeted the receptionist and headed down the hall toward my office, when I heard another prosecutor exclaim in anger, "I cannot believe what he's doing here! I've had it with these little games!" He was referring to a series of odd requests from Colonel Brownback and his assistant, Colonel Hodges.

For the past few weeks, they had inundated the lawyers with hypothetical questions. The questions concerned issues that could eventually arise at trial, but hadn't yet, and may never. It is unconventional to ask prosecutors and defense counsel to draft mock motions about hypothetical matters not yet raised in trial. We all wondered what bearing, if any, they would have on the trial. Lawyers don't ordinarily respond to hypothetical questions in a vacuum and out of the trial context.

One seasoned prosecutor, who was an Air Force Reservist, opined, "These questions are ridiculous, and we shouldn't even respond. Wait until the issues arise at trial, and then respond on the record." I agreed. There's no way we, the prosecution, could benefit from this time-consuming, hypothetical exchange.

One prosecutor, who had previously appeared before Judge Brownback, explained that Brownback often held extensive off-the-record sessions, in an attempt to orchestrate the trial. This prosecutor thought these sessions were harmless, and believed the judge was just being proactive and "getting ahead of the issues." Another thought that we should respond because the judge was giving each party a chance to "shape the battle-field." Nonetheless, some prosecutors disagreed. Judges don't "get ahead" of trials. As Chief Justice Robertson has said, judges are like umpires who objectively call balls and strikes. They're not supposed to be on the pitcher's mound.

Judge Brownback and his assistant Colonel Hodges became little dictators. Brownback asked complicated questions that called for essay answers but he wanted simple answers. For example, he asked, "Can the Military Commission determine POW status?" Colonel Hodges rejected answers that he didn't like. He admonished parties with statements like, "We want a yes or no answer," and even warned that "failing to respond by 1700 (5:00 p.m.) today waives your opportunity to be heard on this matter." Yes, he said that prosecutors would forever waive their right to make arguments at trial if they failed to participate in the hypothetical exchange about legal issues divorced from factual context.

For weeks, we struggled with these questions, spent hours in divisive discussions, and tried to predict what impact our answers may have on upcoming trials. I don't think defense counsel participated. If they did, I never saw their responses.

A Little Note Leads to a Big Discovery

After one discussion about Judge Brownback and Colonel Hodges' controversial tactics, another lawyer walked into my office and put a folded piece of paper in my hand. I looked at him and was about to ask what it was, but he signaled that I shouldn't. Instead, he said, "Just read it," and then he walked away. I opened the paper and it was the citation to a 2001 case called *U.S. v. Quintanilla*.[1]

I read this case, which led me to others that discussed Mr. Hodges and Judge Brownback, and not in a favorable light. I learned that military appellate courts have overturned both Brownback and Hodges for significant judicial errors.

The appellate court overturned Judge Brownback's conviction of a death-penalty case *only three months* before he was appointed to hear cases before the Military Commissions; Judge Hodges was overturned in October 2001 for

---

1. *U.S. v. Quintanilla*, 56 M.M. 37 (Decided Oct. 19, 2001).

failing to recuse himself in a case where he left the bench and physically assaulted a witness. I am not making this up. He physically assaulted a witness! First, though, let us turn to Judge Brownback.

Brownback presided in a case where the soldier-defendant had concealed himself in the wooded area of Fort Bragg (an army post in North Carolina), armed with a weapon, and waited for his fellow soldiers to form up for their early-morning exercises.[2] The soldier defendant then opened fire, injuring 17 soldiers and killing one. The defendant pled guilty, and the jury sentenced him to death. On appeal, lawyers for the convicted soldier argued that Judge Brownback had unfairly denied defense counsel a meaningful opportunity to consult with psychiatric experts for a professional opinion about the defendant's mental state and competence. The appellate court concluded that such consultation could have led to a life sentence instead of the death penalty for the convicted soldier.

The appellate court conducted its own investigation and learned that the defendant suffered from significant mental impairment, was "delusional," had undergone therapy for homicidal thoughts, was "chronically and seriously mentally ill," and that his crimes were "causally related to his mental illness." Prosecutors had said about the defendant, "Prepare for Insanity Defense! This guy is nutty [sic] than a fruit cake."[3]

Given these facts, the appellate court decided that Judge Brownback abused his discretion by denying the defense's request. The court called his ruling "an error of constitutional magnitude," and found that his ruling "adversely impacted the fairness of the trial" in several respects.[4] The appellate court's decision that Judge Brownback abused his discretion was upheld by a higher court on August 16, 2005.

The appellate court opinion includes affidavits by defense counsel, which offer insight into the proceedings. According to the affidavits, Judge Brownback wanted to move the case along quickly,[5] wasn't receptive to reasonable requests from defense,[6] and often engaged in informal, off-the-record sessions with

---

2. *U.S. v. Kreutzer*, 59 M.J. 773 (Army Ct. Crim. Appl. 2004), aff'd, 61 M.J. 293 (Armed Forces, Aug. 16, 2005).

3. Id. at 777.

4. Id. at 779.

5. *Id.* at 805, James C. Gibson states, "I got the strong impression that the judge was determined to try the case before he was reassigned in the summer 1996 and that he would not have tolerated a delay." James Anthony Martin recalls, "I got the strong impression that the judge wanted the case to move quickly and efficiently." *Id.* at 813.

6. *Id.* at 812, James Anthony Martin recalls that rejecting his reasonable request for a private investigator was "completely illogical, unreasonable and insulting." Instead of a pri-

counsel that excluded the defendant.[7] One attorney explained that Judge Brownback wanted to "ensure that there were no surprises when we were in the courtroom. In retrospect, I should have formally objected to the large number of substantive issues that were discussed in 802s [off the record sessions], and I probably should have sought a writ at the appellate courts to force the judge to stay on the record."[8]

Now, of all the active duty military judges, or those retired military judges who now practice law or preside as judges in their civilian capacity—of all these judges, why would the Appointing Authority pick Brownback as the judge? Is he of the caliber of the Nuremberg Judge, Francis Biddle, Former U.S. Attorney General? What was Judge Brownback doing before he returned to the military to preside over this case? We know that he was retired, not practicing law, and not a member of the bar.[9] So, why did DoD pick Brownback, whose decision in a death penalty case was reversed on appeal, which led to an unfair death sentence? We do not know.

Colonel Hodges Leaves the Bench and Assaults a Witness

Now, let us turn to the *Quintanilla* case. In that case, a military appellate court overturned Retired Army Colonel Keith Hodges (assistant to Colonel

---

vate investigator, defense counsel was assigned an investigator from the same military police office at Fort Bragg that had investigated and helped prosecute the original case.

7. *Id.* at 804, James C. Gibson stated "I became very concerned about the large number of R.C.M. 802 (off record) sessions with the military judge. I also felt that I was being rushed to trial, and that more time was needed to prepare for trial.

Id. at 813, James Anthony Martin recalls being called into the Judge's office to talk "informally" about the case. He also remembers 802 sessions and opines, "Now I know that, during capital litigation, it is poor practice to have a session in which there is no record for review or to have a session in which the client is not present. There were many informal sessions, including some before referral, in which things related to the case were discussed with the judge and prosecutors."

Id. at 815, Stephen Stokes recalls, "It was not unusual for Judge Brownback to have 802 sessions. I am not sure that everything that should have been on the record was on the record in SGT Kreutzer's case."

8. *Id.* at 804, Affidavit of James C. Gibson.

9. John Hendren, *Lawyer Questions Tribunal's Qualifications*, L.A. Times, August 24, 2004, *stating*, "Hamdan's military lawyer, Navy Cmdr. Charles Swift, immediately challenged Army Col. Peter Brownback's ability to preside over the five-member panel. Swift said Brownback is not qualified to practice law because he is not a member of the Bar in his native Virginia."

Brownback) in October 2001.[10] In a fifty-page opinion, the U.S. Court of Appeals for the armed forces examined and discussed multiple errors made by Judge Hodges in the court martial of Staff Sergeant Quintanilla, accused of several offenses related to inappropriate sexual contact.[11]

The court ultimately concluded that Judge Hodges failed to ensure an accurate record at trial and should have recused himself after having an out-of-court physical altercation with a witness and after he engaged in ex-parte conversations with the prosecutor.

Here is what happened. Mr. Bernstein ran a local pizza parlor and employed JB and CS, two high school students. The students both knew the defendant and told Mr. Bernstein in separate accounts that the defendant, Staff Sergeant Quintanilla, sexually victimized them. Mr. Bernstein then noticed Staff Sergeant Quintanilla spending time with another 15-year old child. Because of the reports from his high-school employees and Staff Sergeant Quintanilla's outward habit of spending time with young boys, Mr. Bernstein contacted military authorities. Mr. Bernstein's report precipitated a criminal investigation against Staff Sergeant Quintanilla that uncovered several other child-victims. Eventually, military prosecutors brought charges against Staff Sergeant Quintanilla that led to the criminal trial at issue here.

At trial, the defense counsel attacked Mr. Bernstein's credibility, alleging that he had manipulated his impressionable, teen-age employees into making false statements against Staff Sergeant Quintanilla. Defense referred to Mr. Bernstein as the "key to the whole thing" in its opening statement.[12] Therefore, Mr. Bernstein, the citizen whistle-blower, became a central figure in the trial.

On August 20th, 1996, the trial against Staff Sergeant Quintanilla got underway. The trial record evidences multiple recesses, and references to off-the-record altercations between Judge Hodges and Mr. Bernstein. According to Judge Hodges account, he overheard the bailiff comment that one of the witnesses did not wish to testify. Judge Hodges then took matters into his own hands, left the bench, confronted witnesses in the witness room, and then returned the bench. Moments later, when prosecutors still weren't ready to proceed, Judge Hodges again left the bench and proceeded to the witness room. He explained, "I didn't want any more lawyers to leave the courtroom because I was having trouble keeping track of them. I was ready to put transponders on them."[13]

---

10. *U.S. v. Quintanilla*, 56 M.J. 37 (Decided Oct. 19, 2001).

11. Specifically, the defendant was charged with forcible sodomy of a child under the age of sixteen, indecent assault, and indecent acts.

12. *Quintanilla*, at 47.

13. *Quintanilla*, at 53.

While in the witness room, Judge Hodges admitted to using the word f*** directed at witness Bernstein, and touching him on the chest. Others, including the prosecution, Mr. Bernstein, and JB characterized Judge Hodges' actions as "emotional and confrontational."[14] Bernstein filed a police report, in which he alleges Judge Hodges told him to get his "f***ing a** in the court room," asked of the witness "who the f***" he was, and then warned Bernstein to "Stay the f*** out of me and [JB's] business." Bernstein also alleges Judge Hodges physically assaulted him by smacking his chest four or five times with an open hand.[15]

After the incident, Judge Hodges revisited his altercation with Bernstein several times during the trial. At one point Hodges stated, "The fact that I want to move this trial along got me the great pleasure of having Mr. Bernstein slander my reputation in the military."[16] In fact, it seemed that the altercation became the central focus of the trial. Judge Hodges asked other witnesses directed questions about Bernstein, including questions about Bernstein's personality style;[17] he questioned random, unsworn spectators about Bernstein,[18] and even suggested defense counsel should "call other persons to testify about whether Bernstein had influenced witnesses outside the courtroom."[19]

Eventually, the prosecutor requested that Judge Hodges recuse himself, alleging that he was seeking to force an acquittal in order to avoid a verbatim record that would reveal his misconduct.[20] Judge Hodges failed to rule on the motion, but stated, "That's so ridiculous I'm not even going to address it. Do you have another basis?" He then offered, "I've been accused of many things, but being a gutless judge is not one of them."[21]

The incident between Judge Hodges and Mr. Bernstein resulted in a trial within a trial. Eventually, the defense counsel proposed a stipulation of fact about the altercation "so we can get on with our closing and get this trial into the jury."[22] The prosecution objected to a stipulation, but Judge Hodges warned, "If there was no stipulation, there might be a mistrial that could preclude further proceedings." He told the prosecutor, "I'm going to let you roll this dice

---

14. *Quintanilla*, at 72.
15. *Quintanilla*, at 75.
16. *Quintanilla*, at 55.
17. *Quintanilla*, at 58.
18. *Quintanilla*, at 59.
19. *Quintanilla*, at 57.
20. *Quintanilla*, at 60.
21. *Quintanilla*, at 61.
22. *Quintanilla*, at 65.

any way you want to.... I just want you to think it through."[23] The prosecution finally agreed to stipulate.

Judge Hodges reviewed the stipulation agreed to by the prosecution and defense. He offered amendments to the document. Judge Hodges wanted to delete his name, and insert the phrase "court official" to conceal that he was the one who assaulted the witness. Over objection, Judge Hodges then suggested the phrase "senior field grade judge advocate" or "senior field grade member of the Judge Advocate General's Corps."[24] The parties disagreed and ultimately named Judge Hodges in the stipulation.[25]

The Appellate Court held that Judge Hodges failed to ensure a coherent record of out-of-court confrontations and should have recused himself. The court pointed out that instead of threatening prosecution with a mistrial, the judge could have stepped down and allowed another judge to take over. The court concluded, "The military judge's continued participation in the case, after the development of a stipulation that relied extensively on the judge's personal knowledge of out-of-court events and that placed the judge's stature and credibility in contest with the credibility of a witness, clearly raised questions about his impartiality...."[26]

The Appellate Court also discussed Judge Hodge's alleged bias toward the prosecutor. The record shows that both the defense, *and even the prosecutor*, jointly objected to the way that Judge Hodges favored the prosecution. Judge Hodges volunteered the reason for his bias by asking, "Do you think that I'm sending pheromones?" The defense counsel said, "Yes," and Judge Hodges replied, "I'll fix that."[27]

The Appellate Court also learned that Judge Hodges failed entirely to disclose an ex parte conversation with the prosecutor. In the conversation, the prosecutor urged Judge Hodges to allow Mr. Bernstein to testify on the merits, before testifying about the altercation. Eventually, the judge acquiesced, based on the prosecutor's "expressed fear" that leading off with testimony about the altercation could "detonate Mr. Bernstein's volatile personality and spoil the prosecution's case."[28] The court opined that defense counsel should have been included in the discussion, as it was "clearly a strategic point for the prosecution."[29]

---

23. *Quintanilla,* at 66.
24. *Quintanilla,* at 65.
25. *Quintanilla,* at 67.
26. *Quintanilla,* at 80.
27. *Quintanilla,* at 55.
28. *Quintanilla,* at 79.
29. *Quintanilla,* at 78.

At trial, Judge Hodges justified his actions by stating, "I don't care—I had my last promotion 3 years ago. Okay. When they don't want me on the bench anymore, I got a job, and I know when to retire."[30]

In addition to a lengthy recitation of the facts, the appellate court spent several pages of the opinion discussing the appropriate decorum and temperament of trial judges, stating that a judge should "be exemplar of dignity and impartiality" and should "exercise restraint over his or her conduct and utterances" and "suppress personal predilections, and control his or her temper and emotions."[31]

The Chief Prosecutor at Nuremberg was a sitting U.S. Supreme Court Justice, Robert Jackson, who took a leave of absence from the bench, and the American judge was Francis Biddle, former U.S. Attorney General.[32]

Against that historical backdrop, it is unclear why the Department of Defense appointed two judges with inelegant judicial records to adjudicate the first War Crimes Tribunals since WWII. Only a few years earlier, they both committed significant judicial errors—in Colonel Brownback's case it erroneously led to a death penalty sentence for one soldier! Surely, considering the great legal minds of our day, the government could select judges with more distinguished judicial records to ensure that the proceedings are fair.

---

30. *Quintanilla,* at 52.

31. *Quintanilla,* at 43.

32. Joseph E. Persico, Nuremberg, Infamy on Trial, (Penguin Books, 1995).

CHAPTER THIRTY

Should the U.S. Government Allow Detainees to Represent Themselves?

The Military Commissions Procedures that the Department of Defense issued provided greater rights than any that have come before, and they provide more discovery than U.S. defendants receive in U.S. federal courts. However, in one instance, they denied detainees an important fundamental right—the right to self-representation.

The right to represent oneself (often referred to as "going pro se") is firmly rooted in both U.S. and international law. In 1975, Anthony Faretta, a California defendant charged with grand theft, refused his appointed defense counsel, arguing that he'd rather represent himself. The trial court denied Faretta's request and appointed him a public defender on grounds that Faretta, who had no legal training, could not possibly understand the law to defend him against the criminal charges. Despite assistance from his defense attorney, the jury convicted Faretta.

Faretta, still maintaining his right to self-representation, appealed his case to the California Supreme Court, and eventually the U.S. Supreme Court. The Supreme Court agreed with Faretta, and reaffirmed the defendant's right to self-representation, opining that the trial court improperly foisted defense counsel on Mr. Faretta. The Supreme Court recognized that pro-se defendants are often significantly disadvantaged, but at their own choosing. The correct answer is not to force defendants into an attorney/client relationship against their will; but rather to advise them of the risks associated with going pro-se. The decision ultimately rests with the defendant—and only the defendant. The Court recognized that imposing counsel on an unwilling defendant results in a chilly relationship between the two, and dampens their communication so significantly that the defendant may be better off representing himself.

The Court stated, "It is undeniable that in most criminal prosecutions defendants could better defend with counsel's guidance than by their own unskilled efforts. But when the defendant will not voluntarily accept representation by counsel, the potential advantage of a lawyer's training and experience can be realized, if at all, only imperfectly. To force a lawyer on a defendant can only lead him to believe that the law contrives against him. Personal liberties are not rooted in the law of averages. The right to defend is personal. The defendant, and not his lawyer or the State, will bear the personal consequences of a conviction. It is the defendant, therefore, who must be free personally to decide whether, in his particular case, counsel is to his advantage."[1]

The 1975 *Faretta* case is the cornerstone in American jurisprudence that protects a defendant's right to represent himself. This standard is not unique to American law, but instead is recognized internationally. The *Faretta* court observed that no modern-day justice system denies defendants the right to represent themselves. In fact, the only body to do so existed from 1487–1641, a medieval English court known for unfair rulings and swift, harsh punishment—the Star Chamber. Even war crimes trials, such as those that occurred in Nuremburg and Rwanda, have consistently recognized the right of self-representation.

One detainee pending trial before a military commission, Mr. Al Bahlul, asserted this right. His request to represent himself is hardly novel, but one easily granted by reviewing both international and American jurisprudence. Defense counsel in the Al Bahlul case objected to their designation as defense counsel, and requested the Military Commission to honor his request.

The prosecution did not object to Al Bahlul representing himself if the judge appointed stand-by counsel. Therefore, both prosecution and defense *agreed* that the law affords an undeniable right to self-representation. Nonetheless, Colonel Brownback denied the request and ordered detailed defense counsel (counsel appointed by the court) to represent Al Bahlul—despite the complicating fact that the defendant refused to speak with his assigned defense counsel at all. Under *Faretta*, unskilled self-representation is far superior to any defense that his detailed defense counsel can muster without any cooperation or communication with his client. In this case, Al Bahlul responded to Judge Brownback's ruling by taking-off his translation headset and "boycotting" the proceedings.

To support his ruling, Judge Brownback concluded, without evidence, that Mr. Al Bahlul was "incompetent." However, he makes this determination without examining the defendant, or providing any basis for why he believes Al Bahlul to be "incompetent." He only provides remarkably circular reasoning for his decision: "He is not competent to go pro se because he has said on the record in open court that he is boycotting the proceedings and that he will not

---

1. *Faretta v. California*, 422 U.S. 806, 834 (1975).

participate in the proceedings. Obviously a person who will not participate in the proceedings cannot represent himself."[2] He maintains this basis, despite the fact that defense counsel directs his attention to the obvious—that the defendant boycotted the proceedings because Judge Brownback denied his request for self-representation.

There are not gradations of competence in courts of law. The standard for legal competence is relatively low. If a defendant can understand the charges against him, then a court considers him "competent" to stand trial and "competent" to enter a plea. If Judge Brownback truly believes that the defendant lacks competence, then under the law, Judge Brownback should not accept his plea, or even allow the court to try him. One cannot be "competent" in one realm of the proceeding, but "incompetent" in another.

A complicating factor is that earlier the Appointing Authority issued an advisory opinion in which he concluded that the Military Commission rules do not afford the right of self-representation, citing "procedural complexities" as a justification for denying self representation, a basis clearly denied by the Supreme Court in *Faretta*. With this decision "on the books" of military commission law, one assumes that Judge Brownback relied on the decision as precedent in his ruling before the commission.

Judge Brownback stated, "A lot of research has been done on this [self-representation issue] and the answer received is that they stay as they are. I can't change that." However, it is unclear why Judge Brownback then goes on to independently conclude, for different reasons, that no such right exists.

Defense counsel did not object, or ask for clarification of what role the Appointing Authority's opinion played in Judge Brownback's ultimate decision to deny defendant's request, nor did the prosecution. Strangely, in their briefs to the Appointing Authority, the two sides concurred that the defendant had a right to self-representation, but failed to restate their arguments on the record before Judge Brownback. In fact, the prosecutor's comment suggested a change in his position. He said, "He [Mr. Al Bahlul] also stated that he is not going to accept our rules and our laws which of course is something that you would have to accept at any court or proceeding in order to represent yourself...."[3]

If that were true, no defendant could ever argue that a court lacks jurisdiction—also an instance where the defendant "doesn't accept" the rules and laws of a court. Furthermore, this statement seems inconsistent with the prosecu-

---

2. *US v. Al Bahlul*, Trial Transcript at 66, Jan. 11, 2006.

3. *U.S. v. Ali Hamza Ahmad Sulayman Al Bahlul*, Trial Transcript, at 67, January 11, 2006.

tion's earlier brief to the appellate authority acknowledging the right of self-representation, with stand-by counsel.

What was clear at the closing of the January 2006 hearing was that detailed defense counsel would represent the accused, over defense objection and prosecution's tacit acquiescence.

Finally, late in 2006, the U.S. Congress intervened and granted detainees the right to represent themselves before military commissions.[4] It understood what the Department of Defense did not, that it makes sense to follow long-standing legal principles.

Judge Brownback Wore Two Hats

Colonel Brownback on various occasions seemed to vacillate between the role of judge and defense counsel. He acted with some trepidation and erred on the side of defense, even when the facts and the law direct otherwise. Another aspect of the of Al Bahlul case demonstrates this point. The government accused Al Bahlul of supporting Al Qaeda and creating propaganda videos encouraging their viewers to kill Americans. When brought before the commission for his preliminary hearing in 2004, he voluntarily attempted to confess his crimes before the court, on the record. He stated, "I am from al Qaida, and the relationship between me and September 11th..."[5] But before the accused could finish his statement, Judge Brownback interrupted him, telling him to stop and explaining to the members, "none of this is evidence in any way."[6] The prosecution objected. Then Judge Brownback told Al Bahlul to go on, but Al Bahlul had lost his train of thought and did not finish his sentence or otherwise explain his relationship to September 11th.

During a later session, Colonel Brownback silenced the defendant three times, and at one point tellingly stated, "I'm not going to let you harm yourself in my courtroom."[7] Although the defendant understood the risks and consequences of his statements and knew that he was on trial for alleged war crimes, Judge Brownback stopped him from doing what defendants do every day in U.S. courtrooms—confessing! At one point the defendant even *thanked* Colonel

---

4. Military Commissions Act of 2006, Pub. L. No. 109-366, 120 Stat. 2600, 10 USC 948a, §949a(1)(D) (2006).

5. *U.S. v. Ali Hamza Ahmad Sulayman Al Bahlul*, Trial Transcript at 11, August 26, 2004 and January 11, 2006 sessions.

6. *Id*. at 11.

7. Id. at 54–55.

Brownback for helping him, and asked Colonel Brownback to hold up his hand and signal to the defendant each time he was about to say something suggesting his guilt.[8] Colonel Brownback did not object to this role, and the defendant proceeded to express nine reasons why he believed the Military Commission process was unfair and why he wanted to represent himself. The prosecution showed remarkable restraint and did not object to the hand-signal agreement between the judge and the defendant. Even the defendant understood that he was being aided by the judge, hence his expression of gratitude to Judge Brownback.

Judge Brownback again acted as Al Bahlul's defense counsel later in this same proceeding. Near the end of the hearing, without prompting by either side, Judge Brownback observed a disparity in the number of prosecutors versus defense counsel. Four attorneys were at the prosecution table, and only one attorney appeared at defense table. Without considering the obvious reason for a disparity—that Al Bahlul didn't want representation *at all*—the judge, on his own, without any urging from the defense attorney, suggested that the scales were tipped in favor of the prosecution, who out-manned defense counsel four to one. He advised defense counsel to request additional support.[9] Ironically, defense counsel offered a number of reasons why he needed additional time to prepare the case—and never suggested that he needed additional counsel. Instead, he cited the fact that the government recently appointed him, and he spent most of December representing a criminal defendant in Oklahoma. Furthermore, he explained that before coming on active duty he did not have an opportunity to familiarize himself with the rules governing commissions, because he was closing a number of cases in his civilian job as a federal public defender.[10] That is—defense counsel never even hinted that he was outmanned. The judge usurped defense counsel by independently observing a discrepancy that neither party had raised. The prosecution did not object.

---

8. Id. at 55. Accused stating, "I want to thank the judge for what he said now about not allowing me to harm myself in his court. And this is something very positive from the judge.... And if I speak about some points and the judge sees that they are harmful to me and since the judge is the one who directs this court and he knows everything about it, and if the judge raises his hand I will stop speaking."

9. Id. at 112.

10. Id. at 79.

CHAPTER THIRTY-ONE

Setting the Record Straight

While the government expended time drafting new rules, responding to unusual requests from Judge Brownback, negotiating with other agencies to get evidence declassified, and providing extensive discovery to defense counsel, defense lawyers tried their case in the media. They captured media attention and repeatedly criticized the military for its "kangaroo courts." When prosecutors failed to correct inaccuracies, the defense's allegations intensified and became more frequent.

No Resource Disparity

Defense attorneys for the detainees have repeatedly alleged that there is an uneven playing field—that they are disadvantaged. This simply is not true. There are four full-time JAG officers on the defense team, and by January 2006 they only had nine cases total. For the first two years, each defense attorney had only one case, and time to spare.

A Pentagon official told me that during these two years, one defense attorney spent nearly a month in Yemen, living with the family of the accused and tracing the footsteps of his client. Reportedly, another went back to school earning an LLM (an advanced law degree). Others regularly appeared at speaking engagements and academic panels across the United States. According to the same official, the defense attorneys spent over $60,000 on travel expenses (excluding a daily allowance for food) in the year between 2004 and 2005.

Defense attorneys received legal support from scores of private litigators, including Neil Kaytal, a prominent constitutional law professor at Georgetown University, and top notch "well-heeled lawyers with America's premier corporate firms" who are "at the top of their profession."[1] Manhattan's Constitutional Rights Center leads a team of more than 400 attorneys representing

---

1. Deroy Murdeock, *National Review Online*, January 25, 2006, expanding a piece that appeared in the December 5, 2005 issue of *National Review*.

detainees in court; Mayer, Brown Rowe & Maw, the 11th largest law firm, which grossed $911 million in 2005, consider representing detainees to be their "cutting edge work";[2] Blank Rome, one of the largest law firms in the world, grossing $247.5 million in 2005, represents detainees.[3] This list is not all-inclusive.[4] One attorney in the prominent office of Covington and Burling has donated $27,600.00 of legal work to represent detainees. Another contributed over $200,000.00 of free legal work to defend a charged detainee.[5]

The defense counsel did not act as though they were out-numbered. Despite their outside teaching and speaking obligations, the defense team inundated the court with over sixty motions in each case. Often the motions were unnecessary. For instance, Hicks' defense team filed a lengthy motion to prohibit prosecutors from forcing the defendant to wear prison clothes at his trial. The motion was unnecessary because the accused was never required to wear a prison uniform to hearings. In fact, he wore an $800.00 Brooks Brothers Suit—paid for by the U.S. government. Importantly, prosecution had never objected to the accused wearing civilian clothing, so the motion was plainly unnecessary and triggered only by defense's imagination.

If any disparity exists, and I don't think it does, it is nonetheless justified. There is always a discrepancy between defense and prosecution personnel and resources. This is because the prosecution bears the burden of proof, while defense has no burden.

Further, in military courts martial, the prosecution is responsible for nearly every logistical aspect of trial, from coordinating travel for witnesses to ensuring that technical equipment functions as it should. These duties apply in military commissions as well. In fact, prosecution coordinates clothing for the defendant, and Judge Brownback admonished prosecutors when one detainee opted to wear a t-shirt to his trial. Other duties fall to the prosecution that ordinarily wouldn't.

For instance, officials in Guantanamo Bay were uncooperative in serving charges on detainees, claiming it made them appear impartial. Because the U.S. detention camp refused to cooperate with U.S. prosecutors trying detainees held there, a prosecutor was forced to fly from Washington, D.C. to

---

2. *Id.*

3. *Id.*

4. *Id.* Other firms include Covington and Burling; Dorsey and Whitney, Holland and Hart, Hunton and Williams; and Paul Weiss.

5. *Fergus Shiel, Hicks' lawyer denied legal aid funding*, THE AGE (Melbourne, Australia) January 10, 2006 (explaining that a request for additional funding was denied, but explaining that his firm had contributed $200,000.00 of legal work for the detainee.).

Guantanamo Bay for the explicit purpose of hand-delivering charges to detainees. This unnecessary trip cost the prosecution valuable time and resources. It sent a full time lawyer to Florida, and then on to Guantanamo Bay just to hand the detainee a charge sheet. In any other situation, prison officials would simply deliver the charges.

Despite these facts, when asked about the alleged disparity, the DoD spokesperson stated that the defense team was supported by "law students" and "other things" and said that she "didn't think there are 17 prosecutors" but didn't know for sure.

Defense Counsel Did Not Have Conditional Appointments

On June 15, 2005, Lieutenant Commander Charles Swift, defense counsel for detainee Hamdan, testified before the Senate Judiciary Committee on Detainees.[6] He alleged that his appointment was conditional, and for the limited purpose of "negotiating a guilty plea" to an unspecified offense, and that Hamdan's access to counsel was conditioned on his willingness to plead guilty.

No document supports this outrageous claim. In fact, documents provided by the Appointing Authority's Office prove *otherwise*. A memorandum to Lieutenant Commander Swift, from the Chief Defense Counsel states "… you are hereby detailed as Military Counsel for all matters relating to Military Commission proceedings involving Mr. Salem Ahmed Salem Hamden. Your appointment exists until such time any findings and sentence become final…."[7] Furthermore, Lieutenant Commander Swift requested, and was granted, a specific interpreter to "communicate to Mr. Hamden the legal principles and rights accorded him under Military Commissions so that he may adequately participate and make informed, intelligent decisions regarding his defense."[8] His own request doesn't suggest that his role was limited. Instead, they reveal that Lieutenant Commander Swift was acting as any defense counsel should—in the best interest of his client.

---

6. Lieutenant Commander Charles D. Swift, Defense Council, Office of Chief Justice Counsel, Statement, June 15, 2005, available at http://judiciary.senate.gov/print_testimony.cfm?id=1542&wit_id=4361.

7. Memorandum Detailing Defense Counsel, from Colonel William A. Gunn, Chief Defense Counsel, Office of Military Commissions to Lieutenant Commander Charles Swift, December 18, 2003.

8. Memorandum from Lieutenant Commander Swift to the Appointing Authority, Office of Military Commissions, January 8, 2004.

Defense Lawyers—Not the Prosecutors—
Closed the Trials

Lieutenant Commander Swift also alleged that the government removed his client, Mr. Hamdan, from portions of his trial, and that the prosecution sought to exclude Hamdan from several days of the trial proceedings. However, what he fails to mention is that *he*, defense counsel, and not prosecution, requested the closed session. Lieutenant Commander Swift, not prosecutors, requested to admit classified evidence and close the trial. Prosecutors had no intention of using secret evidence. The one time that Hamdan was excluded from the courtroom was because *his attorney requested that it be done*. Prosecution had nothing to do with that request, but critics blame it for closing the hearing.[9]

Lieutenant Commander Swift's claim that the prosecution also planned to close other portions of Hamdan's case is untrue. The chief prosecutor didn't intend then, or ever, to close the hearing, and went to great lengths to get information *declassified* so that hearings could remain open. In fact, later the chief prosecutor (then Colonel Davis) resigned his post as the chief prosecutor because he disagreed with having closed trials—something the Department of Defense later pressured him to do. He states, "The second reason I resigned is that I believe even the most perfect trial in history will be viewed with skepticism if it is conducted behind closed doors. Telling the world, 'Trust me, you would have been impressed if only you could have seen what we did in the courtroom' will not bolster our standing as defenders of justice. Getting evidence through the classification review process to allow its use in open hearings is time-consuming, but it is time well spent."[10] Prosecutors never supported closed trials. It jumped through hoops to declassify evidence so the trials could remain open and transparent. The truth is that defense counsel created the error it later complained about to the U.S. Supreme Court.

It is unclear why DoD often opted not to respond to criticism brought forth in the media. The DoD acted like a punching bag—receiving punches but putting up no defense. The military has professional Public Affairs Officers (PAOs) whom it trains to interact with the media. By the year 2006, the military assigned approximately 23 public affairs officers to Guantanamo Bay, Cuba, two to CITF, and one to the Office of Military Commissions. Although, oddly, the person assigned to handle public affairs at the Office of Military

---

9. *U.S. v. Hamdan*, Official Transcript of Proceedings, at 81–82, Nov. 8, 2004.

10. Colonel Morris Davis, *AWOL Military Justice, Why the former Chief Prosecutor for the Office of Military Commissions Resigned his Post*, LA TIMES, December 10, 2007.

Commissions was not trained in public affairs. It was a JAG officer with no specialized media training or experience.

Colonel Davis Speaks Up—
Accused No Boy Scout

"Well I woulda been here sooner, except that I fell asleep on the train and woke-up somewhere in the middle of D.C.," he said, through a friendly smile, smoothing his rain soaked hair. Colonel Morris Davis "Mo" joined the prosecution office as the chief prosecutor in fall 2005, when criticism against the military was at an all-time high. On ethics he said, "Just do the right thing, take the high ground, and you can't go wrong."

Colonel Davis jointed the prosecution team with a solid Air Force record. The Air Force commended him for handling high-profile sexual harassment cases at the Air Force Academy, where he served as the legal advisor. He had experience with the press, and understood first-hand how journalists can "spin" a story into a tale.[11]

When Colonel Davis assumed the position, he began responding to one-sided stories and correcting the facts. For instance, one article appeared in the LEGAL TIMES accusing some prosecutors of misconduct based on allegations from a former prosecutor. Colonel Davis responded in writing to clarify that the government had thoroughly investigated the allegations and didn't find any support for them.[12] The response was an important step because it corrected misinformation and cleared prosecutors of alleged wrongdoing. The media and defense team had unfairly and falsely accused military prosecutors of misconduct. But, the government did not allow junior prosecutors to talk to the press. These prosecutors were grateful when Colonel Davis told their side of the story and set the record straight.

In January 2006, Colonel Davis accompanied some of the prosecutors to Guantanamo Bay for preliminary hearings in the cases involving detainee Kadhr and detainee Al Bahlul. Prosecutors accused Kadhr, who was 15 years old at the time of his crime, of attacking and killing an American soldier. Prosecutors accused Al Bahlul of making propaganda videos for Al Qaeda.

Colonel Davis, in an unprecedented move for military commission prosecutors, held a press conference for members of the media who had traveled to

---

11. Colonel Morris D. Davis, *Effective Engagement in the Public Opinion Arena: A Leadership Imperative in the Information Age*, AIR AND SPACE POWER CHRONICLES, 5 November 2004.

12. *Military Prosecutors Took Proper Action*, LEGAL TIMES, Vol. 17, No. 43, Oct. 4, 2005.

Guantanamo Bay in order to observe the hearings. In the conference, he called defense's characterization of Kadhr as a fresh-faced boy scout "nauseating" and further explained that Kadhr was not "tying knots and making s'mores," but, instead was making bombs to kill American soldiers. He defended the commission process, calling it full and fair and at one point stated, "damned if you do and damned if you don't." It was a rare and important step for the prosecution team, who previously took the blows but didn't fight back.

The defense team, realizing that they had awakened a sleeping giant, moved quickly to silence prosecutors by filing a motion claiming that Colonel Davis had committed "prosecutorial misconduct" with his statement and requesting a public retraction of his "inflammatory" statements. Defense argued that the procedural rules bind prosecutors to higher standards, and prohibit them from saying anything bad about the accused. It said that special more lenient rules should apply for defense counsel at Guantanamo Bay. It argued for a double standard.[13]

The prosecution argued that it had "sat quietly while the defense has been doing a public relations battle and assault against us."[14] Colonel Davis went on, "This was the first time that [I] stood up and decided to say, 'Hey, I need to say something back to some of these inflammatory remarks. Your Honor, you are not presiding over a kangaroo court.'"[15]

The judge decided that procedural rules allow Colonel Davis to respond to defense counsel's inaccurate statements and attacks. Importantly, the chief prosecutor had spoken, and the judge had confirmed his right to do so. At this moment, the judge leveled the playing field.[16]

Colonel Davis' stand was an important moment for military prosecutions not only on the ground in Guantanamo Bay, but also miles away in our Washington, D.C. office. Surprisingly, the prosecution team had muted itself for so long that the office hummed with concern about Colonel Davis' remarks. "He's gone too far," some claimed, stating the prosecutors have a higher responsibility to the public. One of the higher-ranking prosecutors even suggested that Pentagon officials would reprimand Colonel Davis for his comments. With-

---

13. *U.S. v. Omar Ahmed Kadhr*, Official Trial Transcript, Vol. 7 at 202, Jan. 11–12, 2006. The Presiding officer stated, "I think we are in agreement that rule, 3.6, [rules governing statements made outside of trial] applies equally to the defense and the government." Defense counsel responded, "No, sir. Respectfully, we are not in agreement."

14. *U.S. v. Omar Ahmed Kadhr*, Official Trial Transcript, Vol. 7 at 211, Jan. 11–12, 2006.

15. *U.S. v. Omar Ahmed Kadhr*, Official Trial Transcript, Vol. 7 at 214–215, Jan. 11–12, 2006.

16. *U.S. v. Omar Ahmed Kadhr*, Official Trial Transcript, Vol. 7 at 228–229. Jan. 11–12, 2006.

out visiting the governing rules, prosecutors were too quick to accept defense's position—that they could talk but the prosecution couldn't.

By March 2006, having lost the argument in court, attorneys affiliated with the defense team petitioned the D.C. bar to revoke Colonel Davis' license to practice law within the District of Columbia. They seem to prefer a one-sided debate.

Eventually, the D.C. bar dismissed the complaint, confirming that prosecutors may respond to defense's troubling allegations. After all, prosecutors have a client too—the U.S. government.

CHAPTER THIRTY-TWO

The Way Forward with Military Commissions

At the Office of Military Commissions, prosecutors come and prosecutors go. Cases move at a glacial pace and prosecutors move on to other duty stations without ever setting foot in the courtroom. To some extent, JAG officers must manage their own careers and maintain a competitive edge so they can promote to a higher rank. Some believed that being a war crimes prosecutor would lessen their chances of being promoted. One explained, "I don't want to be personally associated with a disaster."

While some prosecutors remained fully committed to prosecuting detainees, others equivocated and began to question the legitimacy of war crimes trials. Still others lacked enthusiasm and believed it was only a matter of time before the government would close the Office of Military Commissions.

I was proud to serve at the Office of Military Commissions. I believed then, as I do now, that bringing detainees to justice is the right thing to do. However, I disagreed with unnecessarily delaying trials, changing the rules mid-trial, affording more rights to the detainees than international law required in some instances while denying fundamental rights in others, and failing to object to outlandish defense allegations.

In the summer of 2006, Hamdan's case finally reached the U.S. Supreme Court. The court, in a sharply divided opinion, invalidated military tribunals and said that the President should receive specific approval from Congress before using military tribunals to try suspected criminals. Importantly, it did not say that military commissions are unconstitutional. Instead, it merely called on Congress to approve the rules, or write new ones.

The Supreme Court's decision interrupted military tribunals that were already underway. Immediately, Congress began exploring and debating the proper way to try detainees in Guantanamo Bay. This created a sharp divide between the president's administration and members of Congress over controversial questions, like whether to exclude defendants from portions of their trials and whether to allow coerced evidence.

Eventually Congress adopted a robust set of rules called the "Military Commissions Act of 2006."[1] Generally, the rules disallow information obtained by torture,[2] guarantee defendants the right to represent themselves,[3] guarantee that defendants cannot be excluded from their trials except when they are disruptive and only after being warned by the judge,[4] and protect the sources and methods of classified information.[5] Further, the rules allow defendants to appeal their convictions to the District of Columbia Circuit Court, and *even* the United States Supreme Court.[6]

However, one glaring flaw in the new rules is a provison that leaves open the possibility of using evidence obtained by coercion. I've heard some DOD officials say there is a good reason for the rule. I disagree.[7]

One important question that has been overlooked is whether the government should proceed with military tribunals during a time of war, *at all*. The government plans to resume the Guantanamo trials in the spring or summer of 2008. However, it should consider waiting until the war is over. So long as we are at war with terrorists, perhaps the U.S. has more to lose than gain by trying detainees in Guantanamo Bay.

My experiences with the Criminal Investigation Task Force (the organization responsible for investigating terrorist leads) and the Office of Military Commissions, (the organization responsible for prosecuting detainees held in Guantanamo Bay), demonstrate overwhelmingly that simultaneously fighting a war and prosecuting war criminals simply doesn't work. Ordinarily we would prosecute war criminals after—not during—the war.

---

1. Military Commissions Act of 2006, Pub. L. No. 109-366, 120 Stat. 2600, 10 USC 948a (2006).

2. Military Commissions Act of 2006, Pub. L. No. 109-366, 120 Stat. 2600, 10 USC 948a, 948r(b), *stating*, "A statement obtained by use of torture shall not be admissible in a military commission under this chapter, except against a person accused of torture as evidence that the statement was made."

3. Military Commissions Act of 2006, Pub. L. No. 109-366, 120 Stat. 2600, 10 USC 948a,(b)(D) (2006).

4. Military Commissions Act of 2006, Pub. L. No. 109-366, 120 Stat. 2600, 10 USC 948a, 949d(e) (2006).

5. Military Commissions Act of 2006, Pub. L. No. 109-366, 120 Stat. 2600, 10 USC 948a, 949d(f) (2006).

6. Military Commissions Act of 2006, Pub. L. No. 109-366, 120 Stat. 2600, 10 USC 948a, 950(g) (2006).

7. Military Commissions Act of 2006, Pub. L. No. 109-366, 120 Stat. 2600, 10 USC 948r (b-c) (2006).

Ironically, U.S. officials predicted its fate. On the day that it named the chief prosecutor and defense counsel,[8] a reporter asked, "But wouldn't it be more difficult to find the evidence if you are still involved in a war? And do you see any difficulties, since it is going to be the military is [sic] involved with that?" One prosecutor responded "… there's no doubt that you're right, and there's going to be a lot of difficulties associated with getting evidence that, in many cases, comes from a different country, from where people who are speaking a different language and from places where we're not in the habit with law enforcement investigators to go in and get evidence. So, all of those difficulties will be there."[9]

But, the "difficulties" CITF agents encountered were crippling to cases. It is impossible to gather evidence during an ongoing war. Imagine securing a crime scene in the midst of battle, with flying bullets and fleeing witnesses. Terrorist still occupy safe houses and compounds that CITF agents need to exploit for evidence. Imagine if Nuremberg prosecutors attempted to bring Nazi criminals to justice while Hitler occupied Germany, and concentration camps still existed. Obviously, investigators could not have walked through the gates of Auschwitz, seized evidence, and interviewed witnesses. The Nazis would have executed them. Even after the war, when the Nazis fell and Germany stabilized, it took investigators months to gather evidence, and locate witnesses. Even when CITF locates witnesses, some hesitate to get involved. Their countries and governments are unstable, and they are afraid.

So long as we are at war, classified evidence is still relevant. When the war is over, evidence such as information seized from terrorist camps, the identity of undercover agents, and U.S. secret surveillance techniques won't be as sensitive. Until the war is over and soldiers are safe at home, the U.S. would be foolish to put detainees on trial and reveal classified information to the world (even a summarized, unclassified version that the new rules allow). If it waits until after the war, it can use all of that evidence without risking lives or compromising U.S. intelligence gathering tactics. That is what happened at Nuremberg.

It often doesn't make sense to try war criminals and fight a war simultaneously. There are practical ramifications, too. It makes sense that any fair proceeding will result in some acquittals, some convictions, and a range of sentences commensurate with the crime. At Nuremberg, several Nazi criminals faced the gallows, some were imprisoned for varying lengths of time, and others were acquitted and set free.[10]

---

8. Department of Defense Briefing on Military Commissions, May 22, 2003, 2:00pm, transcript available at www.kuwaitidetainees.org/media/DoD_052293.htm.

9. *Id.*

10. See generally JOSEPH E. PERSICO, NUREMBERG, INFAMY ON TRIAL, 383–433 (Penguin Books) (2005).

What would become of a detainee held in Guantanamo Bay whom the military tries and finds not guilty? Would he get a ticket home? Under the law, the answer is no. Under the law, the U.S. can hold enemy combatants until the end of hostilities. It could hold the detainee as an enemy combatant, despite the finding of not guilty. But the American public objects to holding detainees at all and will not understand holding a detainee found not guilty. It also begs the question, if the U.S can hold the detainee anyway, why try him?

And, what if the detainee is tried before a military commission and found guilty, but sentenced to only a few years imprisonment? When should this term begin to run? If it begins to run immediately, convicted detainees could conceivably complete their sentences and be released before the war is over and, ironically, before enemy combatants who were not prosecuted for war crimes are released. That result obviously doesn't make sense. It seems inconsistent that one is *better off* being tried and found guilty of a war crime than not being tried at all.

Arguably, the term must only begin to run *after* the war is over. But defense attorneys aren't interested in plea bargaining for a shorter sentence without knowing when that sentence will begin to run. We have no idea when the war could end, so his two-year term may not begin running for another 10, 20, 30 years or more. Plea bargains for reduced sentences seem pointless if the agreed sentence only runs at the end of an uncertain time-period.

When the government attempted to try detainees in Guantanamo Bay initially, the cases lacked momentum partially because defense counsel sought to delay them. Defense's interest in speedy trials is conspicuously absent, because their client remains in custody regardless. Defense counsel argued that the U.S. government violated detainees' right to a speedy trial on one hand, but then sought continuances (delays) one after the other. In the Hamdan case, defense counsel passionately alleged speedy trial violations in the morning, and then that very afternoon asked the judge to delay the trial for several months. In another instance, defense counsel sought to delay the trial so he could pick up his dog Hank from his parent's house in Florida. They were going on a cruise and couldn't look after Hank. Defense counsel looked for every reason to delay the trials.

If the Government restarts Military Commissions with congressionally approved rules, this practical problem will still exist, and defense counsel will seek to delay the trials. Nothing motivates them to proceed. Their client is being held regardless of whether there is a trial or not.

Hold Detainees until the War Is Over

But, if the U.S. doesn't try detainees held in Guantanamo Bay, what should it do with them? The answer is a simple one. The normal rule and the historical tradition is to hold detainees until the war is over. Those detainees it believes are war criminals should face trial by Military Commission at the end of the war. There have been exceptions to the normal rule. President F.D.R. prosecuted the Nazi saboteurs while WWII was still raging. The Court approved this in *Ex parte Quirin*. F.D.R. wanted to make an example of these Nazis by promptly trying all of the saboteurs and executing most of them. Yes, there are situations, like *Quirin*, where exigent circumstances authorize war crimes tribunals before the war is over. But that does not apply here, where the judges, the defense counsel, and the appointing authority for the military commission appear to be in no hurry to go to trial.

Some criticize the U.S. for holding detainees in Guantanamo Bay "without charge," suggesting incorrectly that charging detainees is the only legal way to hold them. In fact, the laws of war permit holding one's enemies[11]—and even civilians captured on the battlefield[12]—until the war is over. Even doctors and chaplains, considered "protected persons," can be held until the end of hostilities.[13]

Holding detainees until after the war doesn't mean the U.S. government can hold them *indefinitely*. Neither the Geneva Conventions nor international law provide for such discretion. The U.S. can only hold detainees under a theory that the war will end. Just like every other war, this one will end. We do not know when, and we cannot predict how, but eventually U.S. troops will come home and active hostilities will end.

Stop Exceeding Geneva

Many critics accuse the United States of failing to follow the Geneva Conventions. But these claims are not persuasive to many who have seen conditions at Guantanamo Bay firsthand. The government guarantees each detainee a full eight hours of sleep every night, without interruption. They also receive three *halal* meals (prepared in accordance with Muslim dietary restrictions), five prayers, and at least two hours of outdoor recreation a day, also

---

11. Third Geneva Convention, Relative to the Treatment of Prisoners of War, 12 August 1949, article 118 stating, "Prisoners of war shall be released and repatriated without delay after the cessation of active hostilities."

12. Fourth Geneva Convention, Relative to the Protection of Civilian Persons in Time of War, 12 August 1949, allows civilians taking no active part in hostilities to be detained. They are guaranteed more movement, and interaction, than POWs. Nonetheless, they are detained.

13. Third Geneva Convention, Relative to the Treatment of Prisoners of War, 12 August 1949, article 33. Medical Personnel and Chaplains are retained, and held under the same conditions as Prisoners of War, except that they also enjoy greater freedom of movement in order to administer medical and religious services to other detainees.

without interruption. One journalist recently noted, "One interrogator actually bakes cookies for detainees, while another serves them Subway or McDonald's sandwiches."[14]

Despite the debacle at Camp Bucca, discussed in chapter eight, where detainees used a tent designated as a "mosque" to build a weapons cache and brutally attack soldiers from inside the camp, officials in Guantanamo Bay still deem certain religious items "off-limits" to guards. And, like Camp Bucca, detainees take advantage of these freedoms.

According to the Commander of the Joint Task Force in Guantanamo Bay, Admiral Harris, detainees have organized into a multi-cell Al Qaeda network. Some detainees monitor guards and doctors, and others make weapons.[15] Just like at Camp Bucca, detainees in Guantanamo Bay are resourceful. They've used springs from the faucets, broken light bulbs, and fan blades as weapons. These incidents have risen to eight a day. In one year, detainees stabbed victims with homemade knives 90 times, including cutting a doctor administering aid. Now, doctors wear body armor when they treat detainees.[16]

Detainees have even staged suicide to lure and attack prison guards in Guantanamo, Bay. On May 18, 2006, one detainee made a noose from sheets and attached it to the ceiling. A guard perceived the situation, called for backup, and soldiers stormed into the cell to save the detainee from himself. What they encountered was a slick floor from feces, urine and soapy water mixture, that caused them to fall. Detainees then attacked the guards. Detainees managed to restrain one guard and viciously attacked him with broken light fixtures and security cameras they had torn from the wall. Eventually, the guards gained control of the camp.[17] It was Camp Bucca relived, because the U.S. government does not learn from its mistakes.

And, just like at Camp Bucca, detainees specifically abuse religious freedoms granted them by the government. The commander, Admiral Harris, found prescription pills hidden in the binding of the Holy Quran. Guards didn't find it, because the military forbids them from touching detainees' Qurans.[18]

Many abuses occur right under the commander's nose. Detainees reuse envelopes received from their attorneys to pass messages from one block to another.

---

14. Richard Miniter, *Deadly Kindness*, New York Post, September 15, 2006.

15. *Id.*

16. *Id.*

17. James Taranto, *War Inside the Wire*, The Wall Street Journal, September 16–17, 2006.

18. James Taranto, *War Inside the Wire*, The Wall Street Journal, September 16–17, 2006.

(Most detainees have lawyers, and more than 18,500 letters have been mailed to or from detainees in Guantanamo Bay over the past year.)[19] The military won't let guards look inside these envelopes, citing "attorney-client privilege." This government imposes this restriction on guards, even when it knows the information inside is not attorney-client protected. The Camp Commander Admiral Harris takes a black and white approach to the issue, stating, "If it's written correspondence, and it's in the habeas envelope, then we cannot get to it."[20]

Therefore, the government forces U.S. guards into aiding and abetting Al Qaeda's organization and plotting within the walls of its own camp. As one journalist so eloquently observed after an August 2006 visit to Guantanamo Bay, "We should worry less about detainee safety and more about our own."[21]

Geneva makes clear that the U.S. can scale back religious accommodations if detainees do not adhere to disciplinary rules. The military should scale them back. Further, it should adopt a disciplinary system for detainees who break the rules. Many detainees threaten guards, throw urine and feces, and spit at guards with no repercussion. The Geneva Conventions allow camp commanders to establish disciplinary rules and impose punishment for violations. The military should do what the Geneva Conventions permit and impose reasonable punishment for infractions.

Camp discipline should never be left to detainees. At Camp Bucca, in Iraq, the U.S. established separate compounds for Sunni and Shiite prisoners. In the Shiite compound, twenty clerics were in charge of discipline and imposed harsh penalties on detainees who broke the rules. These penalties included denying inmates food and beating the soles of their feet. The U.S. must adopt disciplinary rules that protect both the guards and the detainees from abuse.[22]

Finally, the government should not parole detainees back to the battlefield while we are still at war. While releasing a steady flow of detainees who "no longer pose a threat" counters allegations of indefinite detention, it makes the battlefield more dangerous for U.S. troops and protracts the war. Eventually, a soldier will be killed by a paroled detainee (if it hasn't already happened), and the U.S. will have only itself to blame.

Congress has grappled with "benchmarks" to gauge U.S. success in Iraq and define the war's end. This war is unlikely to culminate in a peace treaty between the U.S. and the world's terrorists, but many have overlooked an obvi-

---

19. *Id.*

20. *Id.*

21. Richard Miniter, *Deadly Kindness*, NEW YORK POST, September 15, 2006.

22. Steve Fainaru and Anthony Shadid, *In Iraq Jail Resistance Goes Underground*, THE WASHINGTON POST, August 24, 2005 at A01.

ous benchmark—the war is not over until U.S. troops are home. Troops are still fighting in Afghanistan and Iraq.

Permanent Investigators, Qualified Judges, and Reasonable Local Rules

Over six years after terrorists attacked the U.S., the government still operates with a *temporary* task force of terrorist investigators. The Criminal Investigation Task Force (CITF) employs talented agents. However, they lack resources, and agents turn over every few months. Both factors seriously impede investigations. CITF should be a permanent task force and should have subpoena power over information held by other intelligence agencies—even when the information is classified. Investigators should continue their investigations, in anticipation of trials at the end of the war.

When the war is over, the government should try suspected terrorists for their war crimes before a military tribunal. It should appoint esteemed judges, like those who participated in Nuremberg, who can assure fair, judicious proceedings. The government should not appoint judges like Colonels Brownback and Hodges, whom appellate courts have reversed for significant judicial error. Doing so would only subject the U.S. to further criticisms and allegations of unfair proceedings and kangaroo courts.

Many of the problems at the Office of Military Commissions stemmed from countless, inconsistent local rules that did not comport with U.S. or international law, or that reinvented longstanding court practices. Evolving rules were confusing, inconsistent, inefficient, and unfair. On account of judge-issued Presiding Officer Memorandums (POMs), we never knew what to expect from one day to the next, and often didn't know whether to rely on domestic or international case law precedent.

In 2006, Congress passed the Military Commissions Act of 2006, and a few months later the military drafted the Manual for Military Commissions. While it is debatable whether military commissions require so many rules, uniform guidelines are a step in the right direction. Hopefully, the new rules will cure earlier procedural problems.

Military Commission Judges should avoid supplementing these new rules with lengthy local rules, and they should do away with the concept of "Presiding Officer Memorandums" (POMs) that require lawyers on both sides to respond to hypothetical scenarios not yet raised at trial. The court should let the case law system work. They should have trials, and the case law that results from those trials will serve to interpret the rules. It cannot "get ahead of the game," as Colonel Brownback tried to do when I worked at the Office of Military Commissions. We cannot know before a trial what issues will be raised and how they will be resolved. We cannot orchestrate these war crimes trials. The government will win some cases, and it will lose some cases, and what will evolve—if the system allows it—is a body of Military Commission Law.

Win the War of Ideas

Nearly three years after the government created the Office of Military Commissions to try terrorists, it suffered attacks from defense counsel in the media— not in a courtroom. However, it was a one-sided debate. Defense counsel, aided by the media, spun complicated legal issues into pithy headlines; while DoD repeatedly bowed out of opportunities to tell its side of the story. Countless news articles, even those waging outright attacks against the DoD, calling the trials *kangaroo courts*, went unanswered. Defense Counsel Major Fleener commented publicly, "the government has made my job really easy,"[23] and he was right. Reckless, unchecked comments misled the U.S. public into believing half-truths about military commissions in the War on Terror.

Beginning in 2005, Chief Prosecutor Colonel Davis made valiant attempts to counter these criticisms. But it was too little, too late. When the U.S. resumes military tribunals, prosecutors should learn from the beating they took in the media and correct inaccurate statements immediately.

Prosecutors weren't the only ones with closed lips. Ironically, even President Bush and Secretary of Defense Rumsfeld sat idly by while critics attacked the war and misrepresented Guantanamo Bay. The administration did not attempt to manage its message or keep the American public informed. Instead, it gave critics the stage. In order to win the War of Ideas, the U.S. must first put its ideas into the marketplace.

We are our own best storytellers, and administration officials are in the best position to keep America informed about their decisions. There are many things the administration could have said, but didn't. For instance, from the very beginning, it called the trials "Military Commissions." True, the term "Military Commission" derives from the Uniform Code of Military Justice (UCMJ), but it is synonymous with "War Crimes Trials." Calling them "commissions" is military jargon, and confusing to the public. The word "commission" usually refers to an investigative body, like the *9-11 Commission*, which investigated the

---

23. Thomas Fleener, Speech delivered at Amnesty International Public Information Forum, Torture and the War on Terror, What you Should Know and What you Can Do, Tuesday March 21, 2006, George Mason University, School of Public Policy.

facts surrounding September 11th, 2001, or the *Federal Trade Commission*, which investigates false advertising. For these reasons, the government should have simply called these trials what they are, "War Crimes Trials," so that Americans would understand what we were doing.

It was too quick to accept inaccurate characterizations. For instance, even the government refers to terrorists in Iraq as "insurgents." That term is inaccurate. They are terrorists, and it should call them terrorists.

Further, when criticism began to mount about holding detainees in Guantanamo Bay, one of the allegations is that the government wanted to hold them *indefinitely*. When the administration failed to respond, the term stuck. Now, four years after the military created the prison camp, news media, and even military personnel, refer to detainees' *indefinite* detention in Guantanamo Bay. The characterization of this mission as indefinite is unrealistic. No war lasts forever. However, we do not have a crystal ball and cannot state a date certain when the war will end. But that is nothing new. Nobody knew that the first Gulf War would only last a few weeks. We never know when a war will end, until it does. The Seven Years' War wasn't called that on day one. True, we don't know when this war will end, but we know that it will. The U.S. doesn't plan to hold detainees forever, and it should make that clear.

The government understands that it must "win the war of ideas," but it is significantly behind in the race. It should step up public affairs efforts, hold press conferences, correct misstatements, and be proactive instead of reactive. It has a good story to tell. It battles brutal terrorists who do not wear uniforms or follow the laws of war, while trying to help a country achieve democracy.

It has helped liberate innocent people from an oppressive regime that governed under archaic, seventh-century principles. Before its fall to U.S. forces, the Taliban rigidly controlled every aspect of life, and prohibited instruments of joy, like music, art, and theatre. It even crushed singing pet canaries because it opposed singing.

The greatest beneficiaries of U.S. support in Iraq and Afghanistan are Muslim women and girls. For instance, the Taliban punished women for wearing shoes that make noise when she walks. And, if caught with painted fingernails, it punished the women offenders by chopping off the tips of her fingers. Now Muslims in Iraq, including women, train alongside U.S. troops to become qualified as police officers.

Because of U.S. support, Iraq has democratic elections, is building hospitals and schools, and allows women and girls to participate in society and even become professionals, politicians, and police officers. Ironically, the U.S. is criticized for violating human rights, while simultaneously liberating people from oppressive regimes and tyrannical leaders. Good stories exist, but the U.S. is an unwilling storyteller.

Staff Sergeant Maupin, Freedom Is Not Free[24]

Aside from telling the good stories, the U.S. government must tell the bad ones too. Citizens should understand the cruelty that drives our enemies and their brutal tactics.

Instead of allowing the debate to center around the treatment of detainees in Guantanamo Bay, the U.S. should remind human rights groups, and the world, about the way our enemy treats U.S. soldiers. Where is the International Committee of the Red Cross for U.S. soldiers?

On April 9, 2004, terrorists in Iraq attacked a convoy and captured Private Matt Maupin, an army reservist and aerospace engineering student at the University of Cincinnati. In high school, Matt was an excellent student and star football player. He joined the army to save money for college, and wound up in Iraq, and in the hands of terrorists.

Images of Matt later appeared on Al Jazeera. He sat in the floor wearing his desert, camouflaged uniform, a floppy desert hat, and an expression full of confusion and fear. Surrounded by mysterious gunmen, with cloths around their faces, he read from a statement, "I am married with a ten-month old son. I came to liberate Iraq, but I did not come willingly because I wanted to stay with my child."

Later terrorists claimed they murdered Maupin. However, It was not until March, 2008 that the Pentagon found his body. It still considered Maupin "missing," and amazingly, it gave him a new title unknown under the Geneva Conventions, "missing/captured" instead of referring to him correctly as a POW. He was one of only four known U.S. POWs in the Iraq war, and the army promoted him twice. By spring 2006, Private Maupin became Staff Sergeant Maupin. But he will never wear the stripes he earned.

His mother, Carolyn Maupin, called Americans to action, "Each day that passes, I believe, draws us closer to resolution as I see yellow ribbons and am reminded of the compassion and humanity of United States citizens. 'Believe in Matt, believe in the U.S. military, believe in prayer' I have found myself saying each time his safety crosses my heart. So for those of you who have a loved one, a friend, a spouse, a child, a neighbor in the U.S. military, I encourage you to believe in them as I do in my son. Freedom is not free—but love lasts forever."[25]

Staff Sergeant Maupin should be a household name. All Americans should know his story. When he was missing, the government should have reminded our enemies, and our critics, that we still waited for word from Iraqi terror-

---

24. More about Staff Sergeant Maupin can be found at the web-site his parents started. It is at www.yellowribbonsupportcenter.com.

25. http://cheddarbay.com/000MattMaupin/mattmaupin.html.

ists about the fate of our beloved missing soldiers. But instead it allowed critics to shift the debate to treatment of detainees in Guantanamo Bay.

*Iraqi army soldiers waiting to vote in Iraqi elections. Notice they are wearing uniforms. DoD
photo by Specialist Charles W. Gill.*

*U.S. Army Sgt. Charles Hummer hands out Iraqi flags in downtown Baghdad. DoD photo by
Norris Jones.*

Army Specialist Shaniece Bannister with Iraqi women before they took their physical readiness part of the Iraqi Police entrance exam. Bannister assists with a screening process to select women candidates for the Iraqi police force. DoD photo by Chief Petty Officer Edward G. Martens.

A soldier comes home after being deployed to Iraq for fifteen months. DoD photo by Tech. Sergeant Brian E. Christiansen, U.S. Air Force.

CONCLUSION

Another September 11th

My story ends, as it began five years earlier, on a sunny September day. I parked my car in the faculty parking lot at the George Mason University Law School, and flung my bag over my shoulder as I walked toward the building. It was my first day of work.

Today, on the anniversary of September 11th, I started my position as the director of a clinic that provides free legal assistance to service members and their families. It seemed like an appropriate way to commemorate this anniversary.

I thought about those who perished five years ago, and I thought about the heroes aboard flight 93, and Staff Sergeant Maupin. I thought about the soldiers I met along the way, such as Private Jessica Lynch, and all the soldiers I never met that did not make it home. I thought about the way our country pulled together in the days after September 11th, and how stores couldn't keep American flags in stock because every American wanted one of his own.

Our country and the world has changed over the last five years. We have felt grief and anger, and even denial, about the horrific attack on our country and our way of life. We are at war, and every day soldiers board planes for faraway places, wondering if they will make it home.

During World War II, Americans showed their support for the war by growing victory gardens. My book is my garden. One of the greatest privileges we enjoy is the freedom of speech and expression. I hope through its pages, you have come to understand the lion we face, the mistakes we've made, and the daily sacrifices that service members make in the name of precious freedom. We soldiers are, and ever will be, *honor bound to defend freedom.*

Military Commissions Act of 2006

10 U.S.C.A. §948b

§948b. Military commissions generally

(a) **Purpose.**—This chapter establishes procedures governing the use of military commissions to try alien unlawful enemy combatants engaged in hostilities against the United States for violations of the law of war and other offenses triable by military commission.

(b) **Authority for military commissions under this chapter.**—The President is authorized to establish military commissions under this chapter for offenses triable by military commission as provided in this chapter.

(c) **Construction of provisions.**—The procedures for military commissions set forth in this chapter are based upon the procedures for trial by general courts-martial under chapter 47 of this title (the Uniform Code of Military Justice). Chapter 47 of this title does not, by its terms, apply to trial by military commission except as specifically provided in this chapter. The judicial construction and application of that chapter are not binding on military commissions established under this chapter.

(d) **Inapplicability of certain provisions.—**

(1) The following provisions of this title shall not apply to trial by military commission under this chapter:

(A) Section 810 (article 10 of the Uniform Code of Military Justice), relating to speedy trial, including any rule of courts-martial relating to speedy trial.

(B) Sections 831(a), (b), and (d) (articles 31(a), (b), and (d) of the Uniform Code of Military Justice), relating to compulsory self-incrimination.

(C) Section 832 (article 32 of the Uniform Code of Military Justice), relating to pretrial investigation.

(2) Other provisions of chapter 47 of this title shall apply to trial by military commission under this chapter only to the extent provided by this chapter.

(e) **Treatment of rulings and precedents.**—The findings, holdings, interpretations, and other precedents of military commissions under this chapter may not be introduced or considered in any hearing, trial, or other proceeding of a court-martial convened under chapter 47 of this title. The findings, holdings, interpretations, and other precedents of military commissions under this chapter may not form the basis of any holding, decision, or other determination of a court-martial convened under that chapter.

(f) **Status of commissions under common Article 3.**—A military commission established under this chapter is a regularly constituted court, affording all the necessary "judicial guarantees which are recognized as indispensable by civilized peoples" for purposes of common Article 3 of the Geneva Conventions.

(g) **Geneva Conventions not establishing source of rights.**—No alien unlawful enemy combatant subject to trial by military commission under this chapter may invoke the Geneva Conventions as a source of rights.

§948c. Persons subject to military commissions

Any alien unlawful enemy combatant is subject to trial by military commission under this chapter.

§948d. Jurisdiction of military commissions

(a) **Jurisdiction.**—A military commission under this chapter shall have jurisdiction to try any offense made punishable by this chapter or the law of war when committed by an alien unlawful enemy combatant before, on, or after September 11, 2001.

(b) **Lawful enemy combatants.**—Military commissions under this chapter shall not have jurisdiction over lawful enemy combatants. Lawful enemy combatants who violate the law of war are subject to chapter 47 of this title. Courts-martial established under that chapter shall have jurisdiction to try a lawful enemy combatant for any offense made punishable under this chapter.

(c) **Determination of unlawful enemy combatant status dispositive.**—A finding, whether before, on, or after the date of the enactment of the Military Commissions Act of 2006, by a Combatant Status Review Tribunal or another competent tribunal established under the authority of the President or the Secretary of Defense that a person is an unlawful enemy combatant is dispositive for purposes of jurisdiction for trial by military commission under this chapter.

(d) **Punishments.**—A military commission under this chapter may, under such limitations as the Secretary of Defense may prescribe, adjudge any punishment not forbidden by this chapter, including the penalty of death when authorized under this chapter or the law of war.

§ 948e. Annual report to congressional committees

(a) **Annual report required.**—Not later than December 31 each year, the Secretary of Defense shall submit to the Committees on Armed Services of the Senate and the House of Representatives a report on any trials conducted by military commissions under this chapter during such year.

(b) **Form.**—Each report under this section shall be submitted in unclassified form, but may include a classified annex.

948h. Who may convene military commissions

Military commissions under this chapter may be convened by the Secretary of Defense or by any officer or official of the United States designated by the Secretary for that purpose.

§ 948i. Who may serve on military commissions

(a) **In general.**—Any commissioned officer of the armed forces on active duty is eligible to serve on a military commission under this chapter.

(b) **Detail of members.**—When convening a military commission under this chapter, the convening authority shall detail as members of the commission such members of the armed forces eligible under subsection (a), as in the opinion of the convening authority, are best qualified for the duty by reason of age, education, training, experience, length of service, and judicial temperament. No member of an armed force is eligible to serve as a member of a military commission when such member is the accuser or a witness for the prosecution or has acted as an investigator or counsel in the same case.

(c) **Excuse of members.**—Before a military commission under this chapter is assembled for the trial of a case, the convening authority may excuse a member from participating in the case.

§ 948j. Military judge of a military commission

(a) **Detail of military judge.**—A military judge shall be detailed to each military commission under this chapter. The Secretary of Defense shall prescribe regulations providing for the manner in which military judges are so detailed to military commissions. The military judge shall preside over each military commission to which he has been detailed.

(b) **Qualifications.**—A military judge shall be a commissioned officer of the armed forces who is a member of the bar of a Federal court, or a member of the bar of the highest court of a State, and who is certified to be qualified for duty under section 826 of this title (article 26 of the Uniform Code of Military Justice) as a military judge in general courts-martial by the Judge Advocate General of the armed force of which such military judge is a member.

(c) **Ineligibility of certain individuals.**—No person is eligible to act as military judge in a case of a military commission under this chapter if he is the accuser or a witness or has acted as investigator or a counsel in the same case.

(d) **Consultation with members; ineligibility to vote.**—A military judge detailed to a military commission under this chapter may not consult with the members of the commission except in the presence of the accused (except as otherwise provided in section 949d of this title), trial counsel, and defense counsel, nor may he vote with the members of the commission.

(e) **Other duties.**—A commissioned officer who is certified to be qualified for duty as a military judge of a military commission under this chapter may perform such other duties as are assigned to him by or with the approval of the Judge Advocate General of the armed force of which such officer is a member or the designee of such Judge Advocate General.

(f) **Prohibition on evaluation of fitness by convening authority.**—The convening authority of a military commission under this chapter shall not prepare or review any report concerning the effectiveness, fitness, or efficiency of a military judge detailed to the military commission which relates to his performance of duty as a military judge on the military commission.

§ 948k. Detail of trial counsel and defense counsel

(a) **Detail of counsel generally.**—(1) Trial counsel and military defense counsel shall be detailed for each military commission under this chapter.

(2) Assistant trial counsel and assistant and associate defense counsel may be detailed for a military commission under this chapter.

(3) Military defense counsel for a military commission under this chapter shall be detailed as soon as practicable after the swearing of charges against the accused.

(4) The Secretary of Defense shall prescribe regulations providing for the manner in which trial counsel and military defense counsel are detailed for military commissions under this chapter and for the persons who are authorized to detail such counsel for such commissions.

(b) **Trial counsel.**—Subject to subsection (e), trial counsel detailed for a military commission under this chapter must be—

(1) a judge advocate (as that term is defined in section 801 of this title (article 1 of the Uniform Code of Military Justice) who—

(A) is a graduate of an accredited law school or is a member of the bar of a Federal court or of the highest court of a State; and

(B) is certified as competent to perform duties as trial counsel before general courts-martial by the Judge Advocate General of the armed force of which he is a member; or

(2) a civilian who—

(A) is a member of the bar of a Federal court or of the highest court of a State; and

(B) is otherwise qualified to practice before the military commission pursuant to regulations prescribed by the Secretary of Defense.

(c) **Military defense counsel.**—Subject to subsection (e), military defense counsel detailed for a military commission under this chapter must be a judge advocate (as so defined) who is—

(1) a graduate of an accredited law school or is a member of the bar of a Federal court or of the highest court of a State; and

(2) certified as competent to perform duties as defense counsel before general courts-martial by the Judge Advocate General of the armed force of which he is a member.

(d) **Chief Prosecutor; Chief Defense Counsel.**—(1) The Chief Prosecutor in a military commission under this chapter shall meet the requirements set forth in subsection (b)(1).

(2) The Chief Defense Counsel in a military commission under this chapter shall meet the requirements set forth in subsection (c)(1).

(e) **Ineligibility of certain individuals.**—No person who has acted as an investigator, military judge, or member of a military commission under this chapter in any case may act later as trial counsel or military defense counsel in the same case. No person who has acted for the prosecution before a military commission under this chapter may act later in the same case for the defense, nor may any person who has acted for the defense before a military commission under this chapter act later in the same case for the prosecution.

§ 9481. Detail or employment of reporters and interpreters

(a) **Court reporters.**—Under such regulations as the Secretary of Defense may prescribe, the convening authority of a military commission under this chapter shall detail to or employ for the commission qualified court reporters, who shall make a verbatim recording of the proceedings of and testimony taken before the commission.

(b) **Interpreters.**—Under such regulations as the Secretary of Defense may prescribe, the convening authority of a military commission under this chapter may detail to or employ for the military commission interpreters who shall interpret for the commission and, as necessary, for trial counsel and defense counsel and for the accused.

(c) **Transcript; record.**—The transcript of a military commission under this chapter shall be under the control of the convening authority of the commission, who shall also be responsible for preparing the record of the proceedings.

§ 948m. Number of members; excuse of members; absent and additional members

(a) **Number of members.**—

(1) A military commission under this chapter shall, except as provided in paragraph (2), have at least five members.

(2) In a case in which the accused before a military commission under this chapter may be sentenced to a penalty of death, the military commission shall have the number of members prescribed by section 949m(c) of this title.

(b) **Excuse of members.**—No member of a military commission under this chapter may be absent or excused after the military commission has been assembled for the trial of a case unless excused—

(1) as a result of challenge;

(2) by the military judge for physical disability or other good cause; or

(3) by order of the convening authority for good cause.

(c) **Absent and additional members.**—Whenever a military commission under this chapter is reduced below the number of members required by subsection (a), the trial may not proceed unless the convening authority details new members sufficient to provide not less than such number. The trial may proceed with the new members present after the recorded evidence previously introduced before the members has been read to the military commission in the presence of the military judge, the accused (except as provided in section 949d of this title), and counsel for both sides.

§ 948q. Charges and specifications

(a) **Charges and specifications.**—Charges and specifications against an accused in a military commission under this chapter shall be signed by a person subject to chapter 47 of this title under oath before a commissioned officer of the armed forces authorized to administer oaths and shall state—

(1) that the signer has personal knowledge of, or reason to believe, the matters set forth therein; and

(2) that they are true in fact to the best of the signer's knowledge and belief.

(b) **Notice to accused.**—Upon the swearing of the charges and specifications in accordance with subsection (a), the accused shall be informed of the charges against him as soon as practicable.

§ 948r. Compulsory self-incrimination prohibited; treatment of statements obtained by torture and other statements

(a) **In general.**—No person shall be required to testify against himself at a proceeding of a military commission under this chapter.

(b) **Exclusion of statements obtained by torture.**—A statement obtained by use of torture shall not be admissible in a military commission under this chapter, except against a person accused of torture as evidence that the statement was made.

(c) **Statements obtained before enactment of detainee treatment act of 2005.**—A statement obtained before December 30, 2005 (the date of the enactment of the Defense Treatment Act of 2005) in which the degree of coercion is disputed may be admitted only if the military judge finds that—

(1) the totality of the circumstances renders the statement reliable and possessing sufficient probative value; and

(2) the interests of justice would best be served by admission of the statement into evidence.

(d) **Statements obtained after enactment of Detainee Treatment Act of 2005.**—A statement obtained on or after December 30, 2005 (the date of the enactment of the Defense Treatment Act of 2005) in which the degree of coercion is disputed may be admitted only if the military judge finds that—

(1) the totality of the circumstances renders the statement reliable and possessing sufficient probative value;

(2) the interests of justice would best be served by admission of the statement into evidence; and

(3) the interrogation methods used to obtain the statement do not amount to cruel, inhuman, or degrading treatment prohibited by section 1003 of the Detainee Treatment Act of 2005.

§ 948s. Service of charges

The trial counsel assigned to a case before a military commission under this chapter shall cause to be served upon the accused and military defense counsel a copy of the charges upon which trial is to be had. Such charges shall be served in English and, if appropriate, in another language that the accused understands. Such service shall be made sufficiently in advance of trial to prepare a defense.

§ 949a. Rules

(a) **Procedures and rules of evidence.**—Pretrial, trial, and post-trial procedures, including elements and modes of proof, for cases triable by military commission under this chapter may be prescribed by the Secretary of Defense, in consultation with the Attorney General. Such procedures shall, so far as the Secretary considers practicable or consistent with military or intelligence activities, apply the principles of law and the rules of evidence in trial by general courts-martial. Such procedures and rules of evidence may not be contrary to or inconsistent with this chapter.

(b) **Rules for military commission.**—(1) Notwithstanding any departures from the law and the rules of evidence in trial by general courts-martial authorized by subsection (a), the procedures and rules of evidence in trials by military commission under this chapter shall include the following:

(A) The accused shall be permitted to present evidence in his defense, to cross-examine the witnesses who testify against him, and to examine and respond to evidence admitted against him on the issue of guilt or innocence and for sentencing, as provided for by this chapter.

(B) The accused shall be present at all sessions of the military commission (other than those for deliberations or voting), except when excluded under section 949d of this title.

(C) The accused shall receive the assistance of counsel as provided for by section 948k.

(D) The accused shall be permitted to represent himself, as provided for by paragraph (3).

(2) In establishing procedures and rules of evidence for military commission proceedings, the Secretary of Defense may prescribe the following provisions:

(A) Evidence shall be admissible if the military judge determines that the evidence would have probative value to a reasonable person.

(B) Evidence shall not be excluded from trial by military commission on the grounds that the evidence was not seized pursuant to a search warrant or other authorization.

(C) A statement of the accused that is otherwise admissible shall not be excluded from trial by military commission on grounds of alleged coercion or compulsory self-incrimination so long as the evidence complies with the provisions of section 948r of this title.

(D) Evidence shall be admitted as authentic so long as—

(i) the military judge of the military commission determines that there is sufficient basis to find that the evidence is what it is claimed to be; and

(ii) the military judge instructs the members that they may consider any issue as to authentication or identification of evidence in determining the weight, if any, to be given to the evidence.

(E)(i) Except as provided in clause (ii), hearsay evidence not otherwise admissible under the rules of evidence applicable in trial by general courts-martial may be admitted in a trial by military commission if the proponent of the evidence makes known to the adverse party, sufficiently in advance to provide the adverse party with a fair opportunity to meet the evidence, the intention of the proponent to offer the evidence, and the particulars of the evidence (including information on the general circumstances under which the evidence was obtained). The disclosure of evidence under the preceding sentence is subject to the requirements and limitations applicable to the disclosure of classified information in section 949j(c) of this title.

(ii) Hearsay evidence not otherwise admissible under the rules of evidence applicable in trial by general courts-martial shall not be admitted in a trial by military commission if the party opposing the admission of the evidence demonstrates that the evidence is unreliable or lacking in probative value.

(F) The military judge shall exclude any evidence the probative value of which is substantially outweighed—

(i) by the danger of unfair prejudice, confusion of the issues, or misleading the commission; or

(ii) by considerations of undue delay, waste of time, or needless presentation of cumulative evidence.

(3)(A) The accused in a military commission under this chapter who exercises the right to self-representation under paragraph (1)(D) shall conform his deportment and the conduct of the defense to the rules of evidence, procedure, and decorum applicable to trials by military commission.

(B) Failure of the accused to conform to the rules described in subparagraph (A) may result in a partial or total revocation by the military judge of the right of self-representation under paragraph (1)(D). In such case, the detailed defense counsel of the accused or an appropriately authorized civilian counsel shall perform the functions necessary for the defense.

(c) **Delegation of authority to prescribe regulations.**—The Secretary of Defense may delegate the authority of the Secretary to prescribe regulations under this chapter.

(d) **Notification to congressional committees of changes to procedures.**— Not later than 60 days before the date on which any proposed modification of the procedures in effect for military commissions under this chapter goes into effect, the Secretary of Defense shall submit to the Committee on Armed Services of the Senate and the Committee on Armed Services of the House of Representatives a report describing the modification.

§ 949b. Unlawfully influencing action of military commission

(a) In general.—

(1) No authority convening a military commission under this chapter may censure, reprimand, or admonish the military commission, or any member, military judge, or counsel thereof, with respect to the findings or sentence adjudged by the military commission, or with respect to any other exercises of its or his functions in the conduct of the proceedings.

(2) No person may attempt to coerce or, by any unauthorized means, influence—

(A) the action of a military commission under this chapter, or any member thereof, in reaching the findings or sentence in any case;

(B) the action of any convening, approving, or reviewing authority with respect to his judicial acts; or

(C) the exercise of professional judgment by trial counsel or defense counsel.

(3) Paragraphs (1) and (2) do not apply with respect to—

(A) general instructional or informational courses in military justice if such courses are designed solely for the purpose of instructing members of a command in the substantive and procedural aspects of military commissions; or

(B) statements and instructions given in open proceedings by a military judge or counsel.

(b) Prohibition on consideration of actions on commission in evaluation of fitness.—In the preparation of an effectiveness, fitness, or efficiency report or any other report or document used in whole or in part for the purpose of determining whether a commissioned officer of the armed forces is qualified to be advanced in grade, or in determining the assignment or transfer of any such officer or whether any such officer should be retained on active duty, no person may—

(1) consider or evaluate the performance of duty of any member of a military commission under this chapter; or

(2) give a less favorable rating or evaluation to any commissioned officer because of the zeal with which such officer, in acting as counsel, represented any accused before a military commission under this chapter.

House of Representatives a report describing the modification.

§ 949c. Duties of trial counsel and defense counsel

(a) Trial counsel.—The trial counsel of a military commission under this chapter shall prosecute in the name of the United States.

(b) Defense counsel.—

(1) The accused shall be represented in his defense before a military commission under this chapter as provided in this subsection.

(2) The accused shall be represented by military counsel detailed under section 948k of this title.

(3) The accused may be represented by civilian counsel if retained by the accused, but only if such civilian counsel—

(A) is a United States citizen;

(B) is admitted to the practice of law in a State, district, or possession of the United States or before a Federal court;

(C) has not been the subject of any sanction of disciplinary action by any court, bar, or other competent governmental authority for relevant misconduct;

(D) has been determined to be eligible for access to classified information that is classified at the level Secret or higher; and

(E) has signed a written agreement to comply with all applicable regulations or instructions for counsel, including any rules of court for conduct during the proceedings.

(4) Civilian defense counsel shall protect any classified information received during the course of representation of the accused in accordance with all applicable law governing the protection of classified information and may not divulge such information to any person not authorized to receive it.

(5) If the accused is represented by civilian counsel, detailed military counsel shall act as associate counsel.

(6) The accused is not entitled to be represented by more than one military counsel. However, the person authorized under regulations prescribed under section 948k of this title to detail counsel, in that person's sole discretion, may detail additional military counsel to represent the accused.

(7) Defense counsel may cross-examine each witness for the prosecution who testifies before a military commission under this chapter.

§ 949d. Sessions

(a) Sessions without presence of members.—(1) At any time after the service of charges which have been referred for trial by military commission under this chapter, the military judge may call the military commission into session without the presence of the members for the purpose of—

(A) hearing and determining motions raising defenses or objections which are capable of determination without trial of the issues raised by a plea of not guilty;

(B) hearing and ruling upon any matter which may be ruled upon by the military judge under this chapter, whether or not the matter is appropriate for later consideration or decision by the members;

(C) if permitted by regulations prescribed by the Secretary of Defense, receiving the pleas of the accused; and

(D) performing any other procedural function which may be performed by the military judge under this chapter or under rules prescribed pursuant to section 949a of this title and which does not require the presence of the members.

(2) Except as provided in subsections (c) and (e), any proceedings under paragraph (1) shall—

(A) be conducted in the presence of the accused, defense counsel, and trial counsel; and

(B) be made part of the record.

(b) **Proceedings in presence of accused.**—Except as provided in subsections (c) and (e), all proceedings of a military commission under this chapter, including any consultation of the members with the military judge or counsel, shall—

(1) be in the presence of the accused, defense counsel, and trial counsel; and

(2) be made a part of the record.

(c) **Deliberation or vote of members.**—When the members of a military commission under this chapter deliberate or vote, only the members may be present.

(d) **Closure of proceedings.**—(1) The military judge may close to the public all or part of the proceedings of a military commission under this chapter, but only in accordance with this subsection.

(2) The military judge may close to the public all or a portion of the proceedings under paragraph (1) only upon making a specific finding that such closure is necessary to—

(A) protect information the disclosure of which could reasonably be expected to cause damage to the national security, including intelligence or law enforcement sources, methods, or activities; or

(B) ensure the physical safety of individuals.

(3) A finding under paragraph (2) may be based upon a presentation, including a presentation ex parte or in camera, by either trial counsel or defense counsel.

(e) **Exclusion of accused from certain proceedings.**—The military judge may exclude the accused from any portion of a proceeding upon a determination that, after being warned by the military judge, the accused persists in conduct that justifies exclusion from the courtroom—

(1) to ensure the physical safety of individuals; or

(2) to prevent disruption of the proceedings by the accused.

(f) **Protection of classified information.**—

(1) National security privilege.—

(A) Classified information shall be protected and is privileged from disclosure if disclosure would be detrimental to the national security. The rule in the preceding sentence applies to all stages of the proceedings of military commissions under this chapter.

(B) The privilege referred to in subparagraph (A) may be claimed by the head of the executive or military department or government agency concerned based on a finding by the head of that department or agency that—

(i) the information is properly classified; and

(ii) disclosure of the information would be detrimental to the national security.

(C) A person who may claim the privilege referred to in subparagraph (A) may authorize a representative, witness, or trial counsel to claim the privilege and make the finding described in subparagraph (B) on behalf of such person. The authority of the representative, witness, or trial counsel to do so is presumed in the absence of evidence to the contrary.

(2) Introduction of classified information.—

(A) Alternatives to disclosure.—To protect classified information from disclosure, the military judge, upon motion of trial counsel, shall authorize, to the extent practicable—

(i) the deletion of specified items of classified information from documents to be introduced as evidence before the military commission;

(ii) the substitution of a portion or summary of the information for such classified documents; or

(iii) the substitution of a statement of relevant facts that the classified information would tend to prove.

(B) Protection of sources, methods, or activities.—The military judge, upon motion of trial counsel, shall permit trial counsel to introduce otherwise admissible evidence before the military commission, while protecting from disclosure the sources, methods, or activities by which the United States acquired the evidence if the military judge finds that (i) the sources, methods, or activities by which the United States acquired the evidence are classified, and (ii) the evidence is reliable. The military judge may require trial counsel to present to the military commission and the defense, to the extent practicable and consistent with national security, an unclassified summary of the sources, methods, or activities by which the United States acquired the evidence.

(C) Assertion of National security privilege at trial.—During the examination of any witness, trial counsel may object to any question, line of inquiry, or motion to admit evidence that would require the disclosure of classified information. Following such an objection, the military judge shall take suitable action to safeguard such classified information. Such action may include the review of trial counsel's claim of privilege by the military judge in camera and on an ex parte basis, and the delay of proceedings to permit trial counsel to consult with the department or agency concerned as to whether the national security privilege should be asserted.

(3) **Consideration of privilege and related materials.**—A claim of privilege under this subsection, and any materials submitted in support thereof, shall, upon request of the Government, be considered by the military judge in camera and shall not be disclosed to the accused.

(4) **Additional regulations.**—The Secretary of Defense may prescribe additional regulations, consistent with this subsection, for the use and protection of classified information during proceedings of military commissions under this chapter. A report on any regulations so prescribed, or modified, shall be submitted to the Committees on Armed Services of the Senate and the House of Representatives not later than 60 days before the date on which such regulations or modifications, as the case may be, go into effect.

§ 949e. Continuances

The military judge in a military commission under this chapter may, for reasonable cause, grant a continuance to any party for such time, and as often, as may appear to be just.

§ 949f. Challenges

(a) **Challenges authorized.**—The military judge and members of a military commission under this chapter may be challenged by the accused or trial counsel for cause stated to the commission. The military judge shall determine the relevance and validity of challenges for cause. The military judge may not receive a challenge to more than one person at a time. Challenges by trial counsel shall ordinarily be presented and decided before those by the accused are offered.

(b) **Peremptory challenges.**—Each accused and the trial counsel are entitled to one peremptory challenge. The military judge may not be challenged except for cause.

(c) **Challenges against additional members.**—Whenever additional members are detailed to a military commission under this chapter, and after any challenges for cause against such additional members are presented and decided, each accused and the trial counsel are entitled to one peremptory challenge against members not previously subject to peremptory challenge.

§949g. Oaths

(a) In general.—

(1) Before performing their respective duties in a military commission under this chapter, military judges, members, trial counsel, defense counsel, reporters, and interpreters shall take an oath to perform their duties faithfully.

(2) The form of the oath required by paragraph (1), the time and place of the taking thereof, the manner of recording the same, and whether the oath shall be taken for all cases in which duties are to be performed or for a particular case, shall be as prescribed in regulations of the Secretary of Defense. Those regulations may provide that—

(A) an oath to perform faithfully duties as a military judge, trial counsel, or defense counsel may be taken at any time by any judge advocate or other person certified to be qualified or competent for the duty; and

(B) if such an oath is taken, such oath need not again be taken at the time the judge advocate or other person is detailed to that duty.

(b) Witnesses.—Each witness before a military commission under this chapter shall be examined on oath.

§949h. Former jeopardy

(a) In general.—No person may, without his consent, be tried by a military commission under this chapter a second time for the same offense.

(b) Scope of trial.—No proceeding in which the accused has been found guilty by military commission under this chapter upon any charge or specification is a trial in the sense of this section until the finding of guilty has become final after review of the case has been fully completed.

§949i. Pleas of the accused

(a) Entry of plea of not guilty.—If an accused in a military commission under this chapter after a plea of guilty sets up matter inconsistent with the plea, or if it appears that the accused has entered the plea of guilty through lack of understanding of its meaning and effect, or if the accused fails or refuses to plead, a plea of not guilty shall be entered in the record, and the military commission shall proceed as though the accused had pleaded not guilty.

(b) Finding of guilt after guilty plea.—With respect to any charge or specification to which a plea of guilty has been made by the accused in a military commission under this chapter and accepted by the military judge, a finding of guilty of the charge or specification may be entered immediately without a vote. The finding shall constitute the finding of the commission unless the plea of guilty is withdrawn prior to announcement of the sentence, in which event the proceedings shall continue as though the accused had pleaded not guilty.

§ 949j. Opportunity to obtain witnesses and other evidence

(a) **Right of defense counsel.**—Defense counsel in a military commission under this chapter shall have a reasonable opportunity to obtain witnesses and other evidence as provided in regulations prescribed by the Secretary of Defense.

(b) **Process for compulsion.**—Process issued in a military commission under this chapter to compel witnesses to appear and testify and to compel the production of other evidence—

(1) shall be similar to that which courts of the United States having criminal jurisdiction may lawfully issue; and

(2) shall run to any place where the United States shall have jurisdiction thereof.

(c) **Protection of classified information.**—(1) With respect to the discovery obligations of trial counsel under this section, the military judge, upon motion of trial counsel, shall authorize, to the extent practicable—

(A) the deletion of specified items of classified information from documents to be made available to the accused;

(B) the substitution of a portion or summary of the information for such classified documents; or

(C) the substitution of a statement admitting relevant facts that the classified information would tend to prove.

(2) The military judge, upon motion of trial counsel, shall authorize trial counsel, in the course of complying with discovery obligations under this section, to protect from disclosure the sources, methods, or activities by which the United States acquired evidence if the military judge finds that the sources, methods, or activities by which the United States acquired such evidence are classified. The military judge may require trial counsel to provide, to the extent practicable, an unclassified summary of the sources, methods, or activities by which the United States acquired such evidence.

(d) **Exculpatory evidence.**—

(1) As soon as practicable, trial counsel shall disclose to the defense the existence of any evidence known to trial counsel that reasonably tends to exculpate the accused. Where exculpatory evidence is classified, the accused shall be provided with an adequate substitute in accordance with the procedures under subsection (c).

(2) In this subsection, the term "evidence known to trial counsel", in the case of exculpatory evidence, means exculpatory evidence that the prosecution would be required to disclose in a trial by general court-martial under chapter 47 of this title.

§ 949k. Defense of lack of mental responsibility

(a) **Affirmative defense.**—It is an affirmative defense in a trial by military commission under this chapter that, at the time of the commission of the acts constituting the offense, the accused, as a result of a severe mental disease or defect, was unable to appreciate the nature and quality or the wrongfulness of the acts. Mental disease or defect does not otherwise constitute a defense.

(b) **Burden of proof.**—The accused in a military commission under this chapter has the burden of proving the defense of lack of mental responsibility by clear and convincing evidence.

(c) **Findings following assertion of defense.**—Whenever lack of mental responsibility of the accused with respect to an offense is properly at issue in a military commission under this chapter, the military judge shall instruct the members of the commission as to the defense of lack of mental responsibility under this section and shall charge them to find the accused—

(1) guilty;

(2) not guilty; or

(3) subject to subsection (d), not guilty by reason of lack of mental responsibility.

(d) **Majority vote required for finding.**—The accused shall be found not guilty by reason of lack of mental responsibility under subsection (c)(3) only if a majority of the members present at the time the vote is taken determines that the defense of lack of mental responsibility has been established.

§ 949l. Voting and rulings

(a) **Vote by secret written ballot.**—Voting by members of a military commission under this chapter on the findings and on the sentence shall be by secret written ballot.

(b) **Rulings.**—

(1) The military judge in a military commission under this chapter shall rule upon all questions of law, including the admissibility of evidence and all interlocutory questions arising during the proceedings.

(2) Any ruling made by the military judge upon a question of law or an interlocutory question (other than the factual issue of mental responsibility of the accused) is conclusive and constitutes the ruling of the military commission. However, a military judge may change his ruling at any time during the trial.

(c) **Instructions prior to vote.**—Before a vote is taken of the findings of a military commission under this chapter, the military judge shall, in the presence of the accused and counsel, instruct the members as to the elements of the offense and charge the members—

(1) that the accused must be presumed to be innocent until his guilt is established by legal and competent evidence beyond a reasonable doubt;

(2) that in the case being considered, if there is a reasonable doubt as to the guilt of the accused, the doubt must be resolved in favor of the accused and he must be acquitted;

(3) that, if there is reasonable doubt as to the degree of guilt, the finding must be in a lower degree as to which there is no reasonable doubt; and

(4) that the burden of proof to establish the guilt of the accused beyond a reasonable doubt is upon the United States.

§ 949m. Number of votes required

(a) **Conviction.**—No person may be convicted by a military commission under this chapter of any offense, except as provided in section 949i(b) of this title or by concurrence of two-thirds of the members present at the time the vote is taken.

(b) **Sentences.**—

(1) No person may be sentenced by a military commission to suffer death, except insofar as—

(A) the penalty of death is expressly authorized under this chapter or the law of war for an offense of which the accused has been found guilty;

(B) trial counsel expressly sought the penalty of death by filing an appropriate notice in advance of trial;

(C) the accused is convicted of the offense by the concurrence of all the members present at the time the vote is taken; and

(D) all the members present at the time the vote is taken concur in the sentence of death.

(2) No person may be sentenced to life imprisonment, or to confinement for more than 10 years, by a military commission under this chapter except by the concurrence of three-fourths of the members present at the time the vote is taken.

(3) All other sentences shall be determined by a military commission by the concurrence of two-thirds of the members present at the time the vote is taken.

(c) **Number of members required for penalty of death.**—

(1) Except as provided in paragraph (2), in a case in which the penalty of death is sought, the number of members of the military commission under this chapter shall be not less than 12.

(2) In any case described in paragraph (1) in which 12 members are not reasonably available because of physical conditions or military exigencies, the convening authority shall specify a lesser number of members for the military commission (but not fewer than 9 members), and the military commission may be assembled, and the trial held, with not fewer than the number of members so specified. In such a case, the convening authority shall make a detailed written statement, to be appended to the record, stating why a greater number of members were not reasonably available.

§ 949 n. Military commission to announce action

A military commission under this chapter shall announce its findings and sentence to the parties as soon as determined.

§ 949 o. Record of trial

(a) **Record; authentication.**—Each military commission under this chapter shall keep a separate, verbatim, record of the proceedings in each case brought before it, and the record shall be authenticated by the signature of the military judge. If the record cannot be authenticated by the military judge by reason of his death, disability, or absence, it shall be authenticated by the signature of the trial counsel or by a member of the commission if the trial counsel is unable to authenticate it by reason of his death, disability, or absence. Where appropriate, and as provided in regulations prescribed by the Secretary of Defense, the record of a military commission under this chapter may contain a classified annex.

(b) **Complete record required.**—A complete record of the proceedings and testimony shall be prepared in every military commission under this chapter.

(c) **Provision of copy to accused.**—A copy of the record of the proceedings of the military commission under this chapter shall be given the accused as soon as it is authenticated. If the record contains classified information, or a classified annex, the accused shall be given a redacted version of the record consistent with the requirements of <u>section 949d</u> of this title. Defense counsel shall have access to the unredacted record, as provided in regulations prescribed by the Secretary of Defense.

§ 949s. Cruel or unusual punishments prohibited

Punishment by flogging, or by branding, marking, or tattooing on the body, or any other cruel or unusual punishment, may not be adjudged by a military commission under this chapter or inflicted under this chapter upon any person subject to this chapter. The use of irons, single or double, except for the purpose of safe custody, is prohibited under this chapter.

§ 949t. Maximum limits

The punishment which a military commission under this chapter may direct for an offense may not exceed such limits as the President or Secretary of Defense may prescribe for that offense.

§ 949u. Execution of confinement

(a) **In general.**—Under such regulations as the Secretary of Defense may prescribe, a sentence of confinement adjudged by a military commission under this chapter may be carried into execution by confinement—

(1) in any place of confinement under the control of any of the armed forces; or

(2) in any penal or correctional institution under the control of the United States or its allies, or which the United States may be allowed to use.

(b) **Treatment during confinement by other than the armed forces.**—Persons confined under subsection (a)(2) in a penal or correctional institution not under the control of an armed force are subject to the same discipline and treatment as persons confined or committed by the courts of the United States or of the State, District of Columbia, or place in which the institution is situated.

Subchapter VI. Post-Trial Procedure and Review of Military Commissions

§ 950a. Error of law; lesser included offense

(a) **Error of law.**—A finding or sentence of a military commission under this chapter may not be held incorrect on the ground of an error of law unless the error materially prejudices the substantial rights of the accused.

(b) **Lesser included offense.**—Any reviewing authority with the power to approve or affirm a finding of guilty by a military commission under this chapter may approve or affirm, instead, so much of the finding as includes a lesser included offense.

§ 950b. Review by the convening authority

(a) **Notice to convening authority of findings and sentence.**—The findings and sentence of a military commission under this chapter shall be reported in writing promptly to the convening authority after the announcement of the sentence.

(b) **Submittal of matters by accused to convening authority.**—(1) The accused may submit to the convening authority matters for consideration by the convening authority with respect to the findings and the sentence of the military commission under this chapter.

(2)(A) Except as provided in subparagraph (B), a submittal under paragraph (1) shall be made in writing within 20 days after the accused has been given an authenticated record of trial under section 949o(c) of this title.

(B) If the accused shows that additional time is required for the accused to make a submittal under paragraph (1), the convening authority may, for good cause, extend the applicable period under subparagraph (A) for not more than an additional 20 days.

(3) The accused may waive his right to make a submittal to the convening authority under paragraph (1). Such a waiver shall be made in writing and may not be revoked. For the purposes of subsection (c)(2), the time within which the accused may make a submittal under this subsection shall be deemed to have expired upon the submittal of a waiver under this paragraph to the convening authority.

(c) **Action by convening authority.**—(1) The authority under this subsection to modify the findings and sentence of a military commission under this chapter is a matter of the sole discretion and prerogative of the convening authority.

(2)(A) The convening authority shall take action on the sentence of a military commission under this chapter.

(B) Subject to regulations prescribed by the Secretary of Defense, action on the sentence under this paragraph may be taken only after consideration of any matters submitted by the accused under subsection (b) or after the time for submitting such matters expires, whichever is earlier.

(C) In taking action under this paragraph, the convening authority may, in his sole discretion, approve, disapprove, commute, or suspend the sentence in whole or in part. The convening authority may not increase a sentence beyond that which is found by the military commission.

(3) The convening authority is not required to take action on the findings of a military commission under this chapter. If the convening authority takes action on the findings, the convening authority may, in his sole discretion, may—

(A) dismiss any charge or specification by setting aside a finding of guilty thereto; or

(B) change a finding of guilty to a charge to a finding of guilty to an offense that is a lesser included offense of the offense stated in the charge.

(4) The convening authority shall serve on the accused or on defense counsel notice of any action taken by the convening authority under this subsection.

(d) **Order of revision or rehearing.**—

(1) Subject to paragraphs (2) and (3), the convening authority of a military commission under this chapter may, in his sole discretion, order a proceeding in revision or a rehearing.

(2)(A) Except as provided in subparagraph (B), a proceeding in revision may be ordered by the convening authority if—

(i) there is an apparent error or omission in the record; or

(ii) the record shows improper or inconsistent action by the military commission with respect to the findings or sentence that can be rectified without material prejudice to the substantial rights of the accused.

(B) In no case may a proceeding in revision—

(i) reconsider a finding of not guilty of a specification or a ruling which amounts to a finding of not guilty;

(ii) reconsider a finding of not guilty of any charge, unless there has been a finding of guilty under a specification laid under that charge, which sufficiently alleges a violation; or

(iii) increase the severity of the sentence unless the sentence prescribed for the offense is mandatory.

(3) A rehearing may be ordered by the convening authority if the convening authority disapproves the findings and sentence and states the reasons for disapproval of the findings. If the convening authority disapproves the finding and sentence and does not order a rehearing, the convening authority shall dismiss the charges. A rehearing as to the findings may not be ordered by the convening authority when there is a lack of sufficient evidence in the record to support the findings. A rehearing as to the sentence may be ordered by the convening authority if the convening authority disapproves the sentence.

§950c. Appellate referral; waiver or withdrawal of appeal

(a) **Automatic referral for appellate review.**—Except as provided under subsection (b), in each case in which the final decision of a military commission (as approved by the convening authority) includes a finding of guilty, the convening authority shall refer the case to the Court of Military Commission Review. Any such referral shall be made in accordance with procedures prescribed under regulations of the Secretary.

(b) **Waiver of right of review.**—(1) In each case subject to appellate review under section 950f of this title, except a case in which the sentence as approved under section 950b of this title extends to death, the accused may file with the convening authority a statement expressly waiving the right of the accused to such review.

(2) A waiver under paragraph (1) shall be signed by both the accused and a defense counsel.

(3) A waiver under paragraph (1) must be filed, if at all, within 10 days after notice on the action is served on the accused or on defense counsel under section 950b(c)(4) of this title. The convening authority, for good cause, may extend the period for such filing by not more than 30 days.

(c) **Withdrawal of appeal.**—Except in a case in which the sentence as approved under section 950b of this title extends to death, the accused may withdraw an appeal at any time.

(d) **Effect of waiver or withdrawal.**—A waiver of the right to appellate review or the withdrawal of an appeal under this section bars review under section 950f of this title.

§950d. Appeal by the United States

(a) **Interlocutory appeal.**—

(1) Except as provided in paragraph (2), in a trial by military commission under this chapter, the United States may take an interlocutory appeal to the Court of Military Commission Review of any order or ruling of the military judge that—

(A) terminates proceedings of the military commission with respect to a charge or specification;

(B) excludes evidence that is substantial proof of a fact material in the proceeding; or

(C) relates to a matter under subsection (d), (e), or (f) of section 949d of this title or section 949j(c) of this title.

(2) The United States may not appeal under paragraph (1) an order or ruling that is, or amounts to, a finding of not guilty by the military commission with respect to a charge or specification.

(b) **Notice of appeal.**—The United States shall take an appeal of an order or ruling under subsection (a) by filing a notice of appeal with the military judge within five days after the date of such order or ruling.

(c) **Appeal.**—An appeal under this section shall be forwarded, by means specified in regulations prescribed the Secretary of Defense, directly to the Court of Military Commission Review. In ruling on an appeal under this section, the Court may act only with respect to matters of law.

(d) **Appeal from adverse ruling.**—The United States may appeal an adverse ruling on an appeal under subsection (c) to the United States Court of Appeals for the District of Columbia Circuit by filing a petition for review in the Court of Appeals within 10 days after the date of such ruling. Review under this subsection shall be at the discretion of the Court of Appeals.

§ 950e. Rehearings

(a) **Composition of military commission for rehearing.**—Each rehearing under this chapter shall take place before a military commission under this chapter composed of members who were not members of the military commission which first heard the case.

(b) **Scope of rehearing.**—

(1) Upon a rehearing—

(A) the accused may not be tried for any offense of which he was found not guilty by the first military commission; and

(B) no sentence in excess of or more than the original sentence may be imposed unless—

(i) the sentence is based upon a finding of guilty of an offense not considered upon the merits in the original proceedings; or

(ii) the sentence prescribed for the offense is mandatory.

(2) Upon a rehearing, if the sentence approved after the first military commission was in accordance with a pretrial agreement and the accused at the rehearing changes his plea with respect to the charges or specifications upon which the pretrial agreement was based, or otherwise does not comply with pretrial agreement, the sentence as to those charges or specifications may include any punishment not in excess of that lawfully adjudged at the first military commission.

§ 950f. Review by Court of Military Commission Review

(a) **Establishment.**—The Secretary of Defense shall establish a Court of Military Commission Review which shall be composed of one or more panels, and each such panel shall be composed of not less than three appellate military judges. For the purpose of reviewing military commission decisions under this chapter, the court may sit in panels or as a whole in accordance with rules prescribed by the Secretary.

(b) **Appellate military judges.**—The Secretary shall assign appellate military judges to a Court of Military Commission Review. Each appellate military judge shall meet the qualifications for military judges prescribed by section 948j(b) of this title or shall be a civilian with comparable qualifications. No person may be serve as an appellate military judge in any case in which that person acted as a military judge, counsel, or reviewing official.

(c) **Cases to be reviewed.**—The Court of Military Commission Review, in accordance with procedures prescribed under regulations of the Secretary, shall review the record in each case that is referred to the Court by the convening authority under <u>section 950c</u> of this title with respect to any matter of law raised by the accused.

(d) **Scope of review.**—In a case reviewed by the Court of Military Commission Review under this section, the Court may act only with respect to matters of law.

§950g. Review by the United States Court of Appeals for the District of Columbia Circuit and the Supreme Court

(a) **Exclusive appellate jurisdiction.**—

(1)(A) Except as provided in subparagraph (B), the United States Court of Appeals for the District of Columbia Circuit shall have exclusive jurisdiction to determine the validity of a final judgment rendered by a military commission (as approved by the convening authority) under this chapter.

(B) The Court of Appeals may not review the final judgment until all other appeals under this chapter have been waived or exhausted.

(2) A petition for review must be filed by the accused in the Court of Appeals not later than 20 days after the date on which—

(A) written notice of the final decision of the Court of Military Commission Review is served on the accused or on defense counsel; or

(B) the accused submits, in the form prescribed by <u>section 950c</u> of this title, a written notice waiving the right of the accused to review by the Court of Military Commission Review under <u>section 950f</u> of this title.

(b) **Standard for review.**—In a case reviewed by it under this section, the Court of Appeals may act only with respect to matters of law.

(c) **Scope of review.**—The jurisdiction of the Court of Appeals on an appeal under subsection (a) shall be limited to the consideration of—

(1) whether the final decision was consistent with the standards and procedures specified in this chapter; and

(2) to the extent applicable, the Constitution and the laws of the United States.

(d) **Supreme Court.**—The Supreme Court may review by writ of certiorari the final judgment of the Court of Appeals pursuant to <u>section 1257 of title 28</u>.

§950h. Appellate counsel

(a) **Appointment.**—The Secretary of Defense shall, by regulation, establish procedures for the appointment of appellate counsel for the United States and for the accused in military commissions under this chapter. Appellate counsel shall meet the qualifications for counsel appearing before military commissions under this chapter.

(b) Representation of United States.—Appellate counsel appointed under subsection (a)—

(1) shall represent the United States in any appeal or review proceeding under this chapter before the Court of Military Commission Review; and

(2) may, when requested to do so by the Attorney General in a case arising under this chapter, represent the United States before the United States Court of Appeals for the District of Columbia Circuit or the Supreme Court.

(c) Representation of accused.—The accused shall be represented by appellate counsel appointed under subsection (a) before the Court of Military Commission Review, the United States Court of Appeals for the District of Columbia Circuit, and the Supreme Court, and by civilian counsel if retained by the accused. Any such civilian counsel shall meet the qualifications under paragraph (3) of section 949c(b) of this title for civilian counsel appearing before military commissions under this chapter and shall be subject to the requirements of paragraph (4) of that section.

§950i. Execution of sentence; procedures for execution of sentence of death

(a) In general.—The Secretary of Defense is authorized to carry out a sentence imposed by a military commission under this chapter in accordance with such procedures as the Secretary may prescribe.

(b) Execution of sentence of death only upon approval by the President.—If the sentence of a military commission under this chapter extends to death, that part of the sentence providing for death may not be executed until approved by the President. In such a case, the President may commute, remit, or suspend the sentence, or any part thereof, as he sees fit.

(c) Execution of sentence of death only upon final judgment of legality of proceedings.—

(1) If the sentence of a military commission under this chapter extends to death, the sentence may not be executed until there is a final judgment as to the legality of the proceedings (and with respect to death, approval under subsection (b)).

(2) A judgment as to legality of proceedings is final for purposes of paragraph (1) when—

(A) the time for the accused to file a petition for review by the Court of Appeals for the District of Columbia Circuit has expired and the accused has not filed a timely petition for such review and the case is not otherwise under review by that Court; or

(B) review is completed in accordance with the judgment of the United States Court of Appeals for the District of Columbia Circuit and—

(i) a petition for a writ of certiorari is not timely filed;

(ii) such a petition is denied by the Supreme Court; or

(iii) review is otherwise completed in accordance with the judgment of the Supreme Court.

(d) **Suspension of sentence.**—The Secretary of the Defense, or the convening authority acting on the case (if other than the Secretary), may suspend the execution of any sentence or part thereof in the case, except a sentence of death.

§950j. Finality or proceedings, findings, and sentences

(a) **Finality.**—The appellate review of records of trial provided by this chapter, and the proceedings, findings, and sentences of military commissions as approved, reviewed, or affirmed as required by this chapter, are final and conclusive. Orders publishing the proceedings of military commissions under this chapter are binding upon all departments, courts, agencies, and officers of the United States, except as otherwise provided by the President.

(b) **Provisions of chapter sole basis for review of military commission procedures and actions.**—Except as otherwise provided in this chapter and notwithstanding any other provision of law (including section 2241 of title 28 or any other habeas corpus provision), no court, justice, or judge shall have jurisdiction to hear or consider any claim or cause of action whatsoever, including any action pending on or filed after the date of the enactment of the Military Commissions Act of 2006, relating to the prosecution, trial, or judgment of a military commission under this chapter, including challenges to the lawfulness of procedures of military commissions under this chapter.

Subchapter VII. Punitive Matters

§950p. Statement of substantive offenses

(a) **Purpose.**—The provisions of this subchapter codify offenses that have traditionally been triable by military commissions. This chapter does not establish new crimes that did not exist before its enactment, but rather codifies those crimes for trial by military commission.

(b) **Effect.**—Because the provisions of this subchapter (including provisions that incorporate definitions in other provisions of law) are declarative of existing law, they do not preclude trial for crimes that occurred before the date of the enactment of this chapter.

§950q. Principals

Any person is punishable as a principal under this chapter who—

(1) commits an offense punishable by this chapter, or aids, abets, counsels, commands, or procures its commission;

(2) causes an act to be done which if directly performed by him would be punishable by this chapter; or

(3) is a superior commander who, with regard to acts punishable under this chapter, knew, had reason to know, or should have known, that a subordinate was about to commit such acts or had done so and who failed to take the necessary and reasonable measures to prevent such acts or to punish the perpetrators thereof.

§950r. Accessory after the fact

Any person subject to this chapter who, knowing that an offense punishable by this chapter has been committed, receives, comforts, or assists the offender in order to hinder or prevent his apprehension, trial, or punishment shall be punished as a military commission under this chapter may direct.

§950s. Conviction of lesser included offense

An accused may be found guilty of an offense necessarily included in the offense charged or of an attempt to commit either the offense charged or an attempt to commit either the offense charged or an offense necessarily included therein.

§950t. Attempts

(a) In general.—Any person subject to this chapter who attempts to commit any offense punishable by this chapter shall be punished as a military commission under this chapter may direct.

(b) Scope of offense.—An act, done with specific intent to commit an offense under this chapter, amounting to more than mere preparation and tending, even though failing, to effect its commission, is an attempt to commit that offense.

(c) Effect of consummation.—Any person subject to this chapter may be convicted of an attempt to commit an offense although it appears on the trial that the offense was consummated.

§950u. Solicitation

Any person subject to this chapter who solicits or advises another or others to commit one or more substantive offenses triable by military commission under this chapter shall, if the offense solicited or advised is attempted or committed, be punished with the punishment provided for the commission of the offense, but, if the offense solicited or advised is not committed or attempted, he shall be punished as a military commission under this chapter may direct.

§950v. Crimes triable by military commissions

(a) Definitions and construction.—In this section:

(1) **Military objective.**—The term "military objective" means—

(A) combatants; and

(B) those objects during an armed conflict—

(i) which, by their nature, location, purpose, or use, effectively contribute to the opposing force's war-fighting or war-sustaining capability; and

(ii) the total or partial destruction, capture, or neutralization of which would constitute a definite military advantage to the attacker under the circumstances at the time of the attack.

(2) **Protected person.**—The term "protected person" means any person entitled to protection under one or more of the Geneva Conventions, including—

(A) civilians not taking an active part in hostilities;

(B) military personnel placed hors de combat by sickness, wounds, or detention; and

(C) military medical or religious personnel.

(3) **Protected property.**—The term "protected property" means property specifically protected by the law of war (such as buildings dedicated to religion, education, art, science or charitable purposes, historic monuments, hospitals, or places where the sick and wounded are collected), if such property is not being used for military purposes or is not otherwise a military objective. Such term includes objects properly identified by one of the distinctive emblems of the Geneva Conventions, but does not include civilian property that is a military objective.

(4) **Construction.**—The intent specified for an offense under paragraph (1), (2), (3), (4), or (12) of subsection (b) precludes the applicability of such offense with regard to—

(A) collateral damage; or

(B) death, damage, or injury incident to a lawful attack.

(b) **Offenses.**—The following offenses shall be triable by military commission under this chapter at any time without limitation:

(1) **Murder of protected persons.**—Any person subject to this chapter who intentionally kills one or more protected persons shall be punished by death or such other punishment as a military commission under this chapter may direct.

(2) **Attacking civilians.**—Any person subject to this chapter who intentionally engages in an attack upon a civilian population as such, or individual civilians not taking active part in hostilities, shall be punished, if death results to one or more of the victims, by death or such other punishment as a military commission under this chapter may direct, and, if death does not result to any of

the victims, by such punishment, other than death, as a military commission under this chapter may direct.

(3) **Attacking civilian objects.**—Any person subject to this chapter who intentionally engages in an attack upon a civilian object that is not a military objective shall be punished as a military commission under this chapter may direct.

(4) **Attacking protected property.**—Any person subject to this chapter who intentionally engages in an attack upon protected property shall be punished as a military commission under this chapter may direct.

(5) **Pillaging.**—Any person subject to this chapter who intentionally and in the absence of military necessity appropriates or seizes property for private or personal use, without the consent of a person with authority to permit such appropriation or seizure, shall be punished as a military commission under this chapter may direct.

(6) **Denying quarter.**—Any person subject to this chapter who, with effective command or control over subordinate groups, declares, orders, or otherwise indicates to those groups that there shall be no survivors or surrender accepted, with the intent to threaten an adversary or to conduct hostilities such that there would be no survivors or surrender accepted, shall be punished as a military commission under this chapter may direct.

(7) **Taking hostages.**—Any person subject to this chapter who, having knowingly seized or detained one or more persons, threatens to kill, injure, or continue to detain such person or persons with the intent of compelling any nation, person other than the hostage, or group of persons to act or refrain from acting as an explicit or implicit condition for the safety or release of such person or persons, shall be punished, if death results to one or more of the victims, by death or such other punishment as a military commission under this chapter may direct, and, if death does not result to any of the victims, by such punishment, other than death, as a military commission under this chapter may direct.

(8) **Employing poison or similar weapons.**—Any person subject to this chapter who intentionally, as a method of warfare, employs a substance or weapon that releases a substance that causes death or serious and lasting damage to health in the ordinary course of events, through its asphyxiating, bacteriological, or toxic properties, shall be punished, if death results to one or more of the victims, by death or such other punishment as a military commission under this chapter may direct, and, if death does not result to any of the victims, by such punishment, other than death, as a military commission under this chapter may direct.

(9) **Using protected persons as a shield.**—Any person subject to this chapter who positions, or otherwise takes advantage of, a protected person with the intent to shield a military objective from attack, or to shield, favor, or impede military operations, shall be punished, if death results to one or more of the victims, by death or such other punishment as a military commission under this chapter may direct, and, if death does not result to any of the victims, by such punishment, other than death, as a military commission under this chapter may direct.

(10) **Using protected property as a shield.**—Any person subject to this chapter who positions, or otherwise takes advantage of the location of, protected property with the intent to shield a military objective from attack, or to shield, favor, or impede military operations, shall be punished as a military commission under this chapter may direct.

(11) **Torture.**—

(A) **Offense.**—Any person subject to this chapter who commits an act specifically intended to inflict severe physical or mental pain or suffering (other than pain or suffering incidental to lawful sanctions) upon another person within his custody or physical control for the purpose of obtaining information or a confession, punishment, intimidation, coercion, or any reason based on discrimination of any kind, shall be punished, if death results to one or more of the victims, by death or such other punishment as a military commission under this chapter may direct, and, if death does not result to any of the victims, by such punishment, other than death, as a military commission under this chapter may direct.

(B) **Severe mental pain or suffering defined.**—In this section, the term "severe mental pain or suffering" has the meaning given that term in section 2340(2) of title 18.

(12) **Cruel or inhuman treatment.**—

(A) **Offense.**—Any person subject to this chapter who commits an act intended to inflict severe or serious physical or mental pain or suffering (other than pain or suffering incidental to lawful sanctions), including serious physical abuse, upon another within his custody or control shall be punished, if death results to the victim, by death or such other punishment as a military commission under this chapter may direct, and, if death does not result to the victim, by such punishment, other than death, as a military commission under this chapter may direct.

(B) **Definitions.**—In this paragraph:

(i) The term "serious physical pain or suffering" means bodily injury that involves—

(I) a substantial risk of death;

(II) extreme physical pain;

(III) a burn or physical disfigurement of a serious nature (other than cuts, abrasions, or bruises); or

(IV) significant loss or impairment of the function of a bodily member, organ, or mental faculty.

(ii) The term "severe mental pain or suffering" has the meaning given that term in section 2340(2) of title 18.

(iii) The term "serious mental pain or suffering" has the meaning given the term "severe mental pain or suffering" in section 2340(2) of title 18, except that—

(I) the term "serious" shall replace the term "severe" where it appears; and

(II) as to conduct occurring after the date of the enactment of the Military Commissions Act of 2006, the term "serious and non-transitory mental harm (which need not be prolonged)" shall replace the term "prolonged mental harm" where it appears.

(13) Intentionally causing serious bodily injury.—

(A) Offense.—Any person subject to this chapter who intentionally causes serious bodily injury to one or more persons, including lawful combatants, in violation of the law of war shall be punished, if death results to one or more of the victims, by death or such other punishment as a military commission under this chapter may direct, and, if death does not result to any of the victims, by such punishment, other than death, as a military commission under this chapter may direct.

(B) Serious bodily injury defined.—In this paragraph, the term "serious bodily injury" means bodily injury which involves—

(i) a substantial risk of death;

(ii) extreme physical pain;

(iii) protracted and obvious disfigurement; or

(iv) protracted loss or impairment of the function of a bodily member, organ, or mental faculty.

(14) Mutilating or maiming.—Any person subject to this chapter who intentionally injures one or more protected persons by disfiguring the person or persons by any mutilation of the person or persons, or by permanently disabling any member, limb, or organ of the body of the person or persons, without any legitimate medical or dental purpose, shall be punished, if death results to one or more of the victims, by death or such other punishment as a military commission under this chapter may direct, and, if death does not result to any of the victims, by such punishment, other than death, as a military commission under this chapter may direct.

(15) **Murder in violation of the law of war.**—Any person subject to this chapter who intentionally kills one or more persons, including lawful combatants, in violation of the law of war shall be punished by death or such other punishment as a military commission under this chapter may direct.

(16) **Destruction of property in violation of the law of war.**—Any person subject to this chapter who intentionally destroys property belonging to another person in violation of the law of war shall punished as a military commission under this chapter may direct.

(17) **Using treachery or perfidy.**—Any person subject to this chapter who, after inviting the confidence or belief of one or more persons that they were entitled to, or obliged to accord, protection under the law of war, intentionally makes use of that confidence or belief in killing, injuring, or capturing such person or persons shall be punished, if death results to one or more of the victims, by death or such other punishment as a military commission under this chapter may direct, and, if death does not result to any of the victims, by such punishment, other than death, as a military commission under this chapter may direct.

(18) **Improperly using a flag of truce.**—Any person subject to this chapter who uses a flag of truce to feign an intention to negotiate, surrender, or otherwise suspend hostilities when there is no such intention shall be punished as a military commission under this chapter may direct.

(19) **Improperly using a distinctive emblem.**—Any person subject to this chapter who intentionally uses a distinctive emblem recognized by the law of war for combatant purposes in a manner prohibited by the law of war shall be punished as a military commission under this chapter may direct.

(20) **Intentionally mistreating a dead body.**—Any person subject to this chapter who intentionally mistreats the body of a dead person, without justification by legitimate military necessity, shall be punished as a military commission under this chapter may direct.

(21) **Rape.**—Any person subject to this chapter who forcibly or with coercion or threat of force wrongfully invades the body of a person by penetrating, however slightly, the anal or genital opening of the victim with any part of the body of the accused, or with any foreign object, shall be punished as a military commission under this chapter may direct.

(22) **Sexual assault or abuse.**—Any person subject to this chapter who forcibly or with coercion or threat of force engages in sexual contact with one or more

persons, or causes one or more persons to engage in sexual contact, shall be punished as a military commission under this chapter may direct.

(23) **Hijacking or hazarding a vessel or aircraft.**—Any person subject to this chapter who intentionally seizes, exercises unauthorized control over, or endangers the safe navigation of a vessel or aircraft that is not a legitimate military objective shall be punished, if death results to one or more of the victims, by death or such other punishment as a military commission under this chapter may direct, and, if death does not result to any of the victims, by such punishment, other than death, as a military commission under this chapter may direct.

(24) **Terrorism.**—Any person subject to this chapter who intentionally kills or inflicts great bodily harm on one or more protected persons, or intentionally engages in an act that evinces a wanton disregard for human life, in a manner calculated to influence or affect the conduct of government or civilian population by intimidation or coercion, or to retaliate against government conduct, shall be punished, if death results to one or more of the victims, by death or such other punishment as a military commission under this chapter may direct, and, if death does not result to any of the victims, by such punishment, other than death, as a military commission under this chapter may direct.

(25) **Providing material support for terrorism.**—

(A) **Offense.**—Any person subject to this chapter who provides material support or resources, knowing or intending that they are to be used in preparation for, or in carrying out, an act of terrorism (as set forth in paragraph (24)), or who intentionally provides material support or resources to an international terrorist organization engaged in hostilities against the United States, knowing that such organization has engaged or engages in terrorism (as so set forth), shall be punished as a military commission under this chapter may direct.

(B) **Material support or resources defined.**—In this paragraph, the term "material support or resources" has the meaning given that term in section 2339A(b) of title 18.

(26) **Wrongfully aiding the enemy.**—Any person subject to this chapter who, in breach of an allegiance or duty to the United States, knowingly and intentionally aids an enemy of the United States, or one of the co-belligerents of the enemy, shall be punished as a military commission under this chapter may direct.

(27) **Spying.**—Any person subject to this chapter who with intent or reason to believe that it is to be used to the injury of the United States or to the advantage of a foreign power, collects or attempts to collect information by clan-

destine means or while acting under false pretenses, for the purpose of conveying such information to an enemy of the United States, or one of the cobelligerents of the enemy, shall be punished by death or such other punishment as a military commission under this chapter may direct.

(28) **Conspiracy.**—Any person subject to this chapter who conspires to commit one or more substantive offenses triable by military commission under this chapter, and who knowingly does any overt act to effect the object of the conspiracy, shall be punished, if death results to one or more of the victims, by death or such other punishment as a military commission under this chapter may direct, and, if death does not result to any of the victims, by such punishment, other than death, as a military commission under this chapter may direct.

§950w. Perjury and obstruction of justice; contempt

(a) **Perjury and obstruction of justice.**—A military commission under this chapter may try offenses and impose such punishment as the military commission may direct for perjury, false testimony, or obstruction of justice related to military commissions under this chapter.

(b) **Contempt.**—A military commission under this chapter may punish for contempt any person who uses any menacing word, sign, or gesture in its presence, or who disturbs its proceedings by any riot or disorder.

President Issues Military Order, November 13, 2001

Detention, Treatment, and Trial of Certain Non-Citizens in the War against Terrorism

By the authority vested in me as President and as Commander in Chief of the Armed Forces of the United States by the Constitution and the laws of the United States of America, including the Authorization for Use of Military Force Joint Resolution (Public Law 107-40, 115 Stat. 224) and sections 821 and 836 of title 10, United States Code, it is hereby ordered as follows:

Section 1. Findings.

(a) International terrorists, including members of al Qaida, have carried out attacks on United States diplomatic and military personnel and facilities abroad and on citizens and property within the United States on a scale that has created a state of armed conflict that requires the use of the United States Armed Forces.

(b) In light of grave acts of terrorism and threats of terrorism, including the terrorist attacks on September 11, 2001, on the headquarters of the United States Department of Defense in the national capital region, on the World Trade Center in New York, and on civilian aircraft such as in Pennsylvania, I proclaimed a national emergency on September 14, 2001 (Proc. 7463, Declaration of National Emergency by Reason of Certain Terrorist Attacks).

(c) Individuals acting alone and in concert involved in international terrorism possess both the capability and the intention to undertake further terrorist attacks against the United States that, if not detected and prevented, will cause mass deaths, mass injuries, and massive destruction of property, and may place at risk the continuity of the operations of the United States Government.

(d) The ability of the United States to protect the United States and its citizens, and to help its allies and other cooperating nations protect their nations and their citizens, from such further terrorist attacks depends in significant part upon using the United States Armed Forces to identify terrorists and those who support them, to disrupt their activities, and to eliminate their ability to conduct or support such attacks.

(e) To protect the United States and its citizens, and for the effective conduct of military operations and prevention of terrorist attacks, it is necessary for individuals subject to this order pursuant to section 2 hereof to be detained, and, when tried, to be tried for violations of the laws of war and other applicable laws by military tribunals.

(f) Given the danger to the safety of the United States and the nature of international terrorism, and to the extent provided by and under this order, I find consistent with section 836 of title 10, United States Code, that it is not practicable to apply in military commissions under this order the principles of law and the rules of evidence generally recognized in the trial of criminal cases in the United States district courts.

(g) Having fully considered the magnitude of the potential deaths, injuries, and property destruction that would result from potential acts of terrorism against the United States, and the probability that such acts will occur, I have determined that an extraordinary emergency exists for national defense purposes, that this emergency constitutes an urgent and compelling government interest, and that issuance of this order is necessary to meet the emergency.

Sec. 2. Definition and Policy.

(a) The term "individual subject to this order" shall mean any individual who is not a United States citizen with respect to whom I determine from time to time in writing that:

(1) there is reason to believe that such individual, at the relevant times, (i) is or was a member of the organization known as al Qaida; (ii) has engaged in, aided or abetted, or conspired to commit, acts of international terrorism, or acts in preparation therefor, that have caused, threaten to cause, or have as their aim to cause, injury to or adverse effects on the United States, its citizens, national security, foreign policy, or economy; or (iii) has knowingly harbored one or more individuals described in subparagraphs (i) or (ii) of subsection 2(a)(1) of this order; and

(2) it is in the interest of the United States that such individual be subject to this order.

(b) It is the policy of the United States that the Secretary of Defense shall take all necessary measures to ensure that any individual subject to this order is detained in accordance with section 3, and, if the individual is to be tried, that such individual is tried only in accordance with section 4.

(c) It is further the policy of the United States that any individual subject to this order who is not already under the control of the Secretary of Defense but who is under the control of any other officer or agent of the United States or any State shall, upon delivery of a copy of such written determination to such officer or agent, forthwith be placed under the control of the Secretary of Defense.

Sec. 3. Detention Authority of the Secretary of Defense. Any individual subject to this order shall be—

(a) detained at an appropriate location designated by the Secretary of Defense outside or within the United States;

(b) treated humanely, without any adverse distinction based on race, color, religion, gender, birth, wealth, or any similar criteria;

(c) afforded adequate food, drinking water, shelter, clothing, and medical treatment;

(d) allowed the free exercise of religion consistent with the requirements of such detention; and

(e) detained in accordance with such other conditions as the Secretary of Defense may prescribe.

Sec. 4. Authority of the Secretary of Defense Regarding Trials of Individuals Subject to this Order.

(a) Any individual subject to this order shall, when tried, be tried by military commission for any and all offenses triable by military commission that such individual is alleged to have committed, and may be punished in accordance with the penalties provided under applicable law, including life imprisonment or death.

(b) As a military function and in light of the findings in section 1, including subsection (f) thereof, the Secretary of Defense shall issue such orders and regulations, including orders for the appointment of one or more military commissions, as may be necessary to carry out subsection (a) of this section.

(c) Orders and regulations issued under subsection (b) of this section shall include, but not be limited to, rules for the conduct of the proceedings of military commissions, including pretrial, trial, and post-trial procedures, modes of proof, issuance of process, and qualifications of attorneys, which shall at a minimum provide for—

(1) military commissions to sit at any time and any place, consistent with such guidance regarding time and place as the Secretary of Defense may provide;

(2) a full and fair trial, with the military commission sitting as the triers of both fact and law;

(3) admission of such evidence as would, in the opinion of the presiding officer of the military commission (or instead, if any other member of the commission so requests at the time the presiding officer renders that opinion, the opinion of the commission rendered at that time by a majority of the commission), have probative value to a reasonable person;

(4) in a manner consistent with the protection of information classified or classifiable under Executive Order 12958 of April 17, 1995, as amended, or any successor Executive Order, protected by statute or rule from unauthorized disclosure, or otherwise protected by law, (A) the handling of, admission into evidence of, and access to materials and information, and (B) the conduct, closure of, and access to proceedings;

(5) conduct of the prosecution by one or more attorneys designated by the Secretary of Defense and conduct of the defense by attorneys for the individual subject to this order;

(6) conviction only upon the concurrence of two-thirds of the members of the commission present at the time of the vote, a majority being present;

(7) sentencing only upon the concurrence of two-thirds of the members of the commission present at the time of the vote, a majority being present; and

(8) submission of the record of the trial, including any conviction or sentence, for review and final decision by me or by the Secretary of Defense if so designated by me for that purpose.

Sec. 5. Obligation of Other Agencies to Assist the Secretary of Defense. Departments, agencies, entities, and officers of the United States shall, to the maximum extent permitted by law, provide to the Secretary of Defense such assistance as he may request to implement this order.

Sec. 6. Additional Authorities of the Secretary of Defense.

(a) As a military function and in light of the findings in section 1, the Secretary of Defense shall issue such orders and regulations as may be necessary to carry out any of the provisions of this order.

(b) The Secretary of Defense may perform any of his functions or duties, and may exercise any of the powers provided to him under this order (other than under section 4(c)(8) hereof) in accordance with section 113(d) of title 10, United States Code.

Sec. 7. Relationship to Other Law and Forums.

(a) Nothing in this order shall be construed to—

(1) authorize the disclosure of state secrets to any person not otherwise authorized to have access to them;

(2) limit the authority of the President as Commander in Chief of the Armed Forces or the power of the President to grant reprieves and pardons; or

(3) limit the lawful authority of the Secretary of Defense, any military commander, or any other officer or agent of the United States or of any State to detain or try any person who is not an individual subject to this order.

(b) With respect to any individual subject to this order—

(1) military tribunals shall have exclusive jurisdiction with respect to offenses by the individual; and

(2) the individual shall not be privileged to seek any remedy or maintain any proceeding, directly or indirectly, or to have any such remedy or proceeding sought on the individual's behalf, in (i) any court of the United States, or any State thereof, (ii) any court of any foreign nation, or (iii) any international tribunal.

(c) This order is not intended to and does not create any right, benefit, or privilege, substantive or procedural, enforceable at law or equity by any party, against the United States, its departments, agencies, or other entities, its officers or employees, or any other person.

(d) For purposes of this order, the term "State" includes any State, district, territory, or possession of the United States.

(e) I reserve the authority to direct the Secretary of Defense, at any time hereafter, to transfer to a governmental authority control of any individual subject to this order. Nothing in this order shall be construed to limit the authority of any such governmental authority to prosecute any individual for whom control is transferred.

Sec. 8. Publication.

This order shall be published in the Federal Register.

GEORGE W. BUSH
THE WHITE HOUSE,
November 13, 2001.

Index